THE DIARY OF
JAMES GALLATIN

James Gallatin

By David 1822

THE DIARY OF JAMES GALLATIN

SECRETARY TO ALBERT GALLATIN
A GREAT PEACE MAKER

1813–1827

EDITED BY
COUNT GALLATIN

WITH AN INTRODUCTION BY VISCOUNT BRYCE

NEW EDITION

NEW YORK
CHARLES SCRIBNER'S SONS
1916

917.3092
G-13d

34489
January 1957

PREFACE

In 1875 my grandfather, James Gallatin, handed me a large sealed packet, telling me it contained his Diary from 1813 until 1827, also many important private documents.

I was not in any case to publish any part of it until 1900. He died the following year. It lay unopened and nearly forgotten until last year. On reading it, I found it of the deepest interest. This decided me (after weeding out large portions and suppressing anything that might offend) to offer it to the public.

It throws a very clear light on the events leading up to the Treaty of Ghent, and on the actual conclusion of that treaty. James accompanied his father, Albert Gallatin, as private and confidential secretary. He was sixteen years of age when the Diary opens.

Albert Gallatin held a unique position. Born at Geneva in 1761, of one of the most aristocratic families, he was left an orphan at an early age, and was brought up by his grandmother, Madame de Gallatin-Vaudenet. She was a woman of very strong character, an intimate friend of the Landgrave of Hesse Cassel, and also of Voltaire.

Albert Gallatin was much influenced by the latter's liberal theories; also he had imbibed the ideas of Rousseau and Condorcet. At the age of nineteen his grandmother informed him that she intended placing him in the army of the Landgrave with the rank of lieutenant-colonel. His answer was, "I will not serve a tyrant." A sharp box on the ears from her decided

v

his future. Without the knowledge of any of his relations, and at that time the possessor of but a small fortune, he suddenly disappeared. The next heard of him was in America.

In this connection the following letter of May 24, 1780, from Benjamin Franklin to Richard Bache, Postmaster-General of the United States, is of interest:

DEAR SON,

Messieurs Gallatin and de Serre, two young gentlemen of Geneva of good families and very good characters, having an inclination to see America, if they should arrive in your City I recommend them to your Civilities, Counsel and Countenance.

I am ever your affectionate father,

B. FRANKLIN.

At the age of forty, Albert Gallatin held the position of Secretary of the Treasury of the United States. This post he held until 1814.

In 1813, an official offer having been made by the Russian Minister, Count Dashkoff, of the mediation of Russia, with a view to making peace between England and the United States, Mr. Madison, the President, sent for Mr. Gallatin and requested him to proceed at once to St. Petersburg as head of a mission, appointing Mr. Adams (Minister to Russia) and Mr. Bayard as the other two delegates.

On April 1, 1813, the Treasury was empty; but, with the assistance of John Jacob Astor,* Gallatin was enabled to make terms with the banking houses of Parish and Girard, and so saved the United States from bankruptcy. It was a bitter pill for the Federalists to swallow that

* John Jacob Astor from Waldorf, Germany. At the age of sixteen he joined his elder brother, a dealer in musical instruments, in London. At the age of twenty with a small pack of furs he started on his own account in New York. Later he carried on a fur trade with the Indians, purchased real estate in New York and accumulated an immense fortune.

three foreigners (Parish was a Bohemian) should have achieved this; it also rather put American patriotism to shame.

As the Diary will show, the mission to Russia was futile. But Gallatin made every effort, and with the aid of his friends, Madame de Staël, Generals Lafayette and Moreau, and Baron Humboldt, he obtained a personal interview with the Emperor Alexander in London. There is no doubt that the latter's influence had great weight. That Albert Gallatin under the greatest difficulties (particularly with his own colleagues) made the Treaty of Peace is now universally acknowledged. His being a foreigner was a great advantage to him as a negotiator in Europe—but placed him at a disadvantage in America.

Lord Castlereagh and the Duke of Wellington were glad to treat with him, and in 1815 he practically completed the Commercial Treaty, though by his tact he allowed Mr. Adams to imagine that he had done so.

He was Minister in France from 1816 until 1823, and was the United States Ambassador in England from 1826 to 1827. He was a man of the most simple tastes but of deep learning. Louis XVIII once laughingly said to him, "Your French is more perfect than mine, but my English is far better than yours."

John Jacob Astor made him the most generous offer of a share in his business, Alexander Baring* did the same; he refused them both with the same answer, "A man holding the position I have must not die rich."

He was offered the Treasury again in 1844. He did not answer the letter, but simply endorsed it, "Folly of which I take no notice."

He died in 1849 at the age of eighty-eight. It was always his wish that my father, his eldest grandson, should return to Geneva, and that his children should not be brought up in America.

* Alexander Baring. First Lord Ashburton.

PREFACE

I was brought up by my grandfather, James Gallatin, the author of this Diary. My father died at Geneva, in 1859.

Gallatin

LONDON,
October 1914.

INTRODUCTION

JUST one hundred years ago three envoys from the United States met, at Ghent, three from Great Britain, in order to negotiate for a peace which should close the aimless and indecisive war which those countries had been waging for two years. After many weeks of wrangling, during which they often despaired of success, they succeeded, and on December 24, Christmas Eve, the treaty of the two nations was signed, which has given one hundred years of a peace several times endangered, but never broken, and now far more likely to continue unbroken than it ever was before.

This result was mainly due to the tact, patience, self-control, and wisdom of Albert Gallatin, one of the American Commissioners, the others being John Quincy Adams, Henry Clay, Bayard and Russell. Born at Geneva in 1761 of an ancient family, originally from Savoy, he had gone to the United States in 1780, had entered Congress in 1795, and had at once risen to distinction there by his remarkable gifts—clearness of thought, power of logical argument, and steadfastness of purpose. As Secretary of the Treasury in the administrations of Jefferson and Madison from 1800 to 1813, he had resumed the wise financial policy of Alexander Hamilton, another naturalized American citizen, and brought the finances of the country into a sounder condition than had ever been seen before. His eldest son, James Gallatin, then a boy of seventeen, acted as his father's secretary in the peace negotiations of 1814, and had already begun, when he accompanied his father to Europe in 1813, a private Diary which he continued during the period (1815–23) when the latter was United States Minister in Paris, and which covers also the period (1826–27) of Albert Gallatin's last special diplomatic mission to England. The latest entry is October 9, 1827.

This Diary, given many years ago by James Gallatin to his grandson, is now published by the latter, Count Gallatin. It is a singularly fresh, frank, and vivid record of the incidents which the young man saw in Holland, France, and England during his stay there, and of the sentiments which those incidents evoked when they happened. Young Gallatin had great advantages as an observer, for while his father's position gave him access to the society of the ruling classes in the countries named, he was himself able to move about more freely than his father could, and see life on its unofficial side. Being moreover a detached observer, and in character and tastes more a Genovese than an American, he was able to survey men and things with an impartially critical eye, which in its youthful confidence spared nobody, except his father, and saw the faults of his American citizens at least as clearly as he did those of Frenchmen or Englishmen.

The intimacy of his daily jottings gives us a lively picture of the Gallatin family. His mother, daughter of a distinguished naval officer, Commander Nicholson, and granddaughter of Sir Francis Nicholson, once Governor of Maryland, was a typical American Protestant and highly estimable Southerner of that time, altogether well regulated, and so loyal to her Puritan piety that she refused to attend on a Sunday any of the State and Court functions which the customs of the Bourbon Restoration allotted to that day. His sister, also well regulated, was not without liveliness and spirit. James, the diarist, is a bright fellow with plenty of humour and by no means well regulated. The ruling figure is, of course, the illustrious father. The picture of his character is all the more interesting because Albert Gallatin was a singularly reserved and to strangers cold and even austere man, the product of generations of Calvinist ancestors, an aristocrat by sentiment, and though by conviction a stern republican, yet under no illusions as to the weak sides of democracy. His perseverance, his high sense of duty, and his clear, strong judgment came out both in the notices of his conduct in difficult moments and in the letters from his pen, some few of which have been very properly inserted in the book. Students of American history will value these familiar glimpses of a man who did not in his own day receive from the general American public the credit which his disinterestedness as well as his abilities deserved. He was not made for popularity, and he certainly never sought it, but those with or under whom he worked recognized his powers, and though there had often been friction between him and John Quincy Adams, that upright and public-spirited man insisted on his accepting the mission to London in 1826, which Gallatin had sought to avoid.

There are in this book many interesting sidelights on the remarkable events and personages of the time. Napoleon Bonaparte (during the Hundred Days) and the Duke of Wellington pass across the stage. Louis the Eighteenth appears frequently, and the Duke of Berri, of whose assassination in 1820 there is a vivid account. So does King George the Fourth and the Tsar Alexander I of Russia, and his Minister Pozzo di Borgo, the only Corsican, except the Bonapartes and Paoli, who has figured in European history since the tenth century. We hear a good deal about Lafayette and Madame de Staël, and Joseph Bonaparte and Madame Patterson Bonaparte (the wife of Jerome Bonaparte), while among the other personages more or less fully touched on, there are Alexander von Humboldt, Lord Castlereagh, Chateaubriand, Talleyrand (of whom there is a good anecdote), Count d'Orsay, Madame Récamier, Count Walevski, George Canning, Lord Goderich, and those two well-

INTRODUCTION

known memoir writers, the Countess de Boigne and
Charles Greville. The anecdotes are often slight but
generally diverting. There is a good deal of scandal, but
it is so softened by the lapse of a century that even the
descendants of the persons implicated need not greatly
care. The anecdotes and the gossip present a lively picture of the society of the time, more dissolute in France,
more intemperate in England, more crude in America.
On the social as well as the political side, the book is a
contribution to history, and Europeans as well as Americans may be glad that the Diary of this youthful diplomatist has not shared the common fate of those to which
young men consign their personal experiences.

JAMES BRYCE.

CONTENTS

PART I

PART II

PART III

PART IV

PART V

LIST OF ILLUSTRATIONS

Dear Son,   Passy, May 24. 1780

    Messieurs Galatin & De Serres, two young
Gentlemen of Geneva, of good Families and very
good Characters; having an Inclination to see
America; if they should arrive in your City. I
recommend them to your Civilities, Counsel and
Countenance... I am ever
        Your affectionate Father

        B Franklin

Richard Bache Esq

PART I

FROM THE RUSSIAN OFFER OF MEDIATION TO THE CONCLUSION OF THE TREATY OF GHENT

MARCH 1813—JANUARY 1815

MARCH 12, 1813

The Russian Minister Count Dashkoff offered mediation, on the part of the Emperor Alexander, to the Secretary of State. Father thinks this very important and of great weight.

MARCH 14

The President has decided to send a Commission to Russia without delay and has requested father to go. He feels that it is his duty. Father rarely talks to anybody now, his mind seems fully occupied with the grave situation. I think I am the only person he confides in. He has decided to take me with him as his Private Secretary.

MARCH 17

Mr. Madison* told father to-day that there was nobody compared to him as a negotiator. It has pleased him greatly. Mr. Bayard† and J. Q. Adams, our Minister at St. Petersburg, form the Commission.

APRIL 21

We sail on May 9.

---

* James Madison, President of the United States for two terms from 1809 until 1817.

† James Ashton Bayard, American Statesman, born 1767, died 1815.

Extract from ALBERT GALLATIN'S *letter of May 5 to his*
BROTHER-IN-LAW

"I have made up my mind that I could in no other manner
be more usefully employed for the present than on the
negotiation of a peace. Peace is at all times desirable.
England must be desirous at this critical moment to have
it in her power to apply her whole force on the continent
of Europe, and the mediation of Russia saves her pride."

Diary resumed:

MAY 9, 1813

We sailed to-day from Newcastle—a ship called the
Neptune, 300 tons—Captain Lloyd Jones, J. A. Bayard,
G. H. Dallas, George Milligan, John Todd, father, and
myself.

MAY 10

Head-winds. I am a bad sailor. I share father's cabin.
He comes in now and then and looks at me gravely. He
says he has no time to think of being sick.

MAY 11

A British frigate at anchor; she sent a boat with a
lieutenant and the captain's compliments to father
saying that he would be pleased to see him on board.
Of course he declined, but sent Dallas and Milligan to
present his compliments. Captain Jones also took
Admiral Warren's passport to have it endorsed. The
frigate is the *Spartan*—her Captain's name is Braynton.

JUNE 20: GOTTENBURG

We anchored in the quarantine grounds this morning.
It being Sunday we only got our permission from Gottenburg to land in the evening. I was only too glad to
jump into a boat and go on shore after having been more
than forty days at sea. We were only allowed on the

quarantine island. Wild roses in profusion. The island
is only a barren rock. Returned on board at 10.30.

JUNE 21

We hired two boats to take us to Gottenburg. We landed
five miles from Gottenburg as the current was so strong.
We fortunately found carriages to take us to the town.
While we waited for them we went into some of the houses;
they are very dirty, horrible smells. All the women are
ugly and blow their noses on their aprons. Such apologies
for carriages—simply open carts, four of them, each
drawn by half-starved ponies; wooden springs to the
carts. The River Gotha full of shipping. We stopped
at the house of a Mr. Dixon a nice Scotsman who had
been American Consul. Several Americans came to see
father.

JUNE 22

Returned to our ship after breakfast—sailed in the
evening. . . . Father found a courier going to England
and entrusted him with a letter to Alexander Baring
which I copied for him.*

JUNE 25: COPENHAGEN

We landed this morning. Went to Bachalan's Hotel.
Father let me go to see all the sights and afterwards
questioned me by way of teaching me history.

JULY 1

We went on board this morning. South-east wind,
which delays us greatly. Father called me on deck;
pointed out where Lord Nelson fought his battle in 1801.
He says all the fortifications are new. It was bom-
barded in September 1807. Most of the houses destroyed
and over two thousand killed. There seem to be

* For the correspondence between Alexander Baring and Albert Gallatin
see Appendix I.

batteries everywhere now and the population is armed. The King lives most simply. The Ministers have merely nominal salaries. Father says he cannot understand England and Russia's conduct toward Norway. It has thrown the nation into the hands of the French against their will. Great poverty and distress and much discontent. The people struck me as most civil; they looked weary and oppressed, but are very sober.

JULY 3

Always head-winds. I do hope we will finish this voyage soon, it is so monotonous. Father wishes me to do a certain amount of work every day. I feel it is good for me and it certainly makes the time pass more rapidly.

JULY 8

Lovely weather but still head-winds. Just called on deck to see the coast of Courland. All on board are getting very weary and impatient to land. Father always keeps his serene temper.

JULY 12

Entered Gulf of Finland. We will soon be at the end of our voyage.

JULY 21: ST. PETERSBURG

After a tedious journey with little to interest one we arrived at St. Petersburg. It is very beautiful. Weather very warm.

JULY 23

Have been sight-seeing all day. St. Petersburg is very fine—great width of the streets and fine palaces. In the evenings father tells me much of Russian history. Mr. Adams* very civil but has a disagreeable manner. He is from New England, a "Yankee."

* John Quincy Adams—1767, died 1848, son of John Adams, second President of the United States.

JULY 25

Father is much disappointed that no steps have been taken by England beyond a note discouraging arbitration altogether. He fears the English Government resent the offer of Russian mediation and that the President was a little hasty in sending the mission.

The Emperor is not at St. Petersburg but with his army fighting Napoleon. He left Count Romanzoff in charge of foreign affairs and has taken Count Nesselrode with him. This father greatly regrets, as Count N. has great influence with the Emperor and thinks it to the interest of Russia to remain in close friendship with England. Count Romanzoff, on the contrary, was the instigator of the offer of mediation on the part of Russia, as he disapproves of the overpowering dominion of England on the sea. . . .

JULY 29

Our position is a very embarrassing one. We plainly see we are not wanted. Romanzoff is pressing the Emperor to renew his offer of mediation to England. . . .

AUGUST 6

Such weary waiting, and all seems so hopeless. My father's wonderful calm and patience surprise one and all. I, of course, being so young, find plenty of amusement here; all is so new to me. To-day, after all correspondence was terminated, father began to talk to me. He warned me as to my future life—that is, if I decided to remain in America—never, above all things, to forget my birth and the duties that birth brings—never to do anything to dishonour a name which for centuries had never borne a stain—always to remember that true nobility was simplicity—always to be civil, particularly to those who were not my equal—to guard against the horde of adventurers who were certain to swarm to America—that the country was so vast that the hidden wealth in minerals, &c. &c., must be enormous—adventurers would come with the lust of gold—men without scruples or conscience or education—that there would be terrible corruption—never to mix myself with any man who did not carry on his business or speculations in an honest manner—far better to die poor and honoured than to sully my name—that the country would suffer for years from corruption—immense fortunes would be made and lost and men of evil repute would, on account of the power of their money, keep corruption and dishonesty afloat. . . .

AUGUST 9

I never saw people drink as the Russians do—a long *buffet* covered with bottles and glasses and caviare. They drink seven or eight glasses of *vodka* (fire water) before going into dinner. I have never touched spirits of any kind. After dinner the young men are all drunk and disgusting. . . .

AUGUST 11

Yesterday the Emperor's answer was communicated to father and the other envoys. He authorizes Romanzoff to renew offer of mediation to England, but to send it direct to London. . . .

AUGUST 24

Count Romanzoff summoned the envoys and read to them the dispatches renewing the offer. Father suggested two or three alterations and they were made. I seem to be writing all day—my head is in a whirl, but I suppose it is a good training for me.

SEPTEMBER 2

Father has written a long letter to-day to General Moreau.* We do our best to amuse ourselves here but it is very

* Jean Victor Moreau, born at Morlaix, Brittany, 1763, killed in battle under the walls of Dresden. He was one of the most illustrious Generals during the Revolution. Arrested by the Order of Bonaparte,

6

weary work, the uncertainty is so great.   Under all this strain father is always calm and shows no signs of anxiety. . . .

SEPTEMBER 12
To-day Count Romanzoff officially recognized father as envoy from America. . . .

GENERAL MOREAU *to* ALBERT GALLATIN *

August 21, 1813

MON CHER MONSIEUR GALLATIN,

Me voilà de nouveau à l'armée, prêt à combattre Bonaparte et le faisant, je vous l'assure, sans la moindre repugnance, bien convaincu que si dans ma petite capacité je puis contribuer à sa chute, je recevrai aussi ma part de remerciements de la France et du monde entier: peu importe la bannière quand on réussit. Si Robespierre avait été tué par les Royalistes, les Republicains les en auraient remercié 24 heures après.

J'ai appris avec bien du chagrin que votre mission n'aurait pas le résultat que nous étions tous promis, malgré la puissante médiation de S.M. Impériale. Les Anglais ne veulent pas traiter de leurs droits maritimes sous aucune médiation. Voilà ce que me dit un de leurs ministres en Allemagne.

Quoique je n'ai pas l'honneur d'être Américain je m'intéresse bien sincèrement au sort d'un pays où j'ai

tried for high treason, found guilty and sentenced to exile. He went to the United States of America in 1804 and remained there until 1813. He joined the army of the Emperor Alexander, and fought against Napoleon.

    * *Translation of Letter of General Moreau to Albert Gallatin*

MY DEAR MR. GALLATIN,
    Here I am back with the army, ready to fight Napoleon, and that, believe me, without the smallest compunction. For I am convinced that if the little I can do in my position contributes to his downfall, I also shall get my share of thanks from France and the whole world. Succeed and it matters little under what flag one fights.

resté si longtemps et où j'ai reçu tant de marques d'amitié.
Je ne suis pas aveugle sur la position actuelle de ce pays,
mais j'aurai toujours de la partialité pour lui. Je
m'intéresserai toujours à son bonheur et à son succès.

Le refus du gouvernement anglais doit vous mettre
dans une situation très-désagréable.

Je vois d'ici les Féderalistes exagérés rire des maux
de leur pays par l'espoir de voir le triomphe de leur
parti, et les exagérés du parti contraire en profiter contre
vous et le Président; car il ne faut pas vous en flatter,
quelque mécontentement que le refus des Anglais de
traiter en Russie puisse occasionner la guerre ne sera pas
nationale; il y'a trop d'égoisme; trop de richesse dans
toutes les classes, et pas assez d'argent dans les caisses
de l'état, pour qu'on puisse espérer un mouvement assez
vigoureux de la nation qui la mette dans une attitude
imposante.

Les Anglais veulent, dit-on, traiter de la paix sans
médiation. Je le crois, mais il est à craindre que la

If it had been the Royalists who slew Robespierre, the Republicans
would have thanked them twenty-four hours after.

I was indeed sorry to hear that in spite of the powerful intervention
of his Imperial Majesty your mission would not meet with the success
that we anticipated. As one of the English ministers in Germany said
to me, "The English will not admit of any mediation when their
rights at sea are under discussion."

I have not the honour to be an American, but I am deeply interested in the fate of a country where I have stayed so long and where
I have received so many marks of kindness. I am far from being
blind to the present position of your country, but I shall always have
an interest in her welfare and success.

The refusal of the English Government must place you in a very
disagreeable position. I can imagine the extreme Federals laughing
at disasters to their country in the hope of a party triumph; while
I can see the Extremists on the other side making capital out of them
to discredit you and the President. There is no use in deceiving
yourself; America may be irritated by the English refusal to treat
under the mediation of Russia, but the war will never be a national
war. There is too much selfishness in every class, too much private
money at stake, and too little in the public Exchequer to permit of

vanité américaine n'accède pas sur-le-champ à cette
façon de faire, et que les malheurs de cette guerre con-
tinuent encore quelque temps.   S'il n'y a pas de commotion intérieure, ce ne sera qu'une perte d'argent, et
la durée de la guerre aura pour les Anglais un grand
désavantage, celui de vous apprendre de vous passer d'eux.
Le pire sera l'avantage que vos enemis particuliers
et ceux du Président en tireront pour vous nuire, vous
accuser de précipitation dans l'envoi de ministres avant
de vous être assurés de l'accession de l'Angleterre.   Il
est beau de commettre de pareilles erreurs.   L'empresse-
ment de faire cesser les maux de la guerre peut éprouver
la censure de la politique, mais certes il méritera, à celui
qui la montre, l'approbation des amis de l'humanité.

Je désirais bien recevoir de vos nouvelles avant votre

any hopes of a national movement strong enough to give to the country
a commanding attitude.

"But England they say wants peace without mediation." I think
so too, but it is to be feared that American pride may prevent an
immediate acceptance of the English proviso, and that the miseries of
this war may continue for some time longer. If the feeling of the
country is not aroused it will be but a waste of money, while England
will also be a loser, for the length of the war will teach you to do
without her.

Worst of all will be the advantage that your own and the President's
personal enemies will gain of damaging you, of accusing you of hasty
action in despatching the mission before you had made certain of the
willingness of England to treat. It is fine to make such mistakes.
Though politicians may blame an eager determination to put an end
to this disastrous war, the determination deserves, as all who support
it deserve, the cordial approval of every friend of humanity.

I would be glad to have some of your news before your return to
America. His Imperial Majesty loads me with proofs of his friendship.
He is kindness itself, and the most honest man of my acquaintance.
He is keenly interested in America, and I am sure that you may
always count on his readiness to use all his influence to bring about
peace. If I can be of any assistance either to yourself personally or
to your mission, pray make use of me, and in the meantime believe
me with kind regards,

Your most humble and obedient servant.   MOREAU.

9

retour en Amérique. S.M. Impériale, l'homme le plus humain et le plus honnête que je connaisse, me comble d'amitié. Il s'intéresse aux Américains et sera toujours prêt, j'en suis sur, à user de toute son influence pour leur procurer la paix. Si je pouvais vous être bon à quelque chose ou pour votre mission ou pour vous-même veuillez disposer de moi et croire aux sentiments de la considération la plus distinguée avec laquelle je suis votre très-humble et très-obéissant serviteur.

MOREAU,
Au Quartier-Général Impérial, Hrushova, 21 Août, 1813.

SEPTEMBER 15: WEDNESDAY

No answer from England. Father greatly distressed at the death of General Moreau.

SEPTEMBER 20

Nothing doing rê mediation; we have to wait patiently for answer. Father thinks nothing can be done in Russia and is anxious to go to England.

SEPTEMBER 25

We amuse ourselves as best we can. It is not the season here. St. Petersburg deserted, hot with wind and dust. I go to the theatre and occasionally dine out. . . .

OCTOBER 19

A thunderclap to-day. Letters from Washington; one announcing officially that the Senate had rejected father's nomination as head of the Commission by one vote. . . .

THE SECRETARY OF STATE *to the* **AMERICAN COMMISSIONERS**

DEPARTMENT OF STATE,
August 5, 1813

GENTLEMEN,

I am very sorry to be under the necessity of communicating to you an event of which there was no anticipation when you left the United States.

The event to which I allude is the rejection by the Senate of the nomination of Mr. Gallatin on the idea that his mission to Russia was incompatible with the office of Secretary of the Treasury.

After the appointment of Mr. Jay, when Chief Justice of the United States, by President Washington, and of Mr. Ellsworth, when holding the same office, by President Adams, by which a member of a separate branch of the Government was brought into an office under the Executive, and after the sanction given in practice as well as by law to the appointment of persons during the absence of a head of a department to perform its duties, it was presumed that there would not be any serious or substantial objection to the employment in a similar service of a member of the Administration itself.

Although this nomination was opposed in the Senate as soon as it was acted on, yet it was not believed that it would be rejected until the vote was taken. At an early stage the President was called on by a resolution of the Senate to state whether Mr. Gallatin retained the office of Secretary of the Treasury, and, in case he did, who performed the duties of that department in his absence. The President replied that the office of Secretary was not vacated by Mr. Gallatin's appointment to Russia, and that the Secretary of the Navy performed its duties in his, Mr. Gallatin's, absence. After this reply, which was given in conformity with the President's own views of the subject, and with those of Mr. Gallatin when he left the United States, it was impossible for the President, without departing from his ideas of propriety in both respects, to have removed Mr. Gallatin from the Treasury to secure the confirmation of his nomination to Russia. It would have been still more improper to have taken that step after the rejection of the nomination. The President resolved, therefore, to leave the mission on the footing on which it was placed by the vote of the Senate by which the nomination of Mr. Adams

11

and Mr. Bayard was confirmed. Whatever has been done jointly under the Commission, given to the three Commissioners by the President when you left the United States, in compliance with your instructions will not be affected by this event.

OCTOBER 22

Father had an interview with Count Romanzoff to-day. The latter begs him to remain in St. Petersburg but he thinks he ought, perhaps, to return at once to the Treasury. He feels now that he can act as he chooses as he is free. His political enemies are gaining power. He is strongly impressed with the idea that he ought to resume the negotiations. . . .

OCTOBER 24

After a stormy interview with Mr. Adams (Adams was the storm) father has decided to take his own course. He is sending Mr. Dallas to London to see Lord Castlereagh, Count Lieven* and Mr. Baring, with the object of being in direct communication with them. . . .

OCTOBER 26

Father thinks of going himself to England or to go direct to the Emperor's headquarters. Count Romanzoff spoke to father a few days since about a Count Joseph Galati, a major-general in the Russian army. He wanted an introduction. He is going to call to-morrow, as he is only passing through St. Petersburg on his way to join the Emperor. . . .

OCTOBER 27

Count Galati called this afternoon. He says he is a branch of our family; that his family were from Savigliano in the Piedmont; that his father was intimate with Count Paul Michael de Gallatin, Councillor of State of

---

* Count Lieven, afterwards Prince Lieven, Russian Ambassador at the Court of St. James.

the Republic of Geneva, who acknowledged relationship. He was very charming, and father does not doubt the relationship. Count Paul Michael was the head of our family and my father was his ward. Count Galati is a great person in Russia. He was in full uniform, covered with orders and stars. He kindly explained them to me. He has the following orders: the Military Orders of St. George and St. Vladimir of Russia, St. Maurice and St. Lazare of Sardinia, and the Sovereign Order of St. Jean of Jerusalem. He so deeply regrets he is leaving to morrow as he wishes us to go to his country house. . . .

OCTOBER 28
Lord Walpole has arrived. Father is greatly annoyed at his openly talking of Count Romanzoff's "intrigues."

OCTOBER 30
Count Romanzoff has just sent father a note informing him that he intended retiring from office but that he will remain Chancellor until he has closed the affairs of the mission.

DECEMBER 1
It seems all the trouble has been made by the Emperor forgetting to communicate a most important note to Count R., which put him in a false position. So after all Lord Castlereagh was not to blame. . . . . .

JANUARY 12, 1814
Father has decided to leave St. Petersburg as there is not a word from the Emperor. . . .

JANUARY 26
We leave to-day. Mr. Bayard accompanies us.

MARCH 5: AMSTERDAM
After a terrible, cold, and weary journey we arrived here last night. . . .

MARCH 6

We learnt with great pleasure to-day that Lord Castle-reagh's offer of direct negotiations has been met by the President by the appointment of a new Commission. Father's name was omitted. It seems the President thinks he is on his way back to take up the Treasury. . . .

MARCH 20

The President has discovered the mistake and appointed Father as one of the Commission. . . .

MARCH 22

Father received to-day the necessary permission from Mr. Baring to visit England. We are leaving imme-diately. . . .

APRIL 9: LONDON

Arrived here to-day.

APRIL 11

Father wants to change the place for the negotiations. He thinks London would be far better. He would then be in direct touch with Lord Castlereagh. We are now comfortably settled in apartments in Seymour Street. I find London very dull in comparison to Paris and St. Petersburg. Our position is not a very pleasant one; we have many invitations, and I think all mean to be civil and kind, but there is always a feeling of constraint. . . . The only house where we seem to be really welcome is Mr. Baring's.

APRIL 13

Father sees a great deal of his old friend Monsieur Dumont.* He brought Jeremy Bentham† to introduce him to-day. We dine with Monsieur D. to-morrow. . . .

* André Dumont, politician, born 1764, died 1836. Banished by Louis XVIII in 1816 under the law against regicides.

† Jeremy Bentham, born 1748, died 1832, a political and philo-sophical writer.

14

APRIL 14

. . . Dined with Lord Bathurst, stiff and formal. . . .

APRIL 15

Oh! the horrors of Sunday in London. It is indeed a day of rest.

Englishwomen are not pretty; they are either coarse or very delicate. Complexions fine but too red. Dress so very badly—no taste. . . .

APRIL 17

I have been nearly every day to the British Museum. Father wanted many works consulted and notes taken. . . .

I looked up Barthélemy de Gallatin.* He was Colonel of the Mounted Grenadiers. He died in 1786 and is buried at Brompton near his country house. I found his name, &c. &c., in an old Army list. He left two daughters. . . .

APRIL 18

I have seen the Prince Regent walking in the Mall. He is handsome. The Queen I have seen several times. She keeps great state. . . .

The following letters of Albert Gallatin to W. H. Crawford and General Lafayette are of interest in connection with the negotiations as showing the diplomatic difficulties with which the mission had to contend.

ALBERT GALLATIN *to* W. H. CRAWFORD†

LONDON, *April* 21, 1814

MY DEAR SIR,

Mr. Bayard and myself left St. Petersburg on January 25, remained four weeks at Amsterdam, and arrived here on the 9th inst. I could not write to you sooner, there having been no communication with Paris

* Barthélemy de Gallatin, Lieut.-Colonel Second Troop of Horse Grenadier Guards, 7th April, 1759. (From the military register for the year 1770.)

† William H. Crawford, Secretary of War in the United States.

from Holland, and Mr. Poletica, who is the bearer of this, having offered the first safe opportunity for a confidential letter.

Messrs. Clay and Russell, who are jointly with Messrs. Adams and Bayard appointed to open a direct negotiation for peace with Great Britain, arrived at Gottenburg on the 12th inst., after a passage of forty-six days; but as they had not reached the town when the last packet sailed, we have not yet received any letter from them, or any American news brought by the vessel in which they came.

There is a newspaper report of Norfolk, under date of February 12, stating that G. W. Campbell was made Secretary of the Treasury, Rush Attorney-General, and that I had been nominated fifth Commissioner to treat of peace with England. My stay in Europe will, of course, depend on the official account which Messrs. Clay and Russell will have brought. You are sufficiently aware of the critical situation in which the restoration of a general European peace has placed our affairs. The numerous English forces in France, Italy, Holland, and Portugal ready for immediate service, and for which there is no further employment in Europe, afford to this Government the means of sending both to Canada and to the United States a very formidable army, which we are not prepared to meet with any regular, well-organized force; and they will also turn against us as much of their superabundant Naval forces as they may think adequate to any object they may have in view. In the prosecution of the war the Ministry would be supported by the general voice of the nation. In the intoxication of an unexpected success, which they ascribe to themselves, the English people eagerly wish that their pride may be fully gratified by what they call the "punishment of America." They do not even suspect that we had any just cause of war, and ascribe it solely to a premeditated concert with Bonaparte at a time when we thought him triumphant and their cause desperate. That such opinions should be almost universally entertained here by the great body of the people is not at all astonishing. To produce such an effect, and thereby render the American war popular, the Ministerial powers have had nothing more to do than to transcribe American Federal speeches and newspapers. If Pickering, Quincy, Strong, Hanson, &c., have not brought a majority of the American people to their side, they have at least fully succeeded here, and had no difficulty in convincing all that part of the English community which derives its information from political journals that we had no cause of complaint, and acted only as allies of Bonaparte. I understand that the members of the Cabinet do not participate in that opinion, but it will certainly require an effort on their part against popular feeling to make peace with America. It must be added that even there (in the Cabinet) a belief is said to be entertained that a continuance of the war would produce a separation of the Union, and perhaps a return of the New England States to the Mother Country. The multitude of persons in the Army or Navy, or connected with the war, attached to the governing party, and whom peace will throw out of employment, will also press on Government; and although it is probable that the immense military and naval establishments of this country will be so far reduced as to enable Government to dispense with the most unpopular war taxes, a prosecution of the war against the United States would afford a convenient pretence for preserving a much more considerable standing force than is necessary and would otherwise be allowed by Parliament. It may, on the whole, be reasonably inferred that the Ministers will be neither disposed to make the least concession—for doing us justice on any point would receive that name—in order to obtain peace, nor at all displeased in case of failure of the negotiations.

The only external check to those dispositions can be

found in the friendly interposition of the Emperor
Alexander, not as a mediator but as a common friend,
pressing on this Government the propriety of an accommodation, and expressing his strong wishes for a general
restoration of peace to the civilized world. I do not
know whether your situation affords you means of
approaching him, and can only state my opinion of the
great importance that an early opportunity should be
taken by you, or any other person you may think fitted
for the object, to call his attention to the situation in
which we are left, and to the great weight which his
opinion in favour of peace on liberal conditions, strongly
expressed to this Government, must necessarily have at
this time. Of his friendly disposition for the United
States there is no doubt; but we may be forgotten;
and it is necessary that he should be apprised of the
hostile spirit which prevails here, and which, if not
balanced by some other cause, may even carry Ministers
beyond their own wishes and views. It should also
be stated that our Government, having accepted one
year ago the Emperor's mediation, and not having supposed that, considering the political connection between
him and Great Britain, she could reject that offer, no
other provision was made on our part to obtain peace
until our Government was apprised in January last of
the rejection of the mediation by England. Thus was a
delay of a year produced, and the opening of our negotiations unfortunately prevented till after England is at
peace with the rest of the world; a circumstance which,
although it does not give us a positive right to claim
the Emperor's interference, affords sufficient ground to
present the subject to his consideration. I entreat you
to lose no time in taking such steps as may be in your
power in that respect, and to write to me whatever you
may think important for the success of the mission
should be known to us. The only modes of safe conveyance which I would recommend would be private American

opportunities, or through the channel of the Russian Secretary of State, or of Mr. Poletica, directing to me under cover of "Count Lieven, Ambassador Extraordinary of H.I.M. the Emperor of all the Russias, London."

I send General la Fayette's patents, which were erroneously put in my hands instead of yours, and which I have had no previous safe opportunity to transmit. My last letters from my family were dated January 23, when they were all well; but I have none of a late date from Government or from any of its members.

I am, my dear sir, with great respect and sincere attachment, truly yours.

ALBERT GALLATIN.

ALBERT GALLATIN *to* GENERAL LAFAYETTE

LONDON, *April 21*, 1814

DEAR SIR,

I regret that your patents should be put in my hands instead of being entrusted to Mr. Crawford, as no safe opportunity has as yet offered itself for their conveyance.

I had the pleasure of seeing very often your friend Tracy at St. Petersburg, and left him there in good health on January 25.

I believe that I am not mistaken in offering you my congratulations on the late events in France. It would certainly have been desirable that the changes should have been produced by the spontaneous will of the French people rather than to appear to have been forced by a foreign army. But if such was to be the mode, you are most singularly fortunate that the Emperor Alexander should have been the agent. With respect to the result itself, I think that every friend of rational liberty and of humanity must rejoice at the overthrow of the detestable tyranny under which you and a great part of Europe groaned, and in the hope that you have at last laid the foundations of institutions probably as free and liberal as you are susceptible of. My attachment to the form

of government under which I was born and have ever
lived never made me desirous that it should, by way of
experiment, be applied to countries which might be better
fitted for a limited monarchy. And if this be that which
suits you best, I think the ancient dynasty in every
respect preferable to a new one. Unfortunately, whilst
the greater part of the civilized world rejoices at the
restoration of a general peace, the United States alone
remain at war, and are placed in a more critical situation
than ever they were since the first years of their revolution. Pride, avarice, and ambition will throw here great
obstacles to an accommodation for which there has ever
been, on our part, the most sincere disposition. I write
to you well knowing your unalterable attachment for
America, and that, if in your power, you will lend your
assistance in promoting that result.

ALBERT GALLATIN.

Diary resumed:

APRIL 23

Father very busy. He has been in close conference with
Lords Castlereagh, Liverpool, and Bathurst. There is
much to be discussed. . . .

APRIL 26

Still waiting to hear when the English Commission think
of starting for Ghent. Father would have much preferred
carrying out the negotiation in London, but our other
Commissioners refused point-blank; they were either
afraid or too proud to come to England. Of course they
look upon father as a foreigner. This has annoyed him
very much. He will, I fear, have a very tough time of it
in keeping his colleagues in unison, although, by the
accident of his being appointed last on the Commission,
he is practically the head of it. This position all the
Commissioners acknowledge with the exception of Mr.
Adams, who is a firebrand. . . .

Father is annoyed at the attitude taken by Messrs. Adams and Clay.* They both have written to him in the same strain refusing to consent to the delegates sitting in London. The reason they both give is that they are plain Americans and that in England they would only be snubbed and treated as colonists, adding: "You are a foreigner, which places you on an entirely different footing."

MAY 2

We dined with Lord Liverpool on Saturday. Nothing new.

MAY 12

I have just written a letter to Mr. Monroe† at father's dictation. He fears that England is determined to isolate the United States and cut her off from the Baltic Powers. This has made him more keen than ever. We remain here until we hear from the Commissioners at Gottenburg, but are ready to leave the moment he hears the English Commissioners are on their way to Ghent.

MAY 22

Father is doing his utmost to obtain the mediation of the Emperor Alexander. The latter he hears is coming to England. He is using all the influence in his power to have a personal interview. . . .

Letter from Gen. Lafayette to Mr. Crawford, giving an account of an interview with the Emperor Alexander and showing the latter's inclination to promote peace.

May 26, 1814

MY DEAR SIR,

I passed the last evening in company with the Emperor Alexander, who, however prepossessed in his favour I may have been, has surpassed my expectations.

* Henry Clay, Orator and Statesman, born in Virginia, U.S.A., 1777, died 1852. Speaker in 1808 in United States Senate.

† James Monroe, Secretary of State, November, 1811, to February, 1815. President of the United States, 1817–1825.

He really is a great, good, sensible, noble-minded man, and a sincere friend to the cause of liberty. We have long conversed upon American affairs. It began with his telling me that he had read with much pleasure and interest what I had sent him. I found ideas had been suggested that had excited a fear that the people of the United States had not properly improved their internal situation. My answer was an observation upon the necessity of parties in a Commonwealth, and the assertion that these were the happiest and freest people upon earth. The transactions with France and England were explained in the way that, although the United States had to complain of both, the British outrages came nearer home, particularly in the affair of impressments. He spoke of the actual preparation and the hostile dispositions of England.

I, of course, insisted on the importance of his mediation, the confidence reposed in him by the United States, who hastened to send Commissioners chosen from both parties, and which he very kindly acknowledged. He said he had twice attempted to bring on a peace. "Do, sir," said I, "make a third attempt; it must succeed; *ne vous arrêtez pas en si beau chemin*. All the objects of a war at an end, the re-establishment of their old limits can be less opposed, as the Americans have gained more than they have lost. A protraction of the war would betray intentions quite perverse and hostile to the cause of humanity. Your personal influence must carry the point. I am sure your Majesty will exert it." "Will," says he, "I promise you I will. My journey to London affords opportunities, and I will do the best I can." I told him I had received a letter from Mr. Gallatin now in London, and we spoke of him, Mr. Adams, Mr. Bayard, and the two new Commissioners. I had also other occasions to speak of America—one afforded me by the Swedish Marshal Stadinck, who mentioned my first going over to that country; another by a well-intentioned observation of Madame de Staël that she had received a letter from my friend Mr. Jefferson, of whom she spoke with great regard. This led to observations relative to the United States and the spirit of monopoly in England, extending even to liberty itself. The Emperor said, they had been more liberal in Sicily than I supposed them. I did not deny it, but expressed my fears of their protecting Ferdinand against the Cortes. His sentiments on the Spanish affairs were noble and patriotic. The slave-trade became a topic upon which he spoke with philanthropic warmth. Its abolition will be an article in the general peace. You see, my dear sir, I had fully the opportunity we were wishing for. If it has not been well improved, the fault is mine. But I think some good has been done. And upon the promise so candid and generous I have full dependence. If you think proper to communicate these details to Mr. Gallatin, be pleased to have them copied. He spoke very well of him, and seemed satisfied with the confidence of the United States and the choice of their representatives to him. By his last accounts Mr. Adams was at St. Petersburg.

The particulars of this conversation ought not, of course, to be published; but you will probably think it useful to communicate to the Commissioners. . . .

JUNE 2

The Emperor is expected in London next week. The European Treaty of Peace has been signed. He comes as the guest of England. This will make it more difficult for father, as the position will be a delicate one. Lord Castlereagh arrives to-day or to-morrow. It seems that the exclusion of all Maritime questions or any interference *re* America was one of the conditions of the Chatellon Conference.

JUNE 4

Father anxious—waiting to hear from General Lafayette. I am just going to Eton to see the festivities.

JUNE 6

He received a letter from M. Lafayette this morning, from Paris. It gave him a brief résumé of his interview with the Emperor Alexander at Madame de Staël's. He begs father if possible to remain in England to have a personal interview with the Emperor, which he says the Emperor promised to grant him—but that it must be of a private nature. He also mentions that Baron Humboldt has also approached his Majesty—and adds that the latter "puts himself at your disposal."

JUNE 10

The Emperor arrived to-day. He is lodged at Leicester House, Leicester Fields. This is the palace that the eldest daughter of James I occupied; she was known as the "One-year Queen of Bohemia." Her daughter was the Electress Sophia, mother of George I. . . .

JUNE 14

The Emperor's aide-de-camp called to-day. He said the Emperor had sent him to say that on June 18 he would receive us privately at 11.30. . . .
As it is a delicate matter there has not been any correspondence on the subject. . . .

JUNE 18

As arranged, his Majesty received father this morning. We went accompanied by Mr. Levitt Harris, a secretary to the St. Petersburg Mission. Our minister offered the loan of his coach. This father thought wise to refuse, and hired a common hackney-coach so as to attract as little attention as possible. The streets were crowded. It is the day of the banquet given by the City of London to the allied Sovereigns. Only father and myself were admitted to his Majesty's presence. There were crowds waiting for audiences. We were passed in at once.

Father was presented and then presented me; then all withdrew except his Majesty. He is a splendid-looking man, was in full uniform and covered with jewelled orders and stars. He was most gracious, and said he had the most friendly feeling toward the United States. He added that he feared his intervention would be of little use—that he had made three attempts since he had been here, but that "England will not admit a third party to interfere in her disputes with you." This he said on account of our former Colonial relations, which are not forgotten. He also expressed an opinion with regard to the conditions of peace, saying: "The difficulty will be with England." He also spoke of Madame de Staël as a woman of "great brain and courage." He congratulated father on being her cousin. Father expressed his deep gratitude to his Majesty for granting him an audience, and the gratitude of the United States for the interest and friendship he had shown. As we withdrew he patted me on the head and said, "You are rather young to be in diplomacy."

I wore a suit of Chinese nankeen, white silk stockings, high white choker, with a breast-pin of seed-pearls mother gave me before I left home. They call my hair auburn— I call it red. I am afraid I looked very young.

Poor Mr. Levitt Harris was furious at not being present, but the Emperor's order was "*Monsieur Gallatin et son fils.*"

JUNE 19: LONDON, SUNDAY

Copied note which the Emperor gave father permission to send. The latter does not think it will have any effect. The illuminations last night were very fine—far surpassing anything I have ever seen. Although father is an "Envoy Extraordinary" here, his position is of such a delicate nature that it is impossible for him to accept any public invitations.

JUNE 20

Lord Castlereagh informed father that the English Mission will start on July 1 for Ghent. . . .

JUNE 21

We leave to-morrow for Ghent by way of Paris, where we will remain for a week if possible. . . .

JUNE 26: PARIS, SUNDAY

We arrived at five o'clock to-day.

JUNE 27

Father had a long visit from General de Lafayette, accompanied by Baron Humboldt.* They were both much pleased that he had had an interview with the Emperor Alexander, but both agree with him that they fear now Russian mediation will be of little use. . . .

JUNE 29

I saw the King to-day driving in state . . . went to the *Français* in the evening—Racine's *Phèdre* very fine. The King and other members of the Royal Family were present.

JUNE 30

I went to Versailles to-day. What memories it awakens, particularly the Petit Trianon! I do not think there is a palace in the world to equal Versailles. I shut my eyes and conjured up Louis XIV and his Court with all its splendours. I was accompanied by a son of the Duc de la Rochefoucauld D'Enville. He is most interesting, and told me many quaint episodes of history. One which impressed and amused me was that when the Electress Sophia, "mother of George I," came on one occasion to visit her sister, the Duchesse d'Orléans, on taking leave of the Queen, etiquette required that she should only raise the skirt of the Queen's robe and kiss it, being only

* Baron Humboldt, born 1767, died 1835. Statesman and Author.

an electress. The Queen, to avoid her doing this, stepped behind a chair, and the electress kissed the chair.

JULY 1

We leave to-morrow for Ghent by easy stages as father is not feeling very well. . . .

JULY 7: GHENT, THURSDAY

We arrived here to-day and are lodged very comfortably in the Hotel d'Alcantara, corner of the Rue des Champs. Ghent looks clean and cheerful. The inhabitants speak only Flemish. All seem employed in commerce. There is an English garrison here; the uniforms make the streets very bright.

They call private residences *hôtels* in this country. The house is large and all the delegates are to lodge here.

JULY 9

No news of the English Mission.

JULY 15

Nothing to do. Mr. Adams in a very bad temper. Mr. Clay annoys him. Father pours oil on the troubled waters. I am now reading a history of the Low Countries. . . . The women are so ugly here. . . .

We had waffles for breakfast—it reminded me of home. It seems they are an old Dutch dish. . . .

AUGUST 7

At last! The British Mission arrived this afternoon. We heard they were coming and I actually saw them arrive. They are lodged in a fine Carthusian monastery. . . .

AUGUST 8

To-day was the first meeting. The British Commissioners, as a base of discussion *re* the treaty—demanded that the Indian tribes should have the whole of the North-Western Territory.

This comprises the States of Michigan, Wisconsin, and Illinois—four-fifths of Indiana and the third of Ohio. That an Indian sovereignty should be constituted under the guarantee of Great Britain: this is to protect Canada. Father mildly suggested that there were more than a hundred thousand American citizens settled in these States and territories. The answer was: "They must look after themselves." Father is not impressed with the British delegates. They are Lord Gambier, Henry Goulburn,* and William Adams—men who have not made any mark and have no influence or weight. He attaches but little importance to them as they are but the puppets of Lords Castlereagh and Liverpool. Father feels he is quite capable of dealing with them. . . .

AUGUST 9

The other demands are of little importance. They consist of Sackett's Harbour and Fort Niagara, so as to have control of the lakes. But all this means the dismemberment of the United States. . . .
Father drafted the rejection of the British "Sine qua non."

AUGUST 10

Father finds greater difficulty with his own colleagues. The accident which placed him at the foot of the Commission placed Mr. Adams at the head of it. Messrs. Clay, Bayard, and Russell let Mr. Adams plainly know that, though he might be the nominal mouthpiece, Gallatin was their leader. Clay uses strong language to Adams, and Adams returns the compliment. Father looks calmly on with a twinkle in his eye. To-day there was a severe storm, and father said, "Gentlemen, gentlemen, we must remain united or we will fail. . . ."

* Henry Goulburn (1784–1856). Member for Horsham, 1808. Under Secretary for Home Affairs, 1810. Under Secretary for War, 1812. Chancellor of the Exchequer to the Duke of Wellington, 1828. Home Secretary, 1835. He was elected member for Cambridge University in 1831.

AUGUST 11

Mr. Adams insisted upon drafting the first dispatch to-day and submitted to the others for a revision. Mr. Bayard used it simply as a foundation for his own draft; after quarrelling they referred to father. He put it into shape, and after endless discussion all the Commissioners ended by adopting it. After this father drafted all other dispatches. He wishes all dispatches to be without any offence to the feeling of the English delegates.

AUGUST 12

He fears negotiations will soon come to an end and has but little hope; he does not think the British Government wish to make peace or they would have sent more powerful delegates.

AUGUST 20

To-day I copied a private note from him to Mr. Monroe: "We will not remain here long, the position is untenable; I am preparing for departure. Our negotiations may be considered at an end. Great Britain wants war in order to cripple us; she wants aggrandisement at our expense. I do not expect to be longer than three months in Europe."
Still lingering on and nothing arrived at. We are kept in absolute ignorance of the cause of the delay. It is most galling. It seems Mr. Goulburn does everything to obstruct matters. This may be to gain time to receive his orders from Lord Castlereagh. . . .

AUGUST 21

We all dine at the Intendant's to-day, the delegates of both sides.
They always entertain here on Sunday—how different from London! It is the gayest day. The working people have a cheerful holiday; in London they show joy by getting drunk. . . .

AUGUST 22

Mr. Clay sat next to Mr. Goulburn; he told father afterwards that he had decidedly made Goulburn understand that we intended to await further instructions from America. Mr. Bayard also had a long conversation after dinner with Mr. Goulburn, but he said he made no impression. . . .

AUGUST 23

Lord Castlereagh arrived here to-day on his way to Vienna.

AUGUST 24

He had a long conference with his delegates, after which he saw father, and was most gracious. I was present. He said he had written to Lord Liverpool. . . .

AUGUST 26

Father much fears that Mr. Adams will do harm. . . .

SEPTEMBER 3

Father is much annoyed with Mr. Goulburn. He saw him to-day. The latter said: "I don't think you have the slightest intention of making peace." Father answered: "Surely you cannot mean this! Why should I have taken the long journey to Russia in 1813 and given up everything else in the one hope of making peace?"

SEPTEMBER 4

We have given notice to our landlord and intend leaving on October 1. Father is quite convinced that Mr. Goulburn has made some serious mistakes and that he has been reprimanded.

SEPTEMBER 5

A note from Lord Bathurst: the pith of it is that it would be more becoming on the part of the United States to agree to surrender the Lakes to England and the North-West Territory to the Indians. . . .

SEPTEMBER 9

Mr. Adams drafted a long reply to it, which he submitted to father, who did not approve of it as it would only add fuel to the fire. He wrote his own reply, and for a wonder Mr. Adams approved of it. . . .

SEPTEMBER 15

There is a continual passing of notes and we still are no nearer a solution. Father is getting rather despondent, but only shows this to me, keeping a cheerful and hopeful demeanour before the others. The Indian Territory question is a great difficulty. Father says if the Indians were included in the peace—and to be in the same position as they were—our Government would break off negotiations. He was of opinion that it would be folly to break up negotiations on that account.
England could not now retreat from the position she had taken up with regard to the Indian Territory with dignity. . . .

SEPTEMBER 20

Father has drafted a reply to the British note. It is to this end, that they were willing to recognize the Indians as an independent nation; they refused to allow them to be included in the treaty in any manner, although they would be allowed their old rights and privileges. . . .

SEPTEMBER 26

The note was signed to-day and sent to Washington. Mr. Goulburn came to see father. He was most gracious and informed him he relied on his tact and good sense that he could treat with him; in fact, that he was not the least like an American. I do not know if father was pleased or not. He says the only Americans are the Red Indians. . . .

SEPTEMBER 30

It seems that Lord Liverpool wishes the offer of the Indian amnesty proffered to be accepted. Lord Bathurst is of the same mind. At last a slight ray of hope that there may be a happy termination.

OCTOBER 3

It is now thought advisable to call for a *projet* of a treaty. Mr. Clay has insisted upon drafting the American reply himself. . . .

OCTOBER 22

The British Commissioners sent a note yesterday; the pith of it is that the basis of *uti possidetis* be admitted and that they would treat on that basis alone. . . .

OCTOBER 24

I copied a short note to-day which was sent to the British Commissioners, drafted by father. It was to the effect that they would not treat on the basis of *uti possidetis* but only on the basis of *status quo ante bellum*, with regard to territory, also asking for a British *projet*. . . .

OCTOBER 29

We are all hard at work framing our *projet*. It is a most difficult task, as both Mr. Adams and Mr. Clay object to everything except what they suggest themselves. Father remains calm but firm and does all he can to keep peace. The articles on impressment, blockade, and indemnities are assigned to Mr. Adams; the boundaries and fisheries to father.

OCTOBER 30

Father to-day drew up an article *re* American rights to fish in British waters and British rights to navigate the

Mississippi, which were confirmed by the treaty of 1783. Mr. Clay objected to them. A long and angry discussion ensued. One question was, what were the fisheries worth? The other the value of the navigation of the Mississippi. Father wishes to save the fisheries; Mr. Clay would not assent to anything. . . .

NOVEMBER 3

This drafting still goes on—endless discussions and violent arguments which I can see father thinks futile, but he never loses patience.

NOVEMBER 5

A vote to-day on father's proposed articles. Mr. Clay and Mr. Russell opposed it; father, Mr. Adams, and Mr. Bayard approved.
So the articles were inserted in the *projet*. We are getting a little more into shape. . . .

NOVEMBER 7

Father is doubtful if the questions of the fisheries and the Mississippi were not made permanent by the treaty of 1783.

NOVEMBER 10

The *projet* signed to-day and sent. The fisheries and Mississippi navigation left out.

NOVEMBER 12

We have to wait patiently for an answer, as all has to be submitted to the superiors in London.

NOVEMBER 26

The British *contre-projet* sent to-day; no allusions to the fishery question. A clause claiming free navigation of the Mississippi. . . .

NOVEMBER 28

A dreadful day. Angry disputes on the *contre-projet*. Father wishes the clause *re* the Mississippi accepted. Mr. Clay would not hear of it. Mr. Adams in opposition to Mr. Clay. Nothing arrived at. . . .

NOVEMBER 28

To-day father received a private dispatch from the Duke of Wellington. I have only just seen it. It is marked "Strictly confidential." It is couched in the most friendly terms, assuring father he has brought all his weight to bear to ensure peace. He goes on to say: "As I gather, Mr. Madison as well as Mr. Monroe gave you full power to act, without even consulting your colleagues on points you considered of importance. I now feel that peace is shortly in view. Mr. Goulburn has made grave errors and Lord Castlereagh has read him a sharp lesson."
Father burnt this dispatch and does not even know that I have recorded it. I wanted to copy it, and was doing so when he took it off the table and burned it. . . .

NOVEMBER 29

Father's proposition to accept the Mississippi clause after prolonged discussion was carried with a clause containing the taking, drying, and curing of fish, as secured by the former Treaty of Peace.

DECEMBER 7

An answer refusing to accept this proposition received to-day. More discussion, everlasting bickering, and matters delayed. Father can no longer support Mr. Adams; he has tried his patience too far.

DECEMBER 12

Another private note from the Duke of Wellington assuring father of his support. He says: "Pray do not take offence at what I say. In you I have the greatest confidence. I hear on all sides that your moderation and sense of justice, together with your good common sense, places you above all the other delegates, not excepting ours. The Emperor Alexander has assured me of this. He says we can place absolute reliance in your word. I have always had the greatest admiration for the country of your birth. You are a foreigner with all the traditions of one fighting for the peace and welfare of the country of your adoption."

Father, I think, was pleased. He is a foreigner and is proud of it. . . .

DECEMBER 22

An answer to-day. The fisheries and Mississippi clauses to be withdrawn and to be referred to further negotiations. It would be withdrawn so as not to be mentioned in the treaty.

Father now sees clearly the avowed wish of the English Government to make peace. . . .

DECEMBER 24

The treaty was signed to-day in the refectory of the monastery. Later on there was a solemn service in the cathedral; it was most impressive. We all attended as well as the Intendant, all the officers and the high officials of Ghent.

CHRISTMAS DAY

The British delegates very civilly asked us to dinner. The roast beef and plum pudding was from England, and everybody drank everybody else's health. The band played first "God Save the King," to the toast of the King, and "Yankee Doodle," to the toast of the President. Congratulations on all sides and a general atmosphere of serenity; it was a scene to be remembered.

God grant there may be always peace between the two nations. I never saw father so cheerful; he was in high spirits, and his witty conversation was much appreciated.

DECEMBER 27

We have now to wait for the ratification of the treaty. Indeed, I find it a great rest for me. I have copied all father's letters as well as all the important ones that he has received. Although I am only seventeen years of age, I feel much older. Mr. Adams has shown great kindness to me. At first I did not like him, but now will be sorry when we part.

JANUARY 1, 1815

I have enjoyed the last week very much. Ghent is *en fête*, dancing nearly every night. . . .

JANUARY 8

The ratification of the treaty completed to-day. A great banquet offered by the town of Ghent takes place to-night. Poor father is not looking forward to it. . . .

JANUARY 9

The banquet was very fine, lasting over five hours— speeches, nothing but speeches and toasts. Father said but a few words, but they were carefully chosen and seemed to go to the hearts of all. He spoke in French and ended in a most witty strain.

JANUARY 10

We are leaving now as soon as possible for Geneva. . . .

The following letters are of interest as a tribute to the part played by Albert Gallatin in the conclusion of the Treaty of Ghent.

HOTEL D'ALCANTARA, GHENT

Where the American commissioners lodged during the negotiations ending in the signing of the treaty of peace,
Dec. 24, 1814

MADAME DE STAËL *to* ALBERT GALLATIN *

COPPET, SUISSE, PAYS DE VAUD,
Ce 31 *Juillet*, 1814

VOUS m'avez permis de vous demander si vous avez quelque succès heureux à espérer de votre mission. Mandez-moi à cet égard, my dear Sir, tout ce qu'il vous est permis de me dire. Je suis inquiète d'un mot de Lord Castlereagh sur la durée de la guerre et je ne m'explique pas pourquoi il a dit qu'il était de l'intérêt de l'Angleterre que le Congrès de Vienne s'ouvrît plus tard. C'est vous, Amerique, qui m'intéresse avant tout maintenant, à part de mes affaires pécuniaires. Je vous trouve à présent les opprimés du parti de la liberté et je vois en vous la cause qui m'attachait à l'Angleterre il y a un an. On souhaite beaucoup de vous voir à Genève et vous y trouverez la République telle que vous l'avez laissée, seulement elle est moins liberale car la mode est ainsi maintenant en Suisse. Aussi les vieux aristocrates se relèvent et se remettent à combattre, en oubliant, comme les géants de l'Arioste, qu'ils sont déjà morts.

* MADAME DE STAËL *to* ALBERT GALLATIN

COPPET, SUISSE, PAYS DE VAUD,
July 31, 1814

YOU gave me permission to ask what hopes you have of the success of your mission. Let me know, my dear sir, all that you are permitted to tell me. I am disturbed by a word that Lord Castlereagh let drop about the duration of the war, and I cannot understand why he said that it was to England's interest that the opening of the Congress of Vienna should be postponed.

It is above all in you—America—that I am interested now apart from the question of my finances. I find you at the moment the oppressed champions of liberty, and it is in you that I find the same cause that attached me to England a year ago.

Every one is very anxious to see you at Geneva, and you will find the Republic there the same as you left it; only it is less liberal—for that is the fashion at the moment in Switzerland. The old aristocrats

J'espère que la raison triomphera, et quand on vous connait on trouve cette raison si spirituelle qu'elle semble la plus forte. Soyez pacifique cependant et sacrifiez aux circonstances. Vous devez vous ennuyer à Gand et je voudrais profiter pour causer avec vous de tout le temps que vous y perdez. Avez-vous quelques commissions à faire à Genève et voulez-vous me donner le plaisir de vous y être utile en quelque chose? Mille compliments empressés.

N. DE STAËL-HOLSTEIN.

Vous savez que M. Sismondi vous à loué dans son discours à St. Pierre.

MADAME DE STAËL *to* ALBERT GALLATIN *

PARIS, RUE DE GRENELLE ST. GERMAIN, No. 105
30 *Septembre*, 1814

JE vous ai écrit de Coppet, my dear Sir, et je n'ai point eu de réponse. Je crains que ma lettre ne vous

too are rising, and entering the arena again, forgetting like Ariosto's giants that they are already dead. I hope Reason will triumph, and to one who knows you, she bears a quality so noble and high-minded that her strength appears supreme. Strive for peace, nevertheless, and be guided by circumstances. You must be wearied at Ghent, and I would fain have the opportunity of passing in converse with you all the time that you are losing there. Have you any commissions that you wish executed at Geneva? If so, pray give me the pleasure of doing you some service.

A thousand compliments.

N. DE STAËL-HOLSTEIN.

You have doubtless heard that M. Sismondi sang your praises in his speech at St. Pierre.

* MADAME DE STAËL *to* ALBERT GALLATIN

PARIS, RUE DE GRENELLE ST. GERMAIN, 105,
September 30.

I WROTE to you from Coppet, my dear Sir, and I have not had any answer from you. I fear my letter has never reached you. Will you soit pas parvenue. Soyez assez bon pour me dire ce que vous pouvez me dire sur la vente de mes fonds en Amerique. Je suis si inquiète que l'idée me venait d'envoyer mon fils en Amérique pour tirer ma fortune de là. Songez qu'elle y est presque toute entière, c'est à dire que j'y ai quinze cents mille francs, soit en terres soit en fonds publiques, soit chez les banquiers. Soyez aussi assez bon pour me dire si vous restez à Gand. Mon fils en allant en Angleterre pourrait passer par chez vous donner mes nouvelles de Paris.

Enfin je vous prie de m'accorder quelques lignes sur tout ce qui m'intéresse. Vous pouvez compter sur ma discrétion et sur ma reconnaissance, et je mérite peut-être quelque bienviellance par mes efforts pour vous servir.

Lord Wellington prétend que je ne le vois jamais sans le prêcher sur l'Amerique. Vous savez de quelle haute considération je suis pénétrée pour votre esprit et votre caractère. Mille compliments.

N. DE STAËL-HOLSTEIN.

be good enough to tell me all you can about the sale of my property in America. I am so anxious that I thought of sending my son to America to withdraw my fortune from that country. Remember that nearly the whole of it is there, that is to say some fifteen hundred thousand francs, in land and public funds or at my bankers.

Be good enough also to tell me if you remain at Ghent. My son could go to see you on his way to England and give you my news from Paris. Lastly, I beg of you to send me a few lines on anything that interests me; you can count on my discretion and gratitude—and I deserve perhaps some kindness for the efforts I have made to serve you.

Lord Wellington pretends that I never see him without preaching to him on the subject of America.

I need not tell you how much I admire your wit and your character. A thousand compliments.

N. DE STAËL-HOLSTEIN.

ALBERT GALLATIN *to* MADAME DE STAËL-HOLSTEIN*

GAND, 4 *Octobre*, 1814

CE n'est que hier, my dear Madam, que j'ai reçu
votre lettre du 23 Septembre; celle que vous m'aviez
fait le plaisir de m'écrire de Coppet m'était bien parvenue; mais malgré la parfaite confiance que vous
m'avez inspirée, il était de mon devoir de ne rien laisser
transpirer de nos négociations; et j'espérais tous les
jours pouvoir vous annoncer le lendemain quelque chose
de positive.   Nous sommes toujours dans le même état
d'incertitude, mais il me paraît impossible que cela
puisse durer longtemps, et je vous promets que vous
serez la première instruite du résultat.   Malgré les
fâcheux auspices sous lesquels nous avions commencé à
traiter, je n'avais point perdu l'espérance de pouvoir
réussir.   Il faut cependant convenir que ce qui s'est
passé à la prise de Washington peut faire naître de
nouveaux obstacles à la paix.   Une incursion momen-
tanée et la destruction d'un Arsénal et d'un frégate ne
sont qu'une bagatelle; mais faire sauter ou brûler les
palais du Congrès et du Président, et les bureaux des
différents départements c'est un acte de Vandalisme dont

* LETTER OF ALBERT GALLATIN *to* MADAME
DE STAËL-HOLSTEIN

GHENT, *October* 4, 1814.

IT was only yesterday, my dear Madam, that I received your letter
of September 30.   The one that you were kind enough to write from
Coppet reached me safely.   But in spite of the perfect confidence
with which you inspire me it was my duty not to let anything transpire
of our negotiations, and I had hopes every day that on the morrow
I should have some definite news to give to you.   We are always in
the same state of uncertainty, but it seems to me impossible that this
can continue for long, and I promise you that you shall be the first to
hear of the result.   Despite the unpropitious auspices under which
we began to treat, I have never lost hope that we shall succeed in
the end.   It must however be admitted that what took place at the
capture of Washington may bring forth further obstacles in the way

la guerre de vingt ans en Europe depuis les frontières
de la Russie jusqu'à Paris et de celles du Danemarc
jusqu'à Naples, n'offre aucun exemple, et qui doit néces-
sairement exaspérer les esprits. Est-ce parceque à
l'exception de quelques cathédrales, l'Angleterre n'avait
aucun édifice public qui pût leur être comparé? Ou
serait-ce pour consoler la populace de la cité de Londres
de ce que Paris n'a été ni pillé ni brûlé?

Tout en vous disant cela, je ne me plains point de la
conduite des Anglais, qui, si la guerre continue, loin de
nous nuire n'aura servi qu'à unir et animer la nation.
Sous ce point de vue, la manière dont on nous fait la
guerre doit pleinement rassurer ceux qui avaient des
craintes mal fondées sur la permanence de notre union
et de notre Gouvernement Féderatif. Et il n'y a qu'une
dissolution totale qui puisse renverser nos finances et
nous faire manquer à nos engagements.

Je comprends cependant fort bien que lorsqu'on n'est
pas Americain, l'on désirerait dans ce moment avoir sa
fortune ailleurs que dans ce pays là; je puis avoir des
préjuges trop favorables et ne voudrais aucunement vous
induire en erreur.

Mais il me semble que vendre vos fonds à 15 ou 20

of peace. A sudden raid and the destruction of an Arsenal and a
frigate are a mere trifle, but to blow up and burn the House of Congress
and the President's Palace, and the offices of the various departments,
is an act of vandalism to which the Twenty Years' War in Europe,
a war that extended from the Russian frontier to Paris, and from
Denmark to Naples, cannot offer a parallel, and which must necessarily embitter the temper. Was it because, with the possible exception
of a few cathedrals, England has not a single building that can compare
with them, or was it to console the populace of the city of London for
the fact that Paris was neither sacked nor burnt?

All the same I am not complaining at all of the conduct of the
English, which, far from hurting us, will, if the war continues, only
serve to unite and to animate our country. From this point of view
their manner of conducting the war must amply reassure all who
cherished groundless fears for the permanence of our Union and our
Federal Government. And nothing short of a total rupture can upset
our finances and make us fail in our engagements. Notwithstanding

pour cent de perte en serait un sacrifice inutile. Ils tomberont probablement encore plus si la guerre continue, mais les intérêts seront toujours fidèlement payés et le capital sera au pair six mois après la paix. Nous nous sommes tirés d'une bien plus mauvaise situation. A la fin de la guerre de l'independance nous n'avions ni finances ni Gouvernement; notre population ne s'élevait qu'à environ trois millions et demi, la nation était extrêmement pauvre, la dette publique était presqu'égale à ce qu'elle est actuellement; les fonds perdaient de 80 à 85 pour cent. Nous n'avons cependant pas fait faillite; nous n'avons pas réduit la dette à un tiers par un trait de plume; avec de l'économie et surtout de la probité, nous avons fait face à tout, remis tout au pair, et pendant les dix années qui avaient précédé la guerre actuelle nous avions payé la moitié du capital de notre ancienne dette.

Au milieu de toutes nos factions, n'importe quel parti ait gouverné, le même esprit les a toujours animés à cet égard. Le même esprit regne encore; nous sommes très

I understand that one who is not an American would prefer to have his fortune at the present moment elsewhere than in that country; I may myself be somewhat prejudiced and under no circumstances would I wish to mislead you. But it is my personal opinion that to sell your investments at a loss of 15 to 20 per cent. would be a useless sacrifice. They will probably fall still further if the war continues, but the interest will always be faithfully paid and the capital will be back at par six months after peace is made. We extricated ourselves from a worse position than the present. At the end of the War of Independence we had neither money nor government; our population did not amount to more than three and a half millions, the country was extremely poor, the national debt was nearly as large as it is at present, and the Funds fell 80 to 85 per cent. Nevertheless we did not go bankrupt, we did not by a stroke of the pen reduce our debt to a third. By economy and, above all, by honesty, we met every obligation, restored all to par value, and in the course of the ten years that preceded the present war paid off half of the capital of our original debt.

In the midst of all our party differences, no matter which party was in power, the same spirit as regards finance has always animated our

riches; nous étions huit millions d'ames au commence-
ment de la guerre, et la population augmente de deux cent
cinquante mille ames par an. Si je n'ai pas entièrement
méconnu l'Amerique, ses ressources et la moralité de sa
politique, je ne me trompe pas en croyant ses fonds
publics plus solides que ceux de toutes les puissances
Européennes. Si cependant vous avez peur, attendez
du moins la conclusion de nos négociations; vous n'avez
pas le temps de faire vendre avant cette époque. Je
serai au reste encore quinze jours au moins à Gand et
donnerai avec grand plaisir à M. votre fils tous les ren-
seignements en mon pouvoir s'il passe par ici en allant
en Angleterre. Je suis très sensible à tout ce que vous
avez fait pour être utile à l'Amérique; je sens encore
plus combien je vous dois; vous m'avez reçu et acceuilli
comme si j'eusse été une ancienne connaissance. Avant
de vous connaître je respectais en vous Madame de Staël
et la fille de Madame Necker, aux écrits et à l'exemple de
qui j'ai plus d'obligation que je ne puis exprimer. Mais
je vous avouerai que j'avais grand peur de vous; une
femme très élégante et aimable et le premier génie de
son sexe; l'on tremblerait à moins; vous eutes à peine

country. The same spirit reigns still. We are very wealthy; at the
beginning of the war our population stood at eight million souls and
it increases at the rate of 250,000 souls every year. If I have not
utterly misunderstood America, her resources and her political morality,
then I am right in believing that her public funds are as good a security
as those of any Power in Europe. If you are still afraid, at least
await the conclusion of these negotiations. You have not time to
sell before. I shall be staying at Ghent for another fortnight at least,
and will be happy to give your son all the information in my power,
if he passes by here on his way to England. I am very sensible of all
the help that you have given to America; and am yet more sensible
of what I owe to you personally. You received and welcomed me
as if I was an old acquaintance. Before I knew you I respected in
you, Madame de Staël, the daughter of Madame Necker, to whose
writings and example I am under a deeper obligation than I am able
to express. But I will confess that I was very much afraid of you.
Before a woman so elegant and so amiable, and the greatest genius of
her sex—one could not but tremble. You had hardly opened your lips

ouvert les lèvres que je fus rassuré, et en moins de cinq minutes je me sentis auprès de vous comme avec une amie de vingt ans. Je n'aurais fait que vous admirer, mais votre bonté égale vos talents et c'est pour cela que je vous aime. Agréez-en, je vous prie, l'assurance et soyez sure du plaisir que me procurerait l'occasion de pouvoir vous être bon à quelque chose.

ALBERT GALLATIN.

ALEXANDER VON HUMBOLDT *to* ALBERT GALLATIN

JE n'ai pas été assez heureux pour vous trouver ce matin, mon illustre ami. J'aurais bien désiré cependant vous parler de mon attachement constant et tendre, de mon vif intérêt pour la paix que vous avez eu la gloire de conclure dans des circonstances difficiles. J'aurais voulu vous féliciter sur cette belle et noble défense de la Nouvelle-Orléans qui fera respecter les armées de la Liberté. Comme les flottes qui voguent sous votre pavillon se sont couvertes de gloire depuis longtemps! Que dans ces temps malheureux mes yeux se fixent avec attendrissement sur ces contrées qui seront bientôt le centre de la civilisation humaine! Je ferais d'autres tentatives pour vous trouver et recommander de nouveau Mr. Warden, mon ami et celui de Messrs. Berthollet, Thenard, Gay Lussac, et de tout ce qui aime les sciences. Je ne puis croire qu'un homme aussi instruit, aussi doux, aussi honnête, aussi attaché aux Etats-Unis, à M. Jefferson et aux doctrines vertueuses puisse être rejetté par votre gouvernement. Je supplie Madame Gallatin d'agréer l'hommage de mon respecteux devouement.

before my confidence returned, and after five minutes in your company I felt that I had been your friend for twenty years. My admiration was yours in any case. But finding your kindness is only equalled by your talents, I cannot but love you. Accept, I pray you, my assurance of this, and believe me when I say that it will always be a pleasure to me to serve you in any way within my power.

ALBERT GALLATIN.

Quel contraste entre cette époque et celle où vous me vites à Londres ennuyé des "Magnanimous Souverains et de la croisade des héros!" *

HUMBOLDT.

QUAI MALAQUAIS, No. 3.
Jeudi. .

*ALEXANDER VON HUMBOLDT *to* ALBERT GALLATIN

I HAD not the pleasure of finding you this morning, my noble friend. Nevertheless I would fain have spoken with you of my constant and sincere attachment and of my keen interest in the peace which you have had the honour to conclude under the most difficult circumstances. I would have liked to congratulate you on your fine and courageous defence of New Orleans, which will gain respect for the armies of Liberty. The fleets which sail under your Flag have indeed for long covered themselves with glory. How tenderly in these unhappy times my eyes gaze on the countries so soon to be the centre of the civilization of the world. I would make other attempts to find you and to recommend again to your notice Mr. Warden, my friend and the friend of Messieurs Berthollet, Thenard and Gay Lussac, as indeed he is of every friend of learning. I cannot believe that a man so full of learning, so gentle and so honourable, so firm a friend of the United States, of Mr. Jefferson and his virtuous doctrines, can be rejected by your Government.

I entreat Madame Gallatin to accept the expression of my respectful homage and devotion.

What a contrast this period presents to the time when you saw me in London, weary of the Magnanimous Sovereigns and the Heroes' Crusade.

HUMBOLDT.

3 QUAI MALAQUAIS,
Thursday.

PART II

JANUARY—JULY 1815

JANUARY 20, 1815: GENEVA

We arrived here to-day. Father was very excited, as it
was his first visit to his native land after so many years
absence.

We went direct to the Gallatin House. The entrance is
in the *Cité*, a steep narrow lane paved with small round
cobble-stones. The house faces on the Rue de la Corratrie.
It is very fine, and belongs to Monsieur Naville, who
married the daughter and heiress of Count Paul Michael
de Gallatin, who was the head of the family. Our coat-
of-arms in stone used to be high up over the door, but
during the Revolution some miscreants destroyed it,
leaving only the two lions the supporters.

JANUARY 21

Crowds of visitors all day to welcome father. Madame
de Staël came from Coppet. She is not handsome, but
such a great charm of manner. She was oddly dressed,
seeming to have one or two skirts on top of the other, a
great pelisse of green cloth lined with sable, on her head
a high green *calèche*. She invited both father and myself
to pay her a visit at Coppet. She is not tall, rather fat,
and has coarse features but splendid eyes.

46

JANUARY 22

This morning the Syndics came in a body to greet father and to congratulate him on the successful termination of the Peace with England. Then Monsieur Sismondi* made a *discours* full of laudation of father, much to the latter's annoyance. After they withdrew Benjamin Constant was announced; he rushed up to father, seized him in his arms, and kissed him on both cheeks. There was some excuse for him as he is a relation of ours.

Large dinner of forty at 3 o'clock, nearly all relatives—Navilles, Saladins, Sellons, Sarrasins, Humberts, Diodatis, de Budés, Pictets, Lullins, &c. &c. I was much struck with their great simplicity and dignity of manner; it was all a revelation to me. The ladies were very plainly dressed with hardly any jewels. So odd, they never change your knife and fork after the fish is served, but have little silver rests by each plate for them. The dinner lasted two hours and a half.

After escorting the ladies to the drawing-room—where all the women kissed their hostess, then kissed each other, and we men kissed their hands. All this was done in a most solemn and dignified manner—then our host, knowing father's habit, conducted him with some of the other guests to the library to smoke.

Father smokes regularly eleven strong cigars a day. After about an hour we adjourned to the large gallery. All the ladies were seated stiffly around the room. Only one person talked at a time. It is called a *salon*. It was interesting at first, but after three hours of it I wished myself in Paris. At 9 o'clock supper was announced. . . .

JANUARY 23

All day paying visits; a quiet evening.

JANUARY 24

We go on a tour of visits, starting on the 26th. I am in love with Geneva, it is so beautiful although it is winter;

* J. C. L. Sismondi, born 1773, died 1842, a Genevan and famous historian.

they tell me I must see it in summer. A large supper to-night—other members of our family and relations, together with Monsieur de Lavalette and Monsieur Bonstetten. . . .

JANUARY 25

A very tiring day, paying visits in the morning. From 5 till 7 o'clock one deputation followed the other to greet father. I think he was bored; I know I was. . . .

JANUARY 26

We started at 10 o'clock and arrived at Château de Rozay, near Rolle. My grandmother was a Mlle Rolaz du Rozay. The château is small with turrets, very old and very comfortable. My two du Rozay cousins, who are about my age, are immensely tall and broad in proportion, one being 6 ft. 4 in., the other an inch taller. It seems that they are always hunting chamois in the mountains. I feel like a dwarf next to them. A portrait of my grandmother as a girl, not pretty; but one of her sisters who married a Prussian, Count Doenhoff, is quite lovely; she was Mistress of the Robes to the Queen of Prussia and a famous beauty. . . .

JANUARY 28: CHATEAU DE ROZAY

We leave here to-morrow and go to the Château d'Allaman.

JANUARY 29: ALLAMAN

Allaman, on the Lake Leman, belongs to Count Sellon (his mother was a Gallatin). A beautiful castle, filled with Gobelin tapestry and furniture; one room all pink tapestry. We dined in the chapel—60 ft. long and 30 ft. wide, stone floor. . . .

JANUARY 30

The family are charming—four daughters, all young.

The youngest is named Hortense. The Queen Hortense*
was her godmother. The latter has stopped for weeks at
Allaman. They have an authentic ghost here, not in
the house but in the park; I hope to see it before I
leave. It is in the form of a monk reading a book. He
is to be seen in one of the alleys of the wood approaching;
as you get quite close he vanishes. All the family have
seen it, as well as hundreds of others. Monsieur de Sellon
stations men with bill-hooks at various places to cut down
branches, as he thinks it but an optical illusion. . . .

JANUARY 31

I saw the ghost at 12.30 to-day. It is certainly extraordinary. They fired point-blank at it without any
effect. . . .

FEBRUARY 1

Too tired to write last night. A beautiful day, bright
sunshine. We have been skating all day. Our visit
terminates to-morrow. To-night a large supper in honour
of Joseph Bonaparte,† the ex-King of Spain, the eldest
brother of Napoleon. He lives at Prangins on the lake.
Monsieur de Sellon had a letter to-day from the Queen
Hortense—he read parts of it aloud to us. Evidently
she is in great trouble.

FEBRUARY 2

Joseph Bonaparte is handsome—acts as if he were still
King of Spain. He arrived with a large suite. We were
presented to him by the Count de Sellon before supper.
He had a long conversation with father on the state of
Europe. He is very rich. He spoke with much feeling

---

* Hortense de Beauharnais, daughter of the Empress Joséphine by
her first husband, married Louis Bonaparte January 3, 1802, was
Queen of Holland and mother of Napoleon III.

† Joseph, the eldest brother of Napoleon, born 1768, died 1844, was
King of Naples and King of Spain.

of Napoleon. He married Julie Clary, the daughter of a
Marseilles tallow-chandler; she had some money. Father
does not like the Bonapartes or their entourage—says
Joseph Bonaparte shows his middle-class bringing up
both in speech and movements, that Napoleon is better
where he is. Although father is representing a republic
and believes in republics, he has a strong affection for
the House of Bourbon. We drove with four horses and
postillions to the Château de Veufflans, above Lausanne.
At the bottom of the hill two more horses were added,
sent by Monsieur de Senarclan. The names are so funny.
Veufflans is superb, built by the Reine Berthe in 1000.
It is in bad repair; it would cost over a million francs
to restore it. After we arrived a deputation presented
an address to father from Lausanne in the name of the
Canton de Vaud. . . .

FEBRUARY 3: VEUFFLANS
I went to-day to the Château de Chillon, near Vevey.
It is most interesting; such a wonderful position, built
out into the lake. It belonged to the Duke of Savoy.
Another dinner lasting two hours, some music, which
was a relief, then talk, talk, talk, and the usual trays
passed round, one closely following the other. I was
glad to get to bed. . . .

FEBRUARY 4
We go to-morrow to Sergy, which belongs to Monsieur
Pictet, another relation. . . .

FEBRUARY 5
A beautiful house. Snowing hard all day. A very large
party but of little interest. . . .

FEBRUARY 6
We left here this morning in a most comfortable sleigh
for Coppet; we had three relays of horses, the last sent

by Madame de Staël. This château is charming—a
wonderful view of the lake and mountains, the latter
covered with snow. A great many people stopping here.
We were very tired after our long cold drive. Madame
de Staël most kind and seems so genuinely glad to welcome
us. Mlle Albertine de Staël, her daughter, is very pretty
and graceful; she is betrothed to the Duc de Broglie.
He looks very untidy and dull but very much in love.
Auguste de Staël, her son, looked very serious. Monsieur
Benjamin Constant, Monsieur Sismondi, Duc and
Duchesse de Duras, Duc and Duchesse de Clermont-
Tonnerre (she is a sister of Monsieur de Sellon), and
Monsieur de Bonstetten are among the guests. Not
such a long dinner. Some music; then the Duc de
Broglie and Mlle de Staël, the Duchesse de Duras and
Monsieur de Montmorency, danced a minuet with great
dignity and grace. As I was very tired father asked
permission for me to retire, so I went to bed early.

FEBRUARY 7: COPPET

A delightful day. Up early. Had my *café au lait* when
I met de Broglie. He kindly proposed to go with me
and show me what was to be seen at Coppet. He improves
on acquaintance. *Déjeuner* at 11.30. Madame de Staël's
first appearance; she does all her correspondence and
writing in bed. She was most animated. Questioned
father about the proceedings at Ghent; congratulated
him, adding: "I had a letter from Milord Wellington
this morning. He praises you, saying you had used
great wisdom and tact." She told us some funny stories
about Madame Patterson Bonaparte, the American wife
of King Jerome, whose wit, beauty, and virtue she
extolled. One story was very funny.* She had given

* The page in the Diary on which this story is written had been
ruined by dampness. In 1869 my grandfather, thinking this was the
story, wrote it on a sheet of paper, pasting it over the ruined sheet.
His memory must have been at fault, as the incident must have oc-
curred much later.   EDITOR.

a dinner at her house in Geneva, to which Madame Bonaparte was invited. Arriving very late, she delayed serving the dinner for over half an hour. On one side of her was a Mr. Dundas, a great gourmand, who was much put out at having to wait. After the soup had been served he turned to Madame Bonaparte and asked her if she had read the book of Captain Basil Hall on America. She replied in the affirmative. "Well, madame, did you notice that Hall said all Americans are vulgarians?" "Quite true," calmly answered Madame Bonaparte, "I am not in the least surprised. If the Americans had been the descendants of the Indians or the Esquimaux there might have been some reason to be astonished, but as they are the direct descendants of the English it is perfectly natural that they should be vulgarians." After this Mr. Dundas did not open his mouth again and left at the first opportunity.

This afternoon we went out in Russian sledges, six of them.

The Marquis of Huntly arrived, and we dined at 5 o'clock. A most interesting evening—our hostess most brilliant. She told us many episodes of the Revolution and the part she had taken in it: how she had helped so many of her friends to escape, having armed herself with passports of different nations; how Napoleon had persecuted her. She also spoke most feelingly of her father with tears in her eyes; it seems she adored him.

FEBRUARY 8: COPPET

The Marquis of Huntly* gave father a copy of a letter given to him by Mr. Barry. It is an account of an interview with Napoleon at Elba—most interesting. He first read it aloud. Madame de Staël could hardly contain herself

* Marquis of Huntly, born 1743, died 1827, afterward Duke of Gordon. At the command of Louis XV he opened the ball at Versailles with the Dauphiness, 1770, and in 1826, at the age of eighty-four, danced with Madame de France, daughter of the Duc de Berri.

and continually interrupted, exclaiming, *"Cet animal; on devrait lui tordre le cou."* Lord Huntly says that one of the reasons she hates Bonaparte so heartily is, when she once asked him whom he considered the greatest women in history he replied, "The women who had the most children." Madame de Staël had only two.

COLONEL BARRY'S LETTER *to* THE MARQUIS OF HUNTLY

"Mr. Douglas* dined with Colonel Barry yesterday. He had just come from the Island of Elba, where he had an audience of nearly two hours with Bonaparte. His account of him is as nearly as follows:

On his arrival in the island he went to General Bertrand (who is a sort of chamberlain) to state that he was a member of the English Parliament and to request permission to pay his respects to the Emperor. General Bertrand was ill, but he received a very civil answer from General Drouet in the affirmative. He was accordingly introduced, and was received with great courtesy. Bonaparte asked several questions about his journey, and then, to the surprise of Mr. D., began to talk in the most unreserved manner of the state of affairs in Europe. He said that he lamented that the present Government had not given up the slave trade—that had he remained in power he would have done so, as it was a system of brigandage by which France was not benefited. He had proposed a plan for the settlement of St. Domingue, to give up the centre of the island to the blacks and to establish factories upon the coast. That he had conceived it would be attended with advantage to allow polygamy amongst the blacks, but upon consulting a certain bishop, *'un bon homme, cet Evêque m'a dit: c'est contraire à la réligion Chrétienne.'* He abused the Emperor Alexander with great violence, said he was *'faux et un fat.*

---

* Mr. Douglas was an M.P., and a violent anti-Bonapartist.

Vous ne pouvez pas avoir une idée de la fausseté de cet homme.' We were right, he said, in supposing that there had been secret articles in the treaty of Tilsit. Alexander was bound by them to go to war with England. *'Cela entra dans mon système!'* He said the Bourbons would repent it if they gave up Belgique.

That he would have given up anything else, but that he knew the French people would not allow him to remain on the throne except as a conqueror. France would not bear to be confined to her ancient limits. He compared her to air compressed within too small a compass, the explosion of which was like thunder. *'Malheur aux Bourbons si jamais ils font la paix sans conserver aucune conquête; il y'a dans la France une jeunesse bouillante de* 100,000 *hommes accoutumés au métier de la guerre.'* He was here evidently carried away by his subject and, suddenly recollecting himself, said: *'Mais ce n'est pas mon affaire—je suis mort.'*

In the course of conversation Prince Metternich was mentioned, and Mr. D. said, *'C'est un bon politique.'* Bonaparte answered: *'Non, c'est un homme très aimable et qui parle très bien en compagnie, mais qui ment toujours; on peut mentir une fois, deux fois, trois fois, mais on ne peut pas mentir toujours, ce n'est pas selon ma politique.'* England was, he said, at the height of her power and glory, but that we must remember that when nations were arrived at that point it was said they were near a decline. That the Continental Powers were jealous of our maritime rights and in time of peace would be as much so as they had been of his territorial acquisitions.

He laughed and joked a great deal about the Pope and the tricks he had played to get him in his power, constantly repeating, *'Moi qui suis le meilleur Catholique du monde; il n'y a pas dans le monde un meilleur Catholique que moi,'* and sentiments of this sort. He said he understood the world had expected that he would

have put a pistol to his head, but no, he had been born
a soldier; had found the "Throne de France" vacant,
circumstances had placed him on it, that he had remained
there fourteen years, and had been obliged to descend
from it. Having borne this '*ce serait un lâche qui ne
pourrait pas soutenir l'existence.*' He was sorry, he said,
at the close of the last campaign, when he had advanced
to Ville Juis, he had not pushed on to Paris. He
had 40,000 of his guards with him who would have
shed the last drop of blood for him, and he thinks his
presence would have raised the people to defend the
town—he wanted so much to do so but was dissuaded
by his generals. He complained bitterly of Marmont.
'Could you have believed it that a man to whom I have
actually given bread would have deserted me in that
manner?' he said; that we had not done justice to the
Americans; that there had never been any treaty between
him and Madison, and they had held as high language
to him as they had done to us. Mr. D. had crossed the
Alps by the passage of the Simplon, one of the most
splendid works of Bonaparte's reign; hearing it, he
made many inquiries about the state of the road, and
appeared minutely acquainted with it and interested on
the subject. This is almost all I can recollect, nearly
the whole of what Mr. D. related to us. He says Bonaparte is in excellent health—not too fat, as he had been
told; very dirty and vulgar in his manner of speaking
and extremely poor.

The French Government have not paid him his pension,
and in consequence he has been obliged to reduce his
household one-half. He had 1200 troops in his pay,
mostly veterans who had followed his fortunes from the
Imperial Guards. Mr. D. says his apparent want of
feeling is beyond anything he could have conceived.
He could not learn anything on the subject of the reports
that he was to leave Elba. Some time ago a felucca
landed in one of the most barren parts of the island and

a messenger was dispatched to Bonaparte; he came down unattended by any servant and received a lady, whom he conducted to a country house of his. She remained there two days, at the end of which time he reconducted her in the same manner. They embraced often at parting. The Elbans think it was Marie Louise, but it is generally supposed to have been a Polish lady to whom he was attached.

Mr. Douglas in the course of conversation two or three times mentioned the Empress, whom he had seen in Switzerland, but Bonaparte took no notice of it and appeared anxious to avoid the subject."

NOTE ON ORIGINAL BY ALBERT GALLATIN

Mr. Douglas's conversation with Bonaparte given to me at Geneva in February, 1815, by the Marquis of Huntly, since Duke of Gordon. . . .

A. G.

Diary continued:

FEBRUARY 8

After dinner Albertine de Staël sang some charming chansonettes, accompanying herself on a spinet. All the chairs were put in a circle and Madame de Staël held forth. She read some letters of Louis XVIII when he was in England. She also told us that it was a fact that the Duc de Berri had married in London the daughter of an English clergyman and had children. Then Monsieur Bonstetten gave a little discourse on Voltaire and Byron, followed by Monsieur Sigismonde. Then father gave a most amusing account of his early life in America and of his first meeting with General Washington in a log-cabin. I saw Madame de S. taking notes on her tablets.

FEBRUARY 9: COPPET

This morning Lord Huntly described the splendours of the ball at Versailles for the marriage of the Dauphin Louis XVI; that the King sent for him and commanded him to open the ball with Dauphine "Marie Antoinette."

Porte e=gradus
a gauche.

BAL PARÉ
à Versailles
POUR LE MARIAGE
De Monseigneur Le Dauphin
Le Mercredi 24 Fevrier
1745.

De Bonneval

CARD TO THE BALL GIVEN AT THE MARRIAGE OF THE DAUPHIN, FATHER OF LOUIS XVI

He saw how delighted I was and sent for me to come to his room. He gave me two of the invitation cards;* they are beautifully engraved. One is in colour, and in the top left-hand corner there is, "*Porte et gradins a gauche*"; in the centre of the coloured design is "*Bal paré à Versailles pour le mariage de Monseigneur Le Dauphin, Le Mercredi, 24. Fevrier*, 1745," signed in the right-hand corner "*De Bonneval*." The other one† is beautifully engraved, is larger, and has the same wording. It was most kind of him. A large dinner at 5 o'clock, to be followed by a comedy written by our hostess. She takes a rôle as well as Monsieur de Montmorency. After breakfast Madame de Staël told father she believed greatly in heredity; undoubtedly he had inherited his talent for finance from their common ancestor Jacques Cœur.‡ More people arriving, I made my escape, and had a good afternoon's skating. The banquet is at 5 o'clock. We are leaving to-morrow, much to my regret.

FEBRUARY 10: COPPET

I was too tired last night to write. I can hardly describe last evening's festivities. Our hostess received her guests at the end of the large *salon*—the Duc and Duchesse

---

* The card printed in colour is for the marriage of the father of Louis XVI. Signed de Bonneval, who was "l'intendant des menus plaisirs du Roi."

† The second card mentioned above is for the ball for the marriage in 1770 of the Dauphin, afterward Louis XVI, and is not signed.

‡ Jacques Cœur, celebrated financier of the fifteenth century. Born at Bourges, died at Chio November 25, 1456. He lent immense sums of money to the King Charles VII of France. His reward was to be arrested on a charge of poisoning Agnes Sorel, the King's mistress. He was condemned to a long imprisonment—this gave the King an excuse to seize the remainder of his property and fortune. Escaping after several years of imprisonment he went to Rome and was taken under the protection of the Pope Nicholas V. He made another enormous fortune by opening the trade of the East. Both Madame de Staël and Albert Gallatin were descended from him.

de Clermont-Tonnerre (she was *née* de Sellon), Count and Countess Cavour, Comtesse de Boigne, and a host of others. We dined thirty. At 8 o'clock more arrivals: Prince Demidoff in a superb sleigh with eight horses harnessed in Russian fashion; he brought the Grand Duke of Mecklenburg-Schwerin, Princess Patiomkin, Princess Galitzin, and Madame Bonaparte. The Grand Duke led in Madame Bonaparte. She is quite beautiful still, was wonderfully dressed, and covered in fine jewels. She kissed me on both cheeks, which made me very shy, but she has known me since I was a child.

At 9 o'clock the comedy was played in the long gallery. It was most witty. Madame de Staël was in white and gold draperies, with a turban with eight or ten white feathers. She really looked handsome. She always has a small branch of laurel in her hand. At the end of the performance, with a curtsey she threw it to father—just the thing to annoy him. Madame Bonaparte gave me a brooch of turquoise for my choker. Supper was served at 10.30, and the guests did not leave until after 1.30 A.M. We leave at 2 o'clock for Sacconex (the de Budés). I watched father carefully and tried to do exactly as he did. All the ladies curtseyed down to the ground to H.R.H.; some of the older ones I thought would never get up again. Why will fat old ladies wear such low waists? I never kissed so many hands in my life, and my neck is quite stiff with bowing.

FEBRUARY 10

We left Coppet after *déjeuner*. Prince Demidoff kindly offered to take us with him, as he was going back to Geneva and Sacconex is on his way. His sleigh is superb; all the rugs are of the finest Russian sable. All assembled in the hall to bid us farewell. Madame de Staël kissed me on both cheeks and gave me a beautifully bound copy of "Corinne" with the dedication "*A Cupidon de la part de l'auteur.*" I really must look a baby. I will never forget my visit to Coppet. We had eight horses harnessed Russian fashion, three relays. Galloped all the way. . . .

FEBRUARY 11: SACCONEX

This is a lovely house and all are so kind. M. de Budé is a cousin of father's. There are two sons—Jules, the younger, full of life. We have been skating. . . .
A large dinner, rather dull. . . .
For three mortal hours in the drawing-room footmen passed tray after tray of *sirops*, wine cakes, &c. &c. People here never seem to stop eating.
Byron called Madame de Staël "old Mother Stale," but nevertheless he said of her "she is vain, but who has better right to be." . . .

FEBRUARY 13: GENEVA

We returned here to-day and are stopping at the Naville's. Father learned to-day that at one time it was the intention of the British Government to send the Duke of Wellington to America, during the Ghent negotiations, to terminate the war. It seems he refused to go, giving his reason that he could not be spared, and at the same time expressing his displeasure at the way Lords Castlereagh, Liverpool, and Bathurst were acting. It seems it was mainly due to him that the English made the concessions they did and brought the matter to a speedy termination. . . .

FEBRUARY 14

Father takes me alone with him to-morrow to spend the day at Ferney. He calls it a pilgrimage. He was often taken to see Voltaire by his grandmother when very young. This afternoon a deputation of Americans residing in Geneva and the Canton de Vaud presented father with an address enclosed in a beautiful casket of enamel. We dined quietly *en famille*.

FEBRUARY 15

Such an interesting day. Sitting in Voltaire's favourite chair at Ferney, I am writing this. We left Geneva early, arriving here for *déjeuner* at 11.30. The owners of Ferney are away, but left orders we were to be entertained. The house is not large, but well situated and comfortable. During *déjeuner* father told me how he used to be brought by his grandmother to Ferney; that he often dined at the tables we were sitting at with the friends of Voltaire—the Marquis de Condorcet,* who wrote the letters of Junius to William Pitt (he was arrested in April 1794 and found dead in his cell at Bourg la Reine on April 8, poisoned by opium, which he always carried in a ring, so cheating the guillotine); the Abbé Galiani, the great wit and *raconteur*, whose indecent stories even Madame Necker forgave (it was he who said the death of Marie Theresa was "like an ink-bottle spilt on the map of Europe"); Diderot the atheist, and Grimm. He said, "I feel them hovering around us now, and can nearly hear their voices."

Then he told me of visits when Voltaire read some new play aloud, or rehearsed with the Duc de Villar and Madame Gallatin (his grandmother)—plays that were acted both at Ferney and Pregny; in fact, he himself had taken the rôle of a negro boy in Oriental dress when he was twelve years old. One Sunday Voltaire took him into the garden and, pointing to the heavens, said, "That is the dome made by the great God—not the God created by man." There was a splendid sunset, and as the sun sank behind the Jura Mountains he said: "Can anything be grander than that?—never to be imitated."—"When I was older he impressed upon me always to be charitable in thought and action, to benefit my fellow-creatures as much as was within my power, always to speak the truth, and never to be afraid to give

* Jean Antoine Nicolas de Caritat, Marquis de Condorcet, born 1743, died 1794.

my opinion." The last time father saw him he was ill;
it was in 1778, the year before he died.   He kissed father
on both cheeks and said, *"Enfin Dieu m'appelle—mais
quel Dieu.   Je n'en sais rien."*   Madame de la Vilette,
his niece, gave father a small bust of her uncle, which I
now have. . . .

Before leaving Ferney I picked some myrtle-leaves
and *pensées* to send to my mother. . . .

After dining at 4 o'clock we returned to Geneva—a
day never to be forgotten.   I am afraid my description
is very poor.

Father is giving sittings to Madame Meunier Romilly
for a portrait for Geneva. . . .

FEBRUARY 16

To-day I visited St. Pierre, the cathedral, also the temple,
and saw the tablet to the victories of the *Escalade* in
1602.   There was a Louis Gallatin killed. . . .

FEBRUARY 17

We went to Pregny, where father was born.   This house,
together with all my father's property, was sold by his
trustees during the Revolution at great sacrifice.   They
thought they were acting wisely in such troubled times.

I went to see father's portrait.   She will only have
time to paint the head and hands, the remainder from
a model.   It looks too old to me.

FEBRUARY 18

We paid a visit to Madame Récamier, who is passing
through Geneva.   She is beautiful, but I could not see
great intelligence in her face; great charm of manner.

We also called on Madame Patterson Bonaparte.   She
was very witty and made father laugh.   She told us how
she first met her husband, Jerome Bonaparte.   He had
gone to America in command of a ship, arriving at
Baltimore.   He was invited to dine with an old French-

man, the Marquis de Poléon, who had escaped with his family from St. Domingo during the massacre on that island; two of his children with their nurses were killed. On account of the troubled state of France, he had thought it wiser to go to America. All the beauties of Baltimore were invited to the dinner—the Catons,* &c. &c. She was looking out of the window overlooking the drive with Monsieur de Poléon's eldest daughter. She continued: "We saw two young men approaching the house. Mlle Pascault exclaimed, pointing to the taller one, 'That man will be my husband.' I answered, 'Very well, I will marry the other one.' Strangely enough, we both did as we had said. Henrietta Pascault married Reubell, son of one of the three directors, and I married Jerome Bonaparte"; adding, "Had I but waited, with my beauty and wit I would have married an English duke, instead of which I married a Corsican blackguard."

We leave to-morrow, much to father's regret. He feels it is his duty to go to England as soon as possible, as there is so much to discuss and settle. This has been his holiday. A large supper of fifty to-night, nearly all relations. I liked them, austere as they were, as they are so fond of father and proud of him.

FEBRUARY 19: BELGARDE

We left at 8 o'clock this morning. Prince Demidoff sent his sleigh and had arranged for four relays of horses. Even at that early hour most of our relations came to wish us "God-speed." Father was touched, I could see it by his eyes. This is our first halting-place. After all, Madame Meunier had only time to paint the head and one hand, which is holding a roll of paper, symbolic of the treaty.

---

* The three beautiful Miss Catons. One married the Duke of Leeds. Another the Marquis of Wellesley, brother of the Duke of Wellington, and the third Lord Stratford.

FEBRUARY 20: BELGARDE

I got up early and went to see the "Bouche du Rhone." The river disappears for over three miles under stone. . . .

FEBRUARY 23: MACON

We arrived here late last night. A charming old town. It is the great wine country. . . .

FEBRUARY 25: DIJON

Not very interesting. Still the wine country. . . .

FEBRUARY 28: FONTAINEBLEAU

What a beautiful place! We are lodged in an inn opposite the palace gates. I went over the château; it is full of interest, of Henry II, Diane de Poitiers, &c. &c. I was shown the apartment that Napoleon gave to the Pope when he made him prisoner. The Pope would not allow a divorce between King Jerome and his wife; that was one of the reasons he brought him to Fontainebleau, as he himself wanted to divorce Josephine. . . .

MARCH 1: PARIS

We started early and arrived for breakfast at Vaux Praslin, a magnificent palace belonging to the Duc de Choiseul. It was built by Fouquet, Marquis de Belle-Isle, Superintendent of Finances to Louis XIV. He entertained the King there in great splendour. . . . The Duc received us most kindly. He is a connexion through the Birons and Marmiers. I never saw such wonderful furniture, tapestries, pictures, &c. &c. The library superb; all the books bound in red morocco with coat-of-arms in gold. Only the family and a nice homely *déjeuner*. Then father returned with the Duc to the library to smoke and to get some political information from him. We left at 3 o'clock for Paris and arrived late. . . .

Oh, beautiful Paris! I am so glad to get back. . . .

MARCH 2: PARIS

The Duc de Choiseul Praslin called to-day and told father his Majesty wished for an interview unofficial. It is a delicate matter, as father feels, until he has been to London, that his mouth is closed. . . .

We are lodged in a quiet little hotel in the Rue de Monsieur. Father will not spend any money unnecessarily as his expenses are paid by his Government. His strong idea is that the representative of a republic should not make any show or be ostentatious, saying, "It is only the vulgar *nouveaux riches* that do that." . . .

MARCH 3, 1815

We were received privately this morning by the King. Only the Duchesse d'Angoulême was present. She looked very sad.

The King moved to the embrasure of a window, motioning to father to follow him; they remained in conversation for a quarter of an hour. Amongst other things his Majesty intimated a wish that father would be sent as Minister to Paris, adding, "You must not forget that your family belonged to France before you belonged to America." The Duchess talked to me most graciously, asked me about my mother, and said, "You are too young to begin political life." I assured her I was seventeen. She exclaimed, "*Mais c'est un bébé.*" . . .

Monsieur David, the great artist, has requested father to allow me to pose to him for Cupid. Father has consented, and I sit to-morrow. . . .

MARCH 4, 1815

A day of great excitement. News has reached Paris that Napoleon had made his escape from Elba and was at a little village called Cannes; that he had been received with acclamation.

The King and Royal Family went to the opera and had a great reception. . . .

"CUPID AND PSYCHE," BY DAVID, FOR WHICH JAMES GALLATIN, ÆT. SIXTEEN, POSED AS CUPID

MARCH 5

Great consternation. Courier after courier arriving;
all news suppressed. . . .

MARCH 6, 1815

No news further than we had yesterday. They say the
King is very calm. I saw him driving in state to-day. . . .
Sat for my portrait—that is, like a model, I had to
pose nude. . . .

MARCH 10

The Emperor is marching on Paris, gathering men on
his way. Some say he has already one hundred thousand. . . .

MARCH 11

All sorts of wild reports: one does not know what to
believe. . . .

MARCH 14

The Emperor was at Grenoble on the 7th with over
one hundred thousand men. . . .

MARCH 16

The Emperor marching steadily on to Paris—acclaimed
everywhere. Father says the Royal Family will leave
Paris in a few days. He has private information, but
has not told me any details. I walk about all day.
Bands of young men shouting "Vive l'Empereur." It
is very exciting. . . .

MARCH 19

The King and Royal Family leave Paris to-night. The
Emperor, with a huge army, is expected at Fontainebleau
to-morrow. The people in the streets look depressed
and uncertain what to do. Father has told me to remain
indoors. . . .

MARCH 20: PARIS, 11.30

The Emperor arrived this evening; most of the Imperial Family were at the Tuilleries to greet him.   All day the greatest confusion—officers and their staff, couriers, messengers, &c., galloping wildly about the streets.

Great carts of baggage and furniture.   It is very amusing: most of the shops closed, the cafés crammed, chairs even put out in the streets.   Orators standing on tables making speeches; roars of "Vive l'Empereur," "Vive le petit Caporal."   I don't know if it is genuine or not, the French are so excitable.   The American Minister sent the Stars and Stripes for father to hang on the balcony, for protection in case of trouble.   I saw the Emperor arrive, thousands and thousands cheering him. I got wedged in the crowd and carried along with it. . . .

MARCH 21

People seem mad with joy.   What turncoats the French are!   Dense crowds surrounding the Tuilleries all day. I saw several of the Imperial Family driving. . . .

MARCH 22

There is to be a gala performance at the opera—the night not yet decided upon.   The Emperor drove out to-day and was received with enthusiasm everywhere.

We are leaving shortly for London.   Father fears there may be trouble, which might delay our journey. . . .

MARCH 23

The performance at the opera to-night.   I am going. . . .

MARCH 24

The scene was superb.   For fully twenty minutes the audience yelled when the Emperor appeared; I yelled too. He is fat, looks very dull, tired, and bored.

I had another sitting to-day for Monsieur David.

MARCH 25

We see but few people; all our friends seem to vanish like magic.

A distracted letter from Madame de Staël to-day. She seems in great trouble about everything, particularly her fortune.

Father will answer her under cover to Monsieur Naville, as he fears a letter addressed to her might not reach her. . . .

MARCH 26

The people are settling down as far as one can see. Father, through Monsieur David, has bought one or two beautiful pictures at a very low sum—a head of a "Madonna" on wood panel cut out of a large picture by Murillo, a fine Paolo Veronese, the subject Queen Esther before Ahasuerus, a portrait of Mlle de Lafayette by Mignard, and a lovely head by Greuze. I don't think father will approve of my picture Monsieur David is painting; it is *L'Amour et Psyche*. I have not seen the model but would like to. She must be very pretty, only seventeen. We are not to pose together. . . .

MARCH 28

My last sitting, as we leave for England in a few days.

MARCH 29

The Emperor sent an aide-de-camp requesting an interview with father, purely on some financial matters. It places him in a most awkward position; he regrets he did not leave for England sooner. . . .

MARCH 30

The audience at 10.30 this morning. I am not to go.

Father was not at all pleased with his interview. He says the Emperor was brusque—that his speech is most vulgar. Joseph Bonaparte was present. I had better quote father's own words: "The Emperor first asked my advice on important financial matters, to which I gave my frank opinion. He then began to question me about Canada, also the slave trade. I replied, 'Sire, my position is such that on these subjects my lips are at present sealed.' He abruptly said, 'Then why did you come here?' Bowing, I answered, 'I obeyed your Majesty's command out of respect for the ruler of France, but as an envoy from the United States to England I am not my own master.' The Emperor, turning his back on me, walked to a window; I having backed out of the room, so ended our interview." . . .

MARCH 31

We are leaving to-morrow for London. Father thinks it is wiser. . . .

APRIL 1: PARIS

We could not start after all—some difficulty about our passports. It seems we cannot leave until the 3rd. Father is much put out. He had a letter to-day from Lord Castlereagh. Mr. Adams is Minister to England. I will be very glad to see him again. . . .

APRIL 2

I saw the Emperor to-day riding with a great staff of officers. He certainly has a most powerful face. I went to the Français last night. We leave early to-morrow. . . .

APRIL 3: MANTES

Our first stopping-place. Arrived in time to go to bed. Ugly country. . . . I wrote a long letter home, as father has an offer to take letters from le Havre. . . .

APRIL 4: LES ANDELYS

A long weary day. There was some mistake about our relay of horses and we were detained three hours. We go by Rouen, as father wants me to see the cathedral. He need not arrive in London until the 10th. . . .

APRIL 5: ROUEN

Arrived here too late to see anything. . . .

APRIL 6: ROUEN

I have been all over the cathedral; it is very beautiful. Joan of Arc was burned here. We leave at 11 o'clock. . . .

APRIL 7: LE HAVRE

We embarked at once. Awfully rough. Such a miserable little packet! Only one cabin, and horrid odours of onions frying. I have gone under. . . .

APRIL 9: DOVER

An awful passage. Father has posted up to London, leaving me here to recover. I will leave to-morrow. . . .

APRIL 10: LONDON

We have been lent such a nice house in St. James's Street and all the servants. I have not seen father yet. . . .

APRIL 11

Mr. Adams does not arrive to take up his post until next month.

Mr. Bayard is appointed Minister to Russia but he is too ill to accept it. He is in Paris. . . .

APRIL 12

I am very busy now as I have all sorts of documents to copy and file. I also have to go with father to take notes. All settling of negotiations is at present entirely carried out by him, so the work is very heavy. Lord Castlereagh is most gracious, even friendly. Our position in London is quite different now; I think I will enjoy myself. Mr. Clay arrives in a few days. The season has not yet commenced but people are returning to town.

I have been specially enjoined not to record any gossip in my diary—to confine it as much as possible to interesting facts. Father dislikes gossip and tittle-tattle, saying it is only fit for idle women. I am having a fine dress made to be presented in May. . . .

APRIL 16: LONDON

I went to St. Paul's Cathedral and the Tower of London to-day; the latter is most interesting.

All we can do now is to go thoroughly into the following matters awaiting Mr. Adams' arrival: Colonial policy; regulating traffic with Canada; opening the St. Lawrence River to us; impressment and blockade in times of war; trade with West Indies and Nova Scotia; trade between India, Europe, and the United States. Father wishes to have everything ready, so as to be able to put matters clearly before the other delegates when all have assembled. Of course, he is anxious to go home, as he has been absent over two years. . . .

APRIL 20: LONDON

We are invited to pay a visit to the Duke of Devonshire at Chatsworth, also to Lord Saye and Sele at Broughton Castle. I went to see a cock-fight yesterday and did not like it; I will not go again. We dine and sup out a great deal. I cannot stand the hours they sit at the table drinking port and Madeira. At some houses they have round shallow silver trays on wheels holding the bottles, which are pushed round the table. I have never been accustomed to drink anything but claret and water, so I have to sit quiet doing nothing and listening to subjects discussed which are far beyond me.

APRIL 26: BROUGHTON CASTLE

This is a most interesting old castle surrounded by a moat with a drawbridge. The hall is full of armour which was fished out of the moat. My bedroom has a sliding panel which opens on the chapel below; other rooms have the same. It is to hear early prayers without leaving one's room. . . .

APRIL 29: CHATSWORTH

We arrived here on Friday. A superb palace. His Grace is so handsome, such great dignity of manner and so kind and gracious. He is only twenty-five. Everything on a splendid scale. They say he will never marry as there is some doubt about his birth—that he is a changeling. We return to London on Tuesday. Father anxious to get back. . . .

APRIL 30: CHATSWORTH

There is a very large party stopping here; I cannot get hold of all the names. One very great lady is the Marchioness of Stafford; she is Countess of Sutherland in her own right. Like all well-born people I have met she is most simple, gracious, and charming. She seems to take an interest in everything and is most kind to me. She took me all over the house, pointing out the pictures and telling me their history. She was a great friend of the unfortunate Queen Marie Antoinette. She has the greatest admiration for Madame de Staël and was much interested in my account of our visit to Coppet. She laughed at the dedication to "Cupidon" in my copy of "Corinne" and calls me "Cupid." I am going to dye my hair black. The ladies are very fine at night and wear wonderful jewels.

We visited some splendid places to-day. Everything is done in such great state. Poor father is so bored; I like it.

MAY 1: CHATSWORTH

We leave to-day. His Grace is putting a fine coach at our disposal with relays of horses all the way to London . . .

MAY 3: LONDON

Mr. Adams arrives shortly. We found quantities of invitations.

Dined with Mr. Alexander Baring. His wife was Miss Bingham from Philadelphia, her father a Senator. Mr. Frederick Robinson,* Vice-President of the Board of Trade, was one of the guests. He takes Lord Gambier's place. He seems most affable—a contrast to Lord Gambier, who reminded me of a fire cracker which would never go off but was always sputtering (I am forbidden to express my opinions). Lord Landsdowne and Lord Grey, very important personages, were also present. We are to be presented privately to the Regent on Saturday. . . .

MAY 5: LONDON, SATURDAY

We were received by the Regent at 12 o'clock. Carlton House is very fine but the furniture, &c., is too showy. The Regent and two of his brothers received us. The former is very handsome and dignified but is fat. He was superbly dressed, his brothers as well. Father made such a contrast in his black shorts, white silk stockings, and black coat with his white choker. The Prince has the most charming manners; he was most affable. I was in my new clothes—yellow breeches, white stockings, and a dark-blue coat embroidered in gold. He patted me on the cheek and said with a laugh, "You will break some hearts." Everything was done with the greatest tact—no mention of politics, simply a wish expressed that we should enjoy our sojourn in England. The audience lasted half an hour.

I forgot to mention that a Royal carriage was sent to take us to the palace. There were three footmen behind and father's *chasseur*, in green with cock's feathers in his hat, stood on the step. We had to have a *chasseur* as father is "Special Ambassador to England." We never

* Frederick John Robinson. Created Viscount Goderich, April 28, 1827, and Earl of Ripon, April 13, 1833.

drive out without him, and when we walk in the Mall he is always behind father. . . .

MAY 9: THURSDAY

Very busy writing. I have been to two balls and a rout. What a funny thing the latter is. You crawl up the staircase, bow to your hosts at the top, and crawl down again with your clothes torn off your back. They call that pleasure. We dine to-morrow with the Duke of Wellington. . . .

MAY 11: SATURDAY

A very fine dinner. Gold and silver plate superb. It lasted four hours. Everybody of note was present— all the Ministry. Of course, I was much interested. I sat next to Lord Grey. He did not talk but snapped out sentences; his mouth is like a mouse-trap. All the servants, they say, were bailiffs. There is so much splendour and so much absolutely degrading poverty in London. Neither in Paris nor Washington have I seen anything of the kind. . . .

MAY 13: MONDAY

Mr. Adams has arrived and we go to serious work. . . .

MAY 15: WEDNESDAY

A very long interview to-day; all delegates present. Mr. Robinson and father continually poured oil on the troubled waters. Serious matters were discussed, then dropped to be brought up again. They meet again on Friday. . . .

MAY 17: FRIDAY

Mr. Adams is really a thorn; he is so absolutely "Yankee" and of a common type. Why he is Minister here I cannot understand. He is totally unfitted for the post. He bursts out at times, upsetting everybody and every-thing. Father looks at him with tightly compressed lips. I fear some day he will wither him; now he only makes a clever joke which restores peace. I can see the contempt on the faces of the English delegates; they are so courteous and civil. . . .

MAY 18

Father had a long personal interview with Lord Castle-reagh to-day. They have both agreed that this is the wiser method to pursue. Lord C. told him they did more in an hour than, when all met, in a week. Father has the same confidence in his lordship's wonderful quickness in grasping matters, also his sound good sense of justice that Lord C. seems to reciprocate.

MAY 20: LONDON

Since the signing of the treaty at Ghent there have been a series of leaders in the *Times* inspired by the war party, of the most bitter character. Of course, they have annoyed me very much. Father has spoken to me several times on the subject with his calm good sense. He says this is inevitable—to be regretted, but unworthy of notice.

Lord Castlereagh has assured him that when he received the news of the signing of the treaty at Vienna he was overjoyed.

The Duke of Wellington and Lord Liverpool have expressed the same sentiments. What has pleased me more than anything else is that these three great men have unreservedly acknowledged that to his good sense, moderation, and firmness the signing of the treaty was due. He has no vanity, but feels it is a reward for all the personal sacrifices he has made.

MAY 23

There is a great activity in military circles; evidently the allies are determined to crush Napoleon once and for all. All this delays us. Father says the climax one way or the other must soon arrive. He is a little anxious, but says little. . . .

MAY 26

Wild rumours of all sorts of what the Emperor is going to do or try to do. Father fears a great financial crisis. . . .

MAY 28

There is but one absorbing topic, "Napoleon"! "Boney"!!!

JUNE 7: LONDON

Father received a detailed account of the great ceremony in the Champs de Mars. There was first a solemn Mass, then the Emperor swore fidelity to the New Constitution. He was dressed in the Imperial robes of state. His brothers wore Court dresses of white velvet embroidered in gold, short capes of the same material powdered with golden bees, and caps with masses of white ostrich feathers. The Emperor distributed the eagles to the various regiments. At that moment a terrific thunderstorm broke and this, together with the repeated salutes of artillery, made a most impressive, if not theatrical, scene. In a box next to the throne were all the Imperial princesses with their children. I wish I had seen all this. . . .

JUNE 12

But little news. Messrs. Bayard and Crawford sail in the *Neptune* on the 18th. Father is forced to remain to sign the treaty. Always some new obstacle crops up. Mr. Adams impossible.

JUNE 15

Great news. Napoleon left Paris last Monday; they say he is marching on Brussels. . . .

JUNE 17

News arrives only to be contradicted, but the fact remains the Emperor is sweeping all before him. Father only seems troubled about the financial crash which is sure to follow if Napoleon is victorious. . . .

JUNE 18

Great anxiety. Consols have fallen terribly. I have never seen greater depression; everybody one sees seems frightened. A rumour to-day that a battle had been fought and that the Duke of Wellington was crushed; to-night that is contradicted. One cannot believe anything. They say Monsieur Rothschild has mounted couriers from Brussels to Ostend and a fast clipper ready to sail the moment something is decisive one way or the other. . . .

JUNE 25, 1815

The last few days have been so intoxicating that I have not had a moment to write in my diary. When the news was confirmed of the great victory of the Duke of Wellington at Waterloo London went mad and I with it. People I had never seen before rushed up to me in the streets and shook me violently by the hand. Father now says we will have a long and lasting peace—that Napoleon will be obliged to abdicate, that his star has fallen. Many people have been ruined and others have made large fortunes. He is a little annoyed at the desertion of Messrs. Bayard and Crawford, who have sailed in the *Neptune,* leaving us to get home as best we can. . . .

JUNE 26

The Emperor has arrived in Paris. It seems he wanted to be killed but his marshals forced him into a carriage, as they feared he might be taken prisoner. . . .

JUNE 27

We are nearing the completion of the Treaty of Commerce, and it is to be signed in a day or two. . . .

JUNE 28

Father had a farewell audience with the Regent. I did not go. Mr. Baring is most kind to us. . . .

JUNE 29

Of course, Mr. Adams is retarding matters with his pig-headedness. Mr. Robinson is so entirely different, so suave and conciliatory. Father is perfectly satisfied with the conditions of the treaty. . . .

JUNE 30

Father has decided to leave London on July 4, on our way home. My mother is not well. We have secured a good ship. . . .

JULY 2

The treaty signed to-day but not without difficulty. Mr. Adams at the last moment wished to make all sorts of alterations. Father agreed to some of them, and Mr. Robinson also; if it had been Mr. Goulburn or Adams they would not have agreed so easily. Mr. Robinson has been most charming in every way. We dine for the last time with Mr. Baring. . . .

JULY 3

We are actually off to-morrow. All the Barings were so kind. The dinner was delightful and we parted with them with deep regret. I will be glad to get home; after all it is my home and I love it. But I want to come back. *Homme propose mais Dieu dispose.*

PART III

THE MINISTRY IN FRANCE

FROM THE RESTORATION OF THE BOURBONS TO THE ASSASSINATION OF THE DUC DE BERRI

NOVEMBER 1815—*JULY* 1820

NOVEMBER 23, 1815: NEW YORK

Much to my regret, father has written to-day declining the mission to France. Lately he seems to have got an idea in his head that he must devote his attention to making money for his children. Mamma is greatly disappointed as well as Frances; they had been looking forward to the gaieties of Paris life after all I had told them. Albert does not care; he would prefer to live in the backwoods.

ALBERT GALLATIN *to* THOMAS JEFFERSON

NEW YORK, *November* 27, 1815

DEAR SIR,

On my return from Washington I found your welcome letter of October 16, which my friends here, daily expecting my return, had kept instead of forwarding it.

Our opinion of Bonaparte is precisely the same. In that Lafayette's and the opinion of every friend of rational liberty in France did coincide. The return of that man was generally considered by them as a curse. Notwithstanding the blunders and rooted prejudices of the Bourbons, the alienation of the army and the absolute want of physical force had made them, upon the whole,

78

harmless, and as soon as the termination of the Congress*
would have left France independent of foreign interference,
they must in the course of things either have been overset
or have governed according to public opinion. After
Bonaparte's restoration, it was hoped to pursue a similar
course; others, placing confidence in the declarations
of the Allies, hoped to get rid both of him and of the
Bourbons. All saw the necessity of defending the
country against foreign invasion, but the fatal catastrophe
was not, to its full extent, anticipated by any. I call it
a catastrophe with an eye only to the present; for,
exhausted, degraded, and oppressed as France now is,
I do not despair of her ultimate success in establishing
her independence and a free form of Government. The
people are too enlightened to submit long to any but a
military despotism. What has lately passed was a scene
in the drama, perhaps necessary to effect a radical cure
of that love of conquest which had corrupted the nation
and made the French oppressors abroad and slaves at
home. As to independence, we have the recent instance
of Prussia, which, with far inferior population, resources,
or intellect, arose in two years from almost annihilation
to the rank of a preponderating Power. But to return
to Bonaparte: I lament to see our republican editors
so much dazzled by extraordinary actions or carried
away by natural aversion to our only dangerous enemy
as to take up the cause of that despot and conqueror,
and to represent him as the champion of liberty who has
been her most mortal enemy, where hatred to republican
systems was founded on the most unbounded selfishness
and on the most hearty contempt for mankind. I really
wish that you would permit me to publish, or rather that
you would publish, your opinions on that subject. This
might have a tendency to correct those which are daily
published, and which do injury to our cause at home,
and to our country abroad.

* At Vienna and the dissolution of the Coalition.

Under different circumstances, without having any wish for a foreign mission or a residence in France, I might have accepted the appointment of Minister there. But, satisfied that nothing can at this moment be effected in that country, and it being very reluctant to my feelings to be on a mission to a degraded monarch and to a nation under the yoke of foreign armies, I thought that I might, without any breach of public duty or of private gratitude, consult my own convenience, and I have accordingly officially informed our Government that I declined altogether the appointment.

ALBERT GALLATIN

NOVEMBER 27

I had a long conversation with father this morning. For the first time he told me of Mr. John Jacob Astor's most generous offer to take him into partnership, with a fifth share in a business whose profits were $100,000 a year. His reasons for refusing were, although he respected Mr. Astor, he never could place himself on the same level with him. I am not surprised, as Astor was a butcher's son at Waldorf—came as an emigrant to this country with a pack on his back. He peddled furs, was very clever, and is, I believe, one of the kings of the fur trade. He dined here and ate his ice-cream and peas with a knife.

DECEMBER 6

He showed me a letter from Mr. Monroe again urging him to accept the French mission. It is in the most flattering terms and begs father not to withdraw from political life—that he is by far the finest diplomatist we have, that anything would be safe in his hands.

I did hope he was going to tell me he would accept, but when I ventured to ask him his answer was: "I must think of making proper provision for my family. I am getting old."

DECEMBER 19

Another letter from Mr. Monroe urging father to reconsider the mission to France. We all want him to, but we know perfectly well it is wise for us not to say anything. I honestly feel I would much prefer to live in either France or England—all is so crude in this country. The two years I spent in Russia, France, and England have unfitted me for America.

DECEMBER 26

Father has just brought another letter to copy.

ALBERT GALLATIN *to* JAMES MONROE

NEW YORK, *December 26, 1815*

DEAR SIR,

I have received your friendly letters of the 4th and 16th instant, and have a grateful sense of the motives which dictated them. I can assure you that I feel a great reluctance to part with my personal and political friends, and that every consideration merely personal to myself and detached from my family urges a continuance in public life. My habits are formed and cannot be altered. I feel alive to everything connected with the interest, happiness, and reputation of the United States. Whatever affects unfavourably either of them makes me more unhappy than any private loss or inconvenience. Although I have nothing to do with it, the continual suspension of specie payments, which I consider as a continued unnecessary violation of the public faith, occupies my thoughts more than any other subject. I feel as a passenger in a storm—vexed that I cannot assist. This I understand to be very generally the feeling of every statesman out of place. Be this as it may, although I did and do believe that for the present at least I could not be of much public utility in France, I did in my private letter to the President place my declining on the ground of private considerations. In

81

that respect my views are limited to the mere means of existence without falling in debt. I do not wish to accumulate any property. I will not do my family the injury of impairing the little I have. My health is frail; they may soon lose me, and I will not leave them dependent on the bounty of others. Was I to go to France, and my compensation and private income (this last does not exceed $2500 a year) did not enable me to live as I ought, I must live as I can. I ask your forgiveness for entering in those details, but you have treated me as a friend and I write to you as such. You have from friendship wished that I would reconsider my first decision, and I will avail myself of the permission. It will be understood that in the meanwhile, if the delay is attended with any public inconvenience, a new appointment may immediately take place. My motive for writing when I did was a fear that, specially with respect to other missions, the belief that I would go to France might induce the President to make different arrangements from those he would have adopted on a contrary supposition. . . .

ALBERT GALLATIN

JANUARY 2, 1816

I really believe he is going to change his mind after all. Mamma does not mention the subject but sighs deeply at intervals. Frances declared at breakfast it was useless for her to go on with her French as they were not going to Paris. . . .

FEBRUARY 2

Hurrah! everything *couleur de rose*. I wrote the letter accepting the French mission for him at his dictation. Mr. Monroe had written him the most pressing letter on the 27th of last month, begging for an immediate reply one way or the other. All I say to them at home is, *"Faites vos paquets, mesdames."* . . .

ALBERT GALLATIN *to* JAMES MONROE
accepting the mission to France

NEW YORK, *February 2,* 1816

DEAR SIR,

I have just received your letter of 27th ult., and have at last concluded to avail myself of the permission given me to accept again the mission to France. I am duly sensible of yours and the President's kindness in having kept the question so long opened, and hope you will find an apology for my hesitation in the importance, at my age, of a decision which must so materially affect the prospects for life of my wife and children. I believe with you that the chance of Congress making any additional allowance to Foreign Ministers is not the better on account either of the present incumbents or of the state of suspense in which some of the important missions are now kept. On what may hereafter be done no reliance can be placed. I calculate only on what now exists, and mean, as I before stated, to regulate my expenses accordingly. If I find it impracticable to live without encroaching on my small property, I will beg permission to return. I believe an additional compensation to be much more important to the United States than to the individual.

I have still some private arrangements to complete, which will not, however, detain me long, and I will be ready to repair to Washington, for the purpose of reading the former correspondence and receiving your instructions, at any time you may be pleased to appoint. It will best suit my convenience to have a short time allowed me on my return from Washington. I will, in the meanwhile, wait for your answer.

I beg you to present Mrs. G.'s and my best respects to Mrs. M. and to Mrs. Hay, and to believe me, with sincere respect and esteem, truly yours.

You will have the goodness to return or destroy the

letter in which I had declined the appointment, as it should not remain on the files of the office.

ALBERT GALLATIN

JAMES MONROE *to* ALBERT GALLATIN

WASHINGTON, *February* 13, 1816

DEAR SIR,

We were much gratified to find by your last letter that you accepted the mission to France. I have not wished to take you from your affairs, which I am convinced must require your unremitted attention before your departure; but I now think that the sooner you come here the better it will be. It is known that you have accepted the mission, and an early visit here will produce a good effect. The prospect of obtaining an augmentation, in the modes heretofore suggested, of the salary is improved by the acceptance; and, being here, the opportunity you will have of conferring with Mr. Clay and Mr. Crawford on the subject, and interesting them in it, will give to our exertions much aid. This you may afford, in the present state, with perfect delicacy. Everything will be done to accommodate your views, in the time of your departure, that circumstances will permit. Your former letter was not filed in the Department. I will return it to you when we meet. Our best regards to Mrs. Gallatin.

With great respect and esteem,

Sincerely yours.

JAMES MONROE

. . . . . .

APRIL 13

Bother! I wish people would let him alone. They now offer him the Treasury; again all our plans are at a standstill.

APRIL 18

He will not accept.   He says his arrangements to go to
France are too far advanced to be changed at this last
moment.   He also has some very important business to
settle in Geneva.   The family *bourse* has accumulated for so long, and now is such a large sum, he thinks
something should be done with it.   He is the only male
Gallatin in the world and the Gallatin women have no
claim to it; there are several of them married in Geneva
of the different branches.   Anyhow, to France we go.

MAY 25

I have been on board the *Peacock* (Captain Rogers),
which is fitting out to take us as soon as possible.   The
captain told me to-day he would be ready June 1, but
from the appearance of things I do not believe he will.

JUNE 2

Of course, the *Peacock* is not ready.   Here we are all
packed up and ready; everything most uncomfortable.

JUNE 7

The captain has promised father that he will be able
to sail in two days.   All our baggage has been put on
board.

JUNE 10: ON BOARD THE *PEACOCK*

We are actually off.   Such a host of friends to bid us
"God-speed."   Mamma in tears, Frances in tears, all
the maids in tears, and all the female relations in tears.
At the present moment mamma and Frances are waving
to the receding shore.   Albert is busy with the chickens,
of which we have a large supply. . . .

JULY 9: PARIS

After a very fast passage here we are in Paris.   I can
hardly believe it is true, and keep rubbing my eyes,
thinking I may be asleep and dreaming.

JULY 10

Father had an interview with the Duc de Richelieu* to-day
at 12 o'clock; I was present to take notes.   He expressed a most friendly feeling that the French Government had for the United States—in fact, was most civil,
even cordial.

He seemed anxious to know what our feelings toward
England were.   Father answered that the two Governments were on excellent terms, but of course there was
irritation between the people, which always existed after
a war—that he regretted that public journals added
fuel to the flame.

The Duke regretted that the newspapers misrepresented
the present government of France.   He could not understand how most of the English and American papers
defended a man who crushed liberty everywhere.

The Duke, on leaving, said His Majesty wished father
to present his letters of credence to-morrow as the Royal
Family were leaving Paris shortly.

JULY 11

I accompanied father to the palace to present his letters.
I was amazed at our reception, both by the King and
the Prince.   Our audience was, of course, private.

Father presented me.   Both the King and the Prince
expressed themselves as most friendly towards the
United States.   "Monsieur,"† the Duc d'Angoulême,
and the Duc de Berri were present.   The King is old
and very fat.   Monsieur is rather handsome; the
Duc d'Angoulême very stern but with a very kind face;

* Duc de Richelieu (Fernand-Emmanuel-Sophie-Septimanio du
Plessis), peer of France.   Minister of Foreign Affairs and President of
the Council September 26, 1815; died May 17, 1822.

† "Monsieur" Charles-Philippe de France, Comte d'Artois, brother
of the King.   He succeeded Louis XVIII as King of France September
16, 1824.   He reigned under the name of Charles X.   His two sons
were the Dukes of Angoulême and Berri.

the Duc de Berri very good-looking and very gay and smiling.

Very great etiquette is maintained. They say the King is more strict than even Louis XIV was. We cut a sorry sight in our plain black coats and breeches with all the splendours of the Court uniforms.

The King asked about mamma's health, how she had borne the journey—is really most kind and gracious. Court coaches were sent for us and took us back. Mr. Sheldon* followed us in the second coach.

JULY 30: 21 RUE DE L'UNIVERSITÉ

I have been all day interviewing servants—tall and short, fat and thin—until I can hardly speak. After sorting out what I considered the best, I had them drawn up for father's approval, which I am glad to say he gave.

Major-domo—Callon by name, a very fine person; two house footmen, Edouard and Alfred; two carriage footmen, Louis and Jean; Chef, Monsieur Ratifar, such a great personage (he brings his own kitchen staff); three maids, all pretty—I chose them. I don't know what mamma will say when she sees them. I hate to look at ugly women.

The house is really very fine *entre cours et jardin.* Furniture old but very good. We have to supply our own plate and linen. We have to make some alterations, so mamma and Frances have gone to the Lussacs at Versailles. I have my own valet, Lucien, aged twenty-five—a very important person he thinks himself, valet to a Secretary of Embassy. He will call me *"Excellence."*

AUGUST 2

All the morning choosing carriages and horses. Of the latter we got two pairs, very fine for the "Berline," which is all glass in front; this will be for Court and

* Mr. Sheldon was one of Albert Gallatin's secretaries.

state occasions. A very strong "Brichka" for everyday use, a nice stout little pair for it. A cabriolet for me; any of the big horses will go in single.

AUGUST 6

We are really in very good order and the servants excellent. Madame Patterson Bonaparte has written from Geneva asking if she might be allowed to pay us a visit of a few days. She is on her way to America. She arrives on the 10th.

NOTE: *The following letter written at this date gives an interesting account of the financial condition of France after Waterloo.*

LETTER *from* ALBERT GALLATIN *to* JAMES MONROE AT WASHINGTON

PARIS, *August* 6, 1816

SIR,

You were informed by my dispatch No. 1 of my arrival in this city on the 9th of last month. On the 11th I had audience of the King, to whom I delivered my letters of credence. The reception, both from him and from the princes, was what is called gracious, and accompanied with the usual expressions of most friendly disposition towards the United States.

My abode here has been too short to enable me to form any opinion of the prospect we have of succeeding in obtaining the indemnities so justly due to our citizens, and I do not wish to enter into the discussion until I have ascertained as far as practicable the disposition of this Government in that respect. Whatever this may be, the situation of their finances will be a formidable obstacle in our way. That there will be a great deficit this and every succeeding year until the foreign contributions are discharged is notorious. The precise amount of that deficit for this year is not so well known, but, from a source entitled to confidence, has been stated to me as exceeding 350 millions of francs. It is not believed that any practical increase of taxes can produce more than 100 millions. The residue, or 250 millions a year for five years, must therefore remain unpaid, or be provided for by creating new stock. That situation would, indeed, be deplorable in a country where there is no public credit, and where the Treasury cannot raise money in any other manner than by selling their 5 per cent. stock at the market rate, which does not now exceed 58 per cent. I still hope that the statement is exaggerated; but the reliance which seems to be placed on the forbearance of the allied Powers confirms the opinion that the internal resources are not sufficient to meet the foreign demands.

It has been suggested to me that some classes of claims, particularly that of vessels burnt at sea, would, if pressed by themselves, have a better chance of being admitted; but, unless otherwise instructed, I will not pursue a course which might injure the general mass of our claims. . . .

ALBERT GALLATIN

AUGUST 7

His Majesty has expressed a wish—in fact, a command— that mamma is to be received in private audience, and has fixed the 9th. Fortunately, she has all her frocks ready. She is to be received in the morning. All the *corps diplomatique* have called, and now it is nothing but returning visits. The de Broglies are still with Madame de Staël at Coppet, but are returning to Paris shortly. The Duc de la Rochefoucauld d'Enville (a distant relation) has been most kind, and has told father what he ought to do and what he ought not to do.

AUGUST 10

Mamma was most graciously received. Father accompanied her. She had to wear full Court dress at eleven in the morning. She was first received by the King, who spoke English to her, much to her relief. When she retired from the presence she was escorted by Madame de Duras to the apartments of the Duchesse d'Angoulême. It seems it was most trying. She has not yet recovered from the fatigue, as she is not strong.

AUGUST 11

Madame Patterson Bonaparte arrived this morning from Geneva. Her baggage nearly filled the antechamber. She is very lovely, but hard in expression and manner. I don't think she has much heart. Her son seems to be her one thought. She had a very long talk with father about his future (her son's); she is most ambitious for him. She even has a list of the different princesses who will be available for him to marry: as he is only ten years old, it is looking far ahead.

I have but little work to do here. I foresee I will soon be in mischief. Paris is indeed the paradise of young men.

AUGUST 12, 1816

Madame Bonaparte's conversation most brilliant. At supper last night she said that when in Paris just after the hundred days, she was at a ball at the British Embassy. She noticed she was much stared at, and that some of the ladies curtsied to her. She asked the Duke of Wellington what it meant, and he told her she was taken for Pauline Bonaparte* as she was so strikingly like her, and that people were so amazed at thinking Pauline Bonaparte would have dared come back to France. The Ambassador came up to her at that moment to lead her to supper. This intrigued the company all the more. She is frightfully vain.

AUGUST 14

Father had an audience of the King this morning. He suddenly said: "I hear that Madame Jerome Bonaparte

---

* Sister of Napoleon, married Prince Borghese.

is with you. Pray express to her our regret she will not come to our Court, but that we know her reasons for not doing so." When father told her she was much gratified, and said, "That Corsican blackguard would not have been so gracious."

AUGUST 15

Madame Bonaparte left to-day for Havre to embark for America. She is such an interesting person, we will miss her. She gave mamma a ruby-velvet frock to cut up for Frances. To father she gave a really beautiful turquoise and diamond brooch. He will never wear it, so I will have it.

AUGUST 17

We are very busy with documents to be copied to send to America. The Duc de Richelieu had a very long conference with father yesterday. The latter likes him so much—admires all his fine qualities, particularly his great simplicity, frugality, and above all his honesty.

AUGUST 23

I drove my new "curricle" for the first time to-day. I do not know which was the most proud, myself, Lucien, or the horse. It is rather difficult to drive a spirited horse and to keep taking off one's hat every moment. I have to be on the *qui vive* not to fail to return a salute; I will do better when I get to know people's faces better, but now I find it most difficult. I saw many lovely ladies, and I flatter myself some of them saw me. I find they notice much more when I am driving than when I am on foot. Moral—always drive.

I have just come back from walking in the gardens of the Palais Royal. How pretty Frenchwomen are! I know I shall get into all sorts of scrapes. I don't remember if I noted our visit to Monsieur de Lafayette. He is stopping with a Mr. Parker some distance from

Paris. He has permission to come to Paris but does not wish to do so at present. His greeting to father was most cordial. We are soon going to see him again. I now find it most difficult to keep up my diary; lately I have neglected it terribly. In the future I will have simply to write when I can find time and from memory. It is work all the morning, receiving for father all kinds and qualities of people; dining out, suppers, theatres, and all sorts and kinds of varied amusements. Hardly time to sleep.

I have made friends with a charming little *danseuse* of the opera, Rosette by name.

. . . . . .

A week since I have been able to take up my pen. On Thursday father and mother were commanded to dine with the King—a very great honour it seems, and one reserved for princes and ambassadors. A rather amusing incident happened. After dinner a small reception was held. Amongst the ladies received was a Comtesse de Boigne.* She is the daughter of the Marquis d'Osmond,† ambassador in England. In a loud tone she expressed her astonishment at the presence of Monsieur Gallatin and his wife to the Prince de Condé.‡ His answer to her was: "His Majesty cannot too highly honour Monsieur Gallatin, as, although representing a new country, his ancestors had served France for generations and one had been a most honoured and intimate friend of Henri IV."§ It seems this got to the King's ears, who was much annoyed, and when Madame de Boigne made her curtsy he turned his back on her. She called on mamma the next day, and was most gracious and asked too many

---

* Charlotte Louise Elénore Adelaide d'Osmond married at the age of sixteen General de Boigne. Separated from him after ten months of married life. He was immensely rich and allowed her a large income.

† Réne Eustache Marquis d'Osmond, Peer of France, Ambassador in England.

‡ Réne de Condé, born 1736, Duc de Bourbon.

§ See Appendix II.

GASPAR GALLATIN
FRIEND OF HENRI IV

questions. They say she is the mistress of the Duc d'Orléans, who is not allowed to come back to France. Madame de Staël has arrived. I went with father to see her to-day; she looks very ill. She had heard of Madame de Boigne's behaviour and was very angry. She said, "That woman is effrontery itself," and "Truth never received her invitation to her christening." Madame Récamier was much amused and told many funny anecdotes about Madame de B. It seems her husband is an Indian nabob who has property at Chambéry. They do not live together but he allows her a large income. Albertine de Broglie was delightful—so glad to see us and is so natural and unaffected. They are looking for a house, but are at present with her mother. . . .

DECEMBER

Poor neglected diary! I have broken with Rosette and now dance with the *jeunes filles du monde*. It is not amusing as I take them back to their mothers when the dance is over. We hardly speak a word. How I hate all this etiquette! We dined yesterday at the Duc de Berri's. They were both most gracious; she is like a spoiled child and has very bad manners. The Duke of Wellington was a guest, and after dinner the Duc de Berri spoke most kindly to me. They say he has many friends in the *coulisse* of the opera. He is so gay and cheerful— such a contrast to his father and uncle. They say the Orléans family will soon return to the Palais Royale and they receive in the most informal manner. A great ball at the Duke of Wellington's. It seems the Royal Family were most rude, but that the duke did not pay any attention and rather put them to shame. Some extraordinary English women were present.

JANUARY 1817

I am trying to collect my senses as it has been nothing but a whirl of gaiety. Father insisted upon having a supper Christmas Day: Madame de Staël, the de Broglies, Pozzo di Borgo, Baron Humboldt, Constant Rebecque, Monsieur la Place, the Duc de Richelieu, Chateaubriand, Duc and Duchesse de Clermont-Tonnerre, Rochefoucauld, his son, and a host of others. We sat down thirty-eight. Albert and Frances were allowed to appear on this occasion. Mamma had a huge Christmas-tree in one of the drawing-rooms. Small souvenirs for all. As Pozzo was cutting off some of the presents the tree caught fire: de Broglie pulled off his coat, I followed suit, and we smothered the fire before it did much damage. At midnight mamma had had prepared "egg nog" and "apple toddy," and we all drank each other's health in American fashion. Madame de Staël looks very ill. After all our guests had left I slipped off to the *Maison Dorée*—quite a different company. I managed to slip into the house at 6 o'clock without any of the servants seeing me.

What gaiety there is in Paris this season of the year! Everybody seems cheerful and happy, and all is ,so bright. Father and I dined on Sunday with the Prince and Princess Galitzin. Katinka Galitzin is pretty and full of fun; we get on capitally. She has much more liberty than French girls, being Russian. The son of the Duc de Caumont la Force is courting her. In the evening a reception at Court. Mamma had excused herself on the plea of illness, but the fact is her religious principles will not allow her to go to any big ball or Court on Sunday. It is a little awkward for father as most of the big Court functions are on Sunday. I forgot to mention the splendid ceremony at Notre Dame on Christmas Eve. The cathedral was in complete darkness save for a few dim lamps. As the bell rang twelve strokes a burst of light and the most beautiful singing I ever heard. The crowd was terrific; several women fainted. I was an hour getting out, so was late for a supper at the *Dorée*. *Toutes ces "petites dames!"*

What a gorgeous New Year! Visits, visits—nothing but visits. My pockets are empty. *Étrennes* for all the servants, presents to all the family, not forgetting my *coulisse* friends, has cleared me out.

Another Court function on Sunday, which, again on the plea of illness, mamma begged to be excused. His Majesty noticed her absence and most graciously inquired if she were seriously ill. Father, who is so absolutely frank, answered: "Sire, I regret that my wife's religious principles prevent her going to any entertainment on Sunday." The King, instead of being annoyed, answered, "Pray convey our respects to Madame Gallatin, and tell her we honour her principles and her courage." Father was much relieved.

JANUARY 9

To our immense surprise, a Court courier arrived this morning to say that his Majesty would in person call at 1.30. No time for any preparations. Father said, "We will receive his Majesty in absolute simplicity, as behoves our republic." He arrived with Monsieur in a very simple coach. Mamma, father, the children, and myself received him under the *perron* in the courtyard. He is very infirm—apologized for not getting out of the carriage. He handed mamma a large roll which was a very fine engraving of himself. Written in English is "To Madam Gallatin, with all the respect due to a woman who has principles. Signed, Louis." He greatly admired Frances, who really promises to be very beautiful. Her complexion, like mamma's, is absolutely perfect. After much bowing, &c. &c., he drove off. It seems no such honour has ever been conferred by him before. Everybody tells father the King pays more attention to him than to anybody else. Comte de Gallatin, our cousin, the Minister from Würtemberg, says he is very jealous. By the way, his story is an odd one. His father was in the service of the Duke of Brunswick when the duke was killed at the Battle of Jena. As he was dying he said to the King of Würtemberg, "I leave to you my most trusted friend." The King took him into his service and created him a Count. Unfortunately, this one only has daughters. We are on the most intimate terms with the family. Poor mamma is quite dazed—the whole system of living is so entirely different from that in America; this, coupled with her want of fluency in French, adds to her troubles. Fortunately, we have been able to obtain the services of an excellent house-keeper, Madame Berthal by name—a Russian who speaks every language under the sun. Nothing ever affects father; he is always pleased, and I have never seen him put out at anything. I really believe if he was given his breakfast at midnight, his dinner at 6 A.M., and his supper at midday he would hardly notice the difference. I have just been seeing the footmen, coachmen, &c., in their new liveries. For ordinary occasions, dark blue plush breeches, yellow waistcoats, and dark blue coats with silver buttons, black silk stockings; state liveries, light blue breeches, white silk stockings, yellow waistcoats, and light blue cloth coats with broad silver braid and silver buttons. The latter is exact, as dark blue does not exist in heraldry.

Father is a little doubtful, fearing Americans may object to so much show, but he feels the Court of France requires it.

Albert's black, Peter, whom we brought from America, showed the cook how to make buckwheat cakes. This came as a complete surprise. Poor mamma burst out crying when she saw them. Frances is taking dancing lessons. I have learnt to cut a "pigeon's wing" and had a great success at the Galitzin's on Sunday evening. . . . Our cousin, Count Gallatin, is most kind; he and his wife have told mamma all that is required of her at Court. We really are in a strange position. Father represents a new republic, and with all his aristocratic relations here much more is expected of mamma, but her manners are so simple and so utterly unaffected that father begs her not to change them in any way.

An accident happened to mamma's *berline* to-day. Turning from the Faubourg St. Honoré into the Rue des Écuries d'Artois, one of the hind wheels caught on the high kerb and was wrenched off. Fortunately, the horses are very quiet and were not frightened. Frances was a little cut by the glass of the window she was sitting by. The English Ambassadress was passing at the time, and very kindly insisted upon taking mamma to the Embassy, which is close by. After having Frances' face seen to she drove mamma home; it was most gracious of her.

. . . . . .

I have made the acquaintance of a young American who is studying painting, Grayson by name. He is going to introduce me to the "*grisette* world"; I am looking forward to it. We go to one of the students' balls on Sunday night. I must keep this very quiet, as I fear father would be much annoyed. He does not mind how much I go out in the *grand monde* but he dislikes anything like low life. He never had a youth himself; he was penned up in Geneva, and when he went to America he lived a simple life in the wild parts. I would not care to do anything to annoy him.

My *grisette* ball was not a success—the fact is, it was not fit for any gentleman to go to; I am not particular but there are limits. The men were much worse than the women. How can they degrade themselves to such an extent! They left nothing to the imagination. I was determined to stop to the end, and even went to supper at a restaurant at the Halle. I will never forget the horrible orgie. There were Russian, Spanish, Italian, and Prussian students; they might have been wild beasts from their behaviour. This has been a lesson to me; I am glad of the experience and will profit by it.

At the Elysée Bourbon last evening there was a little singing vaudeville played by children which was very pretty; then supper, and we danced a *contre-danse*, which gave me a chance to cut my "pigeon's wings." I cut eight in succession when my turn came as advancing cavalier. Madame de Boigne, in that horrid voice of hers, said, *"Très bien, mon jeune Américain."* How I dislike that woman! I cannot help it, she is nothing but pretension. I believe she thinks herself the most important person in France.

I dined at the Russian Embassy yesterday and made such a fool of myself. It was a delightful dinner, and I took in Princess Katinka Galitzin. There was a large *plat monté* of nougat. When it was passed to me the other guests had only taken off some of the ornaments. Princess K. wanted some of the nougat, so I boldly stuck it with a silver fork; I did not think it was so brittle— bang went the whole thing, scattering the nougat in all directions. If the floor had only opened! Bits of the nougat stuck in the ladies' hair, on their necks and shoulders. I was filled with confusion. Pozzo di Borgo exclaimed, *"Voila l'Américain qui attaque la citadelle de Russie."* This caused a general laugh and put every-body in a good humour. I have not got over it yet. I think the ladies forgave me as I am so young.

Mamma is so tiresome. When we were children, every Saturday night we had to take a powder and in the morning a black draught—always administered by mamma in person. She really forgets I am no longer a child; it is all very well for Frances and Albert. I had a bad headache for several days, and asked mamma's maid to give me a powder. To my horror, at 6 o'clock this morning (without knocking) in walked mamma with a black draught in her hand and a frilled nightcap on her head. No use resisting; but as she left the room I said, *"Merci, Madame l'Ambassadrice."* I don't think she quite liked the tone I said it in. . . .

98

TUESDAY

I am in horrible disgrace. The Russian Ambassador gave mamma a beautiful cat. It is always in a large basket in her boudoir. Yesterday some people were coming to *déjeuner*. I was early and alone in the boudoir where we always assemble when *en petite committée*. Mamma had been sent a quantity of Madonna lilies which were in a vase. I do not know what possessed me, but I took one up and commenced to "annunciate" the cat in solemn tones. I had my back to the door, when I suddenly heard my name pronounced—"James," but in such a tone as only mamma can say it. I was saved for the moment by the Duc and Duchesse de Clermont-Tonnerre being announced. I hardly dared speak at table as I knew I was in disgrace. Dear mamma's French is very doubtful, and she never can get a name right. There was a pause in the general conversation. She turned to the duke and said, "How is Madame de Bidé," meaning Madame de Budé, the grandmother of the duchess. This was really too much for me. I exploded, and fortunately choked, and had hurriedly to leave the table. When I returned naturally I apologized, but I might have fallen into the middle of Stonehenge from the expression of their faces. Only dear father had a twinkle in his eye. He I know will get me out of this scrape.

Mamma sent for me before supper and I had a *mauvais quart d'heure*. I humbly apologized and was most repentant. I then threw my arms around her and gave her a good hug. She gave me six tracts, one for each day of the week; I promised to read them. The funniest fact of it is that Mourussa, the cat, gave birth to six kittens in the night. I only suggested to father that one might be called Annunciata. He did not answer but looked out of the window.

I am very sorry for mamma; I can see she is not happy. Father is so occupied that I do not think he

notices it.   It is hard for her: she speaks so little French,
has really no friends whom she cares for, and her position
is a very difficult one.   The Court is so hemmed in by
etiquette to which she is not accustomed.   She does not
understand the ways of Frenchwomen of the *grand
monde* and is continually shocked.   Indeed I am not
surprised the only women she finds anything in common
with are the ladies of the English Embassy and some
of the English residents in Paris.   There are few Americans, and those that are here are mostly in commerce
and without education.   I went with her two days ago
to call on a Mrs. P., the wife of a very rich but common
American.   They have recently bought a very fine hotel
in the Rue de Varennes; they sold all the beautiful old
furniture and have refurnished it in execrable taste, but
she is evidently very proud of it and insisted upon showing
us all the reception-rooms.   In one room there was a
large bronze replica of a statue by "John of Bologna."
For something to say, I admired it.   She folded her
arms and, with a palpable wink, said, "Bologny done it,
but I am going to have pantaloons made for it when I
receive."   Mamma's face was a study.   She relaxed into
a smile when the poor woman offered her molasses candy
and dough-nuts, saying she made them herself to remind
her of home.

Now that the gaieties are over I am hard at work
again; the continual writing, copying of documents,
and so forth is very trying.   Father cannot pin the
Duc de Richelieu down to anything definite.

FEBRUARY

To father's great delight, Lafayette dined here last week,
Baron Humboldt, Madame de Staël, Duc and Duchesse
Plaisance, Monsieur la Place, Pozzo di Borgo, and the
de Broglies.   A rather amusing incident.   We were all
assembled in the drawing-room.   Monsieur de Lafayette
had not arrived.   Monsieur la Place was talking to me

when Lafayette was announced. La Place turned very pale. Just as dinner was announced he went up to father begging leave to retire, as he had been ill and felt very faint. It seems he found it impossible to sit at the same table with Lafayette on account of his relations to the Bourbons. This amused Madame de Staël very much, and I think the dinner was gayer without him. Madame Bonaparte has announced her arrival from America in May.

There has not been a lull in the gaieties, which I thought were over. Invitations keep pouring in. Mamma only accepts those which she is obliged to as it fatigues her so much; father the same, so I have to represent the family on all occasions. When we are at home *en famille*, which both mamma and father prefer, I find it intolerably dull. They both read or write and rarely speak. Frances goes to bed very early, so does Albert. Mamma retires at 10.30; father sits up nearly all night. About 11 o'clock I begin to yawn, and off I go, but not to bed; I generally do not get home until 3 and 4 in the morning. I hate this sort of deception. When I am twenty-one I will openly avow my sins.

Skating all day on the Petit Lac in the Bois de Bologne; I enjoy it immensely. It seems so funny, hardly any of the French ladies can even stand on their skates. The men are really too absurd.

A few Russians and Poles skate well, but all are very cheerful. Large bonfires are lighted on the bank so that we can warm ourselves. The Galitzins brought some punch and cakes. They allow their daughter to skate, so do the Ourousoffs. No French girls, only married women. The G.'s sent two beautiful sledges that a man can push from behind—one in the shape of a springing tiger, and it is lined with tiger-skin and cushions of the same. The other, a large swan, is most graceful; this is lined with blue velvet. They have only just arrived from Russia. We men in turn push the different ladies about on the ice. I don't think I cared much about it. The King's coach passed at the very fast pace that it is always driven; much to our surprise, it returned and stopped for his Majesty to watch us. We—of course, the men—uncovered, but he most graciously sent one of his gentlemen to say that we were not to notice him but go on with our sport, which he wished to watch. He stopped quite half an hour. It is such a pity that the beautiful Bois de Boulogne has been destroyed! Most of the fine trees have been cut down and most of the undergrowth. This was done by the soldiers of the Allies.

I have made some excellent friends of my own age or a little older. The Duc de Guiche, the son of the Duc de Gramont, Rochefoucauld, whom I knew when I was here in 1815, Balliet La Tour, Puységur, are my intimates. I have tried to make friends with some of the attachés of the English Embassy, but I am sorry to say they do not seem to care for us but seem to shun us as if we were at war. Later others may come with a different spirit, as they are often changing. Nobody could be more gracious than the Duke of Wellington. Father had met him so often at Madame de Staël's; she has that wonderful gift of bringing people together and putting them at once at their ease. I had what might have been a most unpleasant adventure last evening. I had noticed several times a very pretty what I thought was a *grisette* in the gardens of the Palais Royal. She didn't seem to mind my rather bold way of staring at her—in fact, she smiled. As I am always ready for adventure, I wrote on a bit of paper asking for a rendezvous. I dropped it just as she was approaching me. I saw her pick it up. She did not look at me, but shortly after a man, raising his hat, handed me a note, only a few words, making an appointment at a house in the Rue St. Honoré for 10.30 in the evening. Naturally I was there. An old woman met me at the door. Putting her finger to her lips and bidding me to follow her, she mounted to the second floor. Letting us in with a key, I found myself in a most beautiful apartment. She threw open the door, and to my amazement there was my *grisette* with a child of about two years on her lap and one a year or so older standing by her side. All were beautifully dressed, and sitting by a little table was a man. He rose, and with a bow said, "Monsieur, you are most welcome to our humble home. My wife has kept the children out of bed expressly for you to see them." Imagine my deep mortification. She is Mademoiselle R—— of the Théâtre Français. It was a lesson I will not forget and which I richly deserved. They both begged me to honour them with a visit at any time. She knew perfectly well who I was. I will certainly not forget them. We are getting very near Lent now, when, of course, we will be very quiet. I love the spring in Paris—the Champs Elysées is so beautiful with the trees and brilliant sunshine. I have been fencing a great deal lately, not that I anticipate a duel; in fact, I would not be allowed to fight on account of father's position— not that I want to in the least, but I think fencing gives great ease, grace, and balance. I took the children on Sunday to Versailles. The great fountains played. I took Frances to see them; they are a wonderful sight. Of course, mamma would not go, as it was Sunday. We lost Albert and did not find him for several hours. When he appeared he had his hat covered with insects and butterflies on pins that he had caught. I made him throw them all away. He is really incorrigible; he ought to be sent to a boarding-school or college.

MARCH 1817

Now that Lent has come we have much more leisure, no Court entertainments of any kind. Father has received an intimation that he will be required to go to the Netherlands in July to help Mr. Eustace in his negotiations *re* indemnity, &c. &c. He does not care much about going but never shirks his duty. I will go with him. Madame de Staël is very ill. She sent for father to-day and had a long conference with him, principally about her property. He had advised her to place all her monetary affairs in the hands of Monsieur Rothschild of London. She did not take his advice at the time and now repents it. It seems she is much troubled about what she should do for Mr. Rocca (her husband). Her great love for her daughter is overwhelming; she wants to leave her the bulk of her property. At one moment—strong woman as she is—she talks of approaching death; the next moment of the house she has taken and the entertainments she intends to give. Madame Récamier has a beautiful hotel in the Rue de (*illegible*). She receives on Thursday evenings, always reclining on a *chaise-longue*. She is certainly very brilliant and witty. She does not like Madame de Boigne and calls her *une prétentieuse*. She says, "Madame de B. only acknowledges two families, that of the Bon Dieu and the Osmonds."

I think I have forgotten to mention the attempt on the life of the Duke of Wellington. As he was driving home in the Champs Elysées a shot was fired, but fortunately missed him—in fact, the bullet has not been found. Some malicious people say he had the shot fired himself. Naturally he has lots of enemies. So great a man as he is can brush such insinuations aside without giving them a thought. He certainly is the most important personage in France at present, and if anything happened to him it would be a dire calamity. Indeed, it is very odd how persistently rude the Royal Family are to him. He never shows the slightest displeasure and is always dignified and courtesy itself. Father has the greatest admiration for him, and believes him to be a born diplomatist as well as a great soldier and leader of men.

I have just heard that a man called Cantillon has been arrested. They say he is but a man of straw and that his arrest was made to appease the English and that he will never be tried. The extraordinary thing is that, with the exception of the Duc de Berri, not one of the Royal Family expressed the slightest sympathy or congratulated the Duke on his escape.

MARCH 26

The Chamber closed to-day. I am getting a little tired of Lent, mamma will keep it so strictly. I see at times it rather annoys father, but he does not say anything. I can never quite make out what his ideas are on religion. He is a Calvinist and was brought up when a child by Mlle Pictet very strictly. I think Voltaire and his ideas greatly influenced him. I do not care what his religion is, nobody could be better than he is. Always so gentle, smoothing over everything and keeping peace, thoughtful for everybody, even for the servants—could there be a better man? I only wish I could approach him in any way. Mamma was a Miss Nicholson; I must have some of the "Old Nick" in me from that side of the family.

MARCH 29

Father to-day told me if I could find an agreeable travelling companion that he would give me the money to go to Bourg to see Jacques Cœur's house, which is so beautiful. I fear my travelling companion must be of the male sex, although father did not stipulate this. It is rather a long journey, quite three days to get there.
I was showing Frances to-day how I could tame her canary. I drew a chalk-line on the table, caught the little bird, and laid him on his back on the line. He remained perfectly quiet. Frances was delighted. She put out her hand to take him up. The poor little thing did not move—he was dead. I was so sorry. Poor Frances cried bitterly. I went out at once and bought her another, but she is not comforted.

APRIL 15

I dined with father at the Duke of Wellington's yesterday. Great magnificence, the plate gold. It is the
Royal plate sent from England for his use. Shoals of
powdered lackeys in the Wellington liveries, eight gold
candelabra on the table. In the centre of the table a
huge gold basin filled with flowers. All the service silver
with the sweets and dessert, and then all was gold.
Prince Talleyrand was present, the Duc de Rohan,
Duchesse de Courlande (niece of Talleyrand, who seems
devoted to him), Duc and Duchesse de Duras, the Galit-
zins, Caumont la Forces, de Broglies, Comte and Comtesse
D'Orsay, Duc and Duchesse de Grammont, Comtesse de
Boigne and her brother Osmond, the English Ambassador,
Chevalier Stuart, Baron Vincent (Austria), the Duc and
Duchesse de Fernan-Nunez (Spain), Baron Fagel (Pays
Bas), Comte and Comtesse Soltz (Prussia), Pozzo di Borgo
(Russia), Marquis Alfieri (Sardinia), Prince Castelcicala
(Deux Siciles), Comte and Comtesse de Gallatin (Würtem-
berg), and a host of others. The Duke was in fine spirits
and received congratulations on all sides.

APRIL

At last the Orléans family have been granted permission
to return to France. They are installed at the Palais
Royal. They were not well received by the King; in
fact, the only members of the Royal Family who greeted
them cordially were the Duc and Duchesse de Berri.
I went officially with father to the Palais Royal after
he had requested an audience. We were received in
the simplest manner possible. They seem like any
ordinary bourgeois family. The Duke* is short, marked

* Louis Philippe d'Orléans, Duc d'Orléans, born September 6, 1773,
reigned as Louis Philippe I, died in England (to which country he fled
in 1848) August 26, 1850. He was the son of Philippe Egalité, Duc
d'Orléans, who voted for the death of Louis XVI.

Bourbon features, decidedly common-looking. The Duchess is not pretty but most gracious and charming, Mademoiselle as well. We stopped quite half an hour, his Highness asking many questions about America, of which he seems to have great knowledge. He spoke of Monsieur de Lafayette and was *au courant* with father's intimacy with him. Driving home, father, who rarely expresses any opinion about people, said, "That man is an intriguer; I would not trust him." We had seen and been presented to him in England three years ago. A Court reception to-morrow.

I had rather an unfortunate adventure some few nights since, but it I hope will never get to father's ears. After going to the opera, a charming little *danseuse*, whose acquaintance I had only just made, asked me if I would sup with her at her apartment. Much to my surprise I found the greatest luxury—some personage evidently in the background. A round table with *couverts* for two. We had just commenced to sup when I heard a noise in the antechamber. My charmer exclaimed, "*Mon Dieu, je suis perdue, cachez-vous.*" I rushed behind a curtain. The door opened, and to my dismay I recognized the voice of the Duc de Berri. He said, "So mademoiselle has an *amant.*" Clare tremblingly answered, "*Non, Monseigneur,* it was only mamma who I was giving a little supper to as you did not arrive." He asked, "What has become of her?" "She has gone, Monseigneur, as she was not properly dressed to receive your Highness." By bad luck I had left my hat on a chair. The Duke picked it up and said with a laugh, "So, madame, *votre mère* wears a man's hat, which she has forgotten." I felt it was time for me to discover myself, no matter what the consequences might be. I stepped out from behind the curtain, saying, "Monseigneur, it is my hat; I am mademoiselle's mother." He broke into fits of laughter, poor Clare into tears. He laughed so heartily that I could not help joining him;

he then became serious and in the kindest manner said, "Young man, you have acted in a most honourable manner not to play eavesdropper. *Tout est pardonné.* Let us sup together." Clare rang and ordered another *couvert* to be laid, and we had a most cheerful supper. When he rose to leave he begged me to accompany him, which, of course, I did. Going down the stairs he took me by the arm and said most kindly, "I am really the one to blame; here we have met as Mr. Smith and Mr. Jones," adding, "in fact, you have unknowingly done me a great favour, as I was most anxious to get rid of Mlle Clare; you have given me the opportunity. I am your debtor, but do not forget I am Mr. Smith." He always speaks English to me, even at Court.

I have not seen Clare again and do not intend doing so. I met the Duc yesterday. He burst out laughing and said, with a twinkle in his eye, "Have you seen your friend, Mr. Jones, lately? Mr. Smith, I hear, has gone back to England."

The Prince de Condé is very ill. His son, the Duc de Bourbon, it seems, leads the most extraordinary life— only cares for people of the lower classes, shows himself in public with the commonest of drabs, hates royalty, and is unfit for decent society.

PARIS

Much to my delight, Lord Huntly (now Duke of Gordon) called to-day. He is very old but looks wonderfully well. He said, "You look a man now; when I last saw you you were a child." He is a very great favourite at Court. Father went again to-day to see Madame de Staël. He came back very depressed, as he fears she will not last long. She was very excited, talking about Jacques Cœur, from whom she is descended through the Gallatins. Cœur was certainly an extraordinary man. I never heard that any of our family benefited by his fortune. I intend some day going to Bourges to see his palace, which they say is the finest Renaissance palace in existence. If Jeanne d'Arc had not had those absurd visions we might be rich. Madame de Staël says that both she and father get their brains from Cœur; they certainly got nothing else. Father does not inherit the latter's love of show. I really believe he would be perfectly happy in one room with any amount of strong segars and a few clever men to discuss abstruse questions with. I am glad to say he has a certain amount of pride, which makes him live in a proper style, which his present position demands.

JULY

Father was sent for this morning as Madame de Staël is worse. He is much distressed, as he has the most profound admiration for her.

JULY 18

Madame de Staël died yesterday. She is to be buried at Coppet; so, at least, is the present intention. We are obliged to leave for Brussels to-morrow, greatly to father's regret, as he would have liked to have paid his last respects to her by going to Coppet for the funeral. He considers her loss a public one, that she was a great power and that she had more influence on public opinion than any other person excepting the actual Ministers in office. Her mind, instead of diminishing with years, improved, and she became more and more brilliant. The Duchesse de Broglie is inconsolable.

I saw Auguste de Staël this morning.

Arrived yesterday in Brussels. Are not well lodged in the Rue de la Loi. Father wishes to confer with Baron Fagel. After a week of idleness the King has decided that the negotiations must be held at the Hague. After all, we need not have come here until much later. We are stopping here for several weeks before going to the Hague. It is extremely dull; everybody out of town, houses shut up, very hot, and absolutely nothing for me to do. Father has given me permission to go to Ostend for some bathing, which I certainly will take advantage of.

JULY 29: OSTEND

Arrived here to-day, a lovely place in the Dunes. I am at a very comfortable hostelry, the Hotel d'Allemagne. The bathing splendid. Full of all the bourgeoisie from Brussels, Ghent, Bruges, &c. &c. Very amusing watching the pacquets coming from England. The people of the place rough Flemish—loud, coarse voices but good-natured and healthy. Fishing is the chief industry.

AUGUST 3

I went to Bruges yesterday and stopped the night—such an interesting place but falling into decay. Wonderful buildings and a beautiful cathedral with such a sweet chime of bells. I have made friends with a nice Englishman, a Mr. Marchmont, who went with me. It is sad to see a place once so opulent and of such importance practically finished. It has played in the past such an important part in history. Ostend interests me on account of the siege. One of our ancestors was killed there. In the "Etrennes de la Noblesse," which is the peerage of France before the Revolution, volume 1778, is the following *anecdote historique:*

"*François de Gallatin fut blessé mortelment au siège d'Ostende—à l'attaque du chemin couvert où il avoit combattu avec la plus grande valeur, à la tête des trois compagnies de Grenadiers du Régiment de la Cour-au-Chantre, qu'il commandoit, et qui y furent écrasés—on lui coupa la cuisse —quelques instants avant sa mort on lui demanda ses derniers volontés pour son fils, encore enfant: 'Qu'il suive mon exemple,' repondit il.*"

Father has written to me to join him at the Hague on August 15, so I will stop here until then. I forgot to mention that when I was at Brussels I visited the plains of Waterloo. I shut my eyes and tried to picture the whole scene of the battle. I cannot but feel pity for the Emperor—to have risen to the great heights that he did and now a prisoner at such a horrible place as St. Helena. He was a very great man and he rose alone without any help. He, I am certain, had great magnetic force. I think his family were a great drag on him. His brothers, with one exception, were full of greed.

My friend Marchmont has not turned out quite as nice as I thought he was. He asked me yesterday if I would lend him one hundred francs, saying he was expecting money from England. He did not turn up at *déjeuner* this morning, and when I asked for him mine host with surprise said, "Did not monsieur know that Monsieur Marchmont left by the packet this morning for England?" With this he handed me a letter— it was only a few lines—which showed me what a dupe I had been: "Young man, never lend money to a stranger in a foreign country," signed "Marchmont." I hope some day to meet my fine gentleman.

AUGUST 15: THE HAGUE

Arrived here last night, but father will not arrive until to-morrow. We are lodged in a very nice house which adjoins one occupied by Mr. Eustace.* We are to eat with him. Lucien is with me. If Brussels was dull, what is this place? It is absolutely dead. Very clean outwardly, but they tell me the people are dirty and that it is all outward show, that the interiors of the houses are very untidy—not a bath in any of the houses and no public baths like in Paris.

* American minister at The Hague.

AUGUST 20

Very little work to do at present. I had to confess to
father how I had been duped at Ostend. He said he
hoped it was a lesson to me, but at once handed me five
napoleons.

AUGUST 28: THE HAGUE

A charming surprise. A Baron Constant Rébecque
whose mother was born Gallatin, called to see father.
They have a beautiful place in the country. He invited
us to stop with him. Father cannot leave but accepted
for me. I go there to-morrow.

SEPTEMBER 2

I came back from the Rébecque's this morning. It is a
lovely place. I was sorry it was not the tulip season as
they have many of them. We shot some hares and foxes;
the latter, it seems, do a lot of damage. What would
they say to this in England, where a fox is sacred?
I must say the Dutch nobility are delightful, so simple and
cordial. I felt at home at once. Madame de Rébecque
was so pleased to see anybody of her name. She said
if father could not spare the time to go and see her she
would go to the Hague to see him. I find all what we
call "hot cakes" in America are of Dutch origin. We
have "waffles" and "griddle cakes" every day for
breakfast. Dutch girls are not pretty. They say they
make good wives. I am not surprised as they cannot
have any other temptations. Two, Mlle von Briennen
and Mlle Bentinck, all round and fat.

THE HAGUE

Hard work now. It seems they laugh at the idea of an
indemnity, which annoys father very much. He feels
his mission is quite useless. We will soon go back to
Paris. I am delighted, as it is not gay here.

SEPTEMBER

We leave on the 22nd. First pay a visit to the Rébecques. Father is the most extraordinary person. After all his trouble coming here, he has only asked for his actual out-of-pocket expenses. Mr. Eustace says it is quite absurd. He cares less for money than anybody I have ever heard of. I only discovered a short time since that he had paid all his grandmother's debts in Geneva. She was a most reckless and extravagant person, and certainly did not consider him in any way.

SEPTEMBER 30: PARIS

Back again in Paris. Mamma and the children are at Fontainebleau. We join them in a few days. Mr. Sheldon must have a holiday, so our stay in the country will be very short. Rumours of a change of Government. The Duke Decazes* is spoken of. They say Monsieur is intriguing against the King.

OCTOBER

Fontainebleau is deadly dull—nothing to do but ride in the forest. Of course, it is very beautiful, but I soon tire of it as I ride alone. The *Chasse* will soon begin, I am glad to say. We have a very comfortable house on the outskirts of the town quite close to the forest.

OCTOBER 12

The Marquis de Breteuil sent me an invitation to hunt with him. I have just come back. It was a *chasse au sanglier*. The wild boars abound in the forest and at times are very dangerous. It was all very new to me and struck me as rather theatrical. The boarhounds were very fine, a large pack—the huntsmen, &c., all

* Monsieur Elie Decazes, born September 28, 1780, died 1860. After the assassination of the Duc de Berri in 1820 he was created duc and given the English Embassy; was a great favorite of Louis XVIII.

in the King's livery. Huge *cors de chasse*, which they put their heads through as one does through a life-preserver; at every opportunity possible they blow blasts on these latter. When a poor "piggy" was killed his dying moments were cheered by a lively tune played on at least six of the horns; still it is an amusement for me. There were several ladies of Court in the Royal Costume at the *Chasse*, which really made a beautiful scene. I expected every moment to see the curtain come down as it does at the play. I believe in the time of Louis XIV they followed the hunt in huge gilt and painted coaches.

NOVEMBER 6

We stopped until the end of October at Fontainebleau and are now again installed in the Rue de l'Université. Paris is very gay. I love the boulevards—so gay and everybody seems so cheerful. What a light-hearted people the French are. I am glad to say mamma seems a little happier. I am sure she will end by liking Paris.

NOVEMBER 9

We have had a sheaf of dispatches from home, which I have to go through and copy. No wonder my handwriting is becoming illegible, my fingers are so cramped. The Caumont la Forces have a large supper to-night to which we are bidden. It has been so dull and cold all day, I think we are going to have a downfall of snow.

NOVEMBER 10

We could hardly get home from the la Forces last night. It had rained a little and then came a frost making the streets like glass; in fact, they call it *ver glas*. The coachman and footman had to get down and lead the horses. I did also, and could hardly keep my own footing. Fortunately, the horses had been roughed. We were quite two hours doing a journey which ordinarily takes less than half an hour. Father has sent to Geneva for a fine gold watch for me for my Christmas present. He certainly spoils me.

I often wonder if anybody got hold of my diary after I am dead what an ass they would think me. I will leave strict instructions to burn it. Frances and I are both learning a new dance, the "Schottische." It is very pretty and quite the fashionable rage.

NOVEMBER 20

I was presented to a Madame Chapelle last night at the opera. She is a daughter of the Regent Orléans and Madame de Genlis. She is not pretty but has great charm of manner—a *grande dame*. She has asked me to call on her. She receives on Friday evening. They say all Paris goes to her. Mamma allowed me to take Frances for a walk on the boulevard yesterday. She is so young it does not make any matter; were she eighteen it would be impossible. Fancy the customs of different countries. Here we are hemmed in by Etiquette. I have a bad toothache and am going to bed.

NOVEMBER 21

I waked this morning and my right cheek felt as if it were going to burst. I got up and looked in the mirror. Horrors, I did not recognize myself! I cannot see my right eye and my cheek is like an apple-dumpling. I am going to send for some leeches. I sent Lucien for my breakfast. Of course mamma thought I was ill and arrived with her medicine-chest. She said in any case a powder would do me good. I put my foot down firmly and said I would not take one. She left the room saying, "It is all biliousness." As if a swollen face was bile! She does annoy me. She even asked me what I had been eating.

NOVEMBER 25

My face quite normal again and I went out to-day. It was very cold, so I thought it best to go quietly and see

Mlle Laflage of the opera. She had a great wood-fire,
and I showed her how to make toast as we do in America.
I did not go home until she had to go to the opera. She
is in the ballet and did not have to leave until 8
o'clock. I got home in time for supper, found the kitchen
chimney on fire, a great crowd, and a "file" passing
buckets all the way from the Seine up one side and down
the other. It was soon put out. Very little damage done
but all the supper ruined. We had to make the best
of it, and ate cake and bread and milk.

DECEMBER 1

Already preparations are being made for Christmas. We
are going to have a Christmas party. I proposed bobbing
for apples and snap-dragon. For once my family
approved of my idea. We are going to have a very
young party for Frances. Mamma enjoys arranging
this sort of thing. I am trying to think of something
new to amuse them. I proposed kiss-in-the-ring and hunt-
the-slipper. Mamma vetoed both as improper—so *voilà*.

DECEMBER 8

Last night a splendid ball at Court. Mamma was very
fine: all Madame de Gallatin-Vaudenet's jewels—which
were all poor father inherited from her; in fact, he had
voluntarily paid all her immense debts—also some fine
lace. Mamma's train was purple velvet with white lace.
The diamonds are all mounted in Louis XV settings.
One huge aigrette with briolet diamonds in her turban,
which was of gold tissue. On her forehead a *ferronnière*
of diamonds—beautiful brooches. Her dress was gold
and purple striped tissue. The Landgrave of Hesse
Cassel gave Madame Gallatin-Vaudenet most of the
jewels.
The Duchesse d'Angoulême was regal in white with
a train entirely of ermine. She was absolutely covered
with jewels—pearls and diamonds. She is the most

royal-looking personage one can possibly imagine. It
was dreadfully crowded. All was over at midnight.

DECEMBER 12

I have decided on my surprise for our Christmas party.
I am having a huge imitation plum-pudding made of
cardboard. It is large enough to hold a little girl of ten
dressed as a fairy. She will distribute flowers and
sweeties. Each package is to have a small flag on it;
the flags are to be of all nations.

DECEMBER 15

Nothing but balls every night. I am quite worn out.
Fortunately there is hardly any work to be done for
father, or I would have to go to bed early.

DECEMBER 24

All is now ready for our Christmas party. The ball-
room looks very nice, and I keep even the stable men
frottéing to get the floor in fine condition. Supper
is to be before we dance and play our *jeux d'innocence.*
Frances is so excited, we will not let her see anything of
our preparation. I tell her unless she keeps quiet she
will have a red nose.

DECEMBER 26

Everything went off capitally. After supper, which
was 8 o'clock, we started our game. Snap-dragon, a
novelty, was a great success. We were allowed to play
kiss-in-the-ring, suppressing the kiss; it was like
"Hamlet" minus the Prince of Denmark. Of course, it
was mamma. My plum-pudding was even a surprise to
mamma. At 11 o'clock I had a great bell rung. In
marched four footmen carrying the pudding on high.
I took a great knife as if to cut it, and, pulling a string
at the same time, it fell open. The little fairy was so
dainty. I had her taught some verses called "Noel,"

which she declaimed as only a child can. After the little packages were distributed, we danced a *contredanse*. The young girls were all so pretty I wanted to kiss them all. The poor little child who was in the plum-pudding burst into tears and would not be comforted. She wanted her mother, who is only a dresser at the opera, and who was to call for her at midnight, not being able to leave her work before then. Mamma took her on her lap and comforted her until she fell asleep from sheer exhaustion. When her mother did arrive, father, with his usual kindness, sent her home in a coach which he had ordered. All the young people loaded her with bon-bons, &c. I gave her a great big doll which I had bought for the purpose. She will be happy when she wakes to-morrow morning.

JANUARY 1, 1818: NEW YEAR'S DAY

After we had all drunk each other's health in egg nog I went out to commence the New Year—I fear badly. I don't think I'll record in my diary where I went.

.   .   .   .   .   .

JANUARY

A delightful dinner and *sauterie* at the Pictet de Rochment's. He is the Bavarian *chargé d'affaires* and a connexion of father's. Mlle Pictet, who brought father up in his early days, was his aunt. Pozzo di Borgo, Comte and Comtesse de Grotz (Hanover), Marquis and Marquise Alfieri (a descendant of the great Italian poet— he represents Sardinia here), Count and Countess Goltz (he represents Prussia), and the Chevalier Stuart, as they call him here, the English Ambassador—in fact, quite a diplomatic gathering. For the *sauterie*, Comte and Comtesse de Gallatin, who brought their two daughters, the Prince and Princesse Castelcicala (Deux Sicèles), the Baillet-Latours, Comte and Comtesse Caumont la Force, the Galitzins. and many others. There was a *pavane*

dance by six young men and six ladies, a *contre-danse*
and several "minuets," then a "Roger de Coverley"
proposed by the English Ambassadress; but few knew
the dance, but on once seeing the four first couples they
quickly acquired it and acquitted themselves very well
amongst much laughter.   When there is a gathering
of young people of this kind it is much gayer.   Even
father, Pozzo di Borgo, and the Chevalier Stuart joined
in the dance.   I had for partner Katinka Galitzin.   My
newly acquired "pigeon's wings" were much applauded.
We supped at midnight.   Mamma slept in the coach
going home.

JANUARY 6

Splendid skating on the *petit lac*, which was reserved.
I got home just in time to dress to go to a twelfth-night
party at Comtesse de Gallatin's.   After cutting the
gateau du roi, Puységur drew the bean in his bit and
Mlle Caumont la Force found the other one.   They
were duly clothed in red velvet mantles trimmed with
ermine, gold paper crowns on their heads, and they
were the reigning king and queen for the evening.   It
was put to the vote for the Court places.   I was voted
to be the Court fool and wore a fool's cap.   As I considered it an insult, I determined to fool to my heart's
content.   After the king and queen had been escorted
in state to their throne the revels commenced.   Minuets,
pavanes, mazurkas, were danced in rapid succession.
Supper was announced at 11 o'clock.   I slipped out
unobserved, got hold of one of the footmen (whose palm
I greased), and got him to get me a large foot-tub full
of warm water; this I had placed facing the throne.
I enlisted the aid of two of my cronies, placed a chair on
either side of the tub, covering the whole with a quilt
which I got my footman to procure for me.   Seating my
friends, one on one side and one on the other, I told
them that sudden death would overtake them if they

dared to move. I returned to the supper-room looking perfectly innocent. We then escorted the king and queen back to their respective thrones. I craved their majesty's permission to try a rebel for *lèse majesté*. They at once granted my fool's request. I then told the trumpeter to sound three times, and the herald to call upon Monsieur d'Osmond* to appear before their majesties to be tried and sentenced. Osmond is full of his own importance. He approached, and was told by me to seat himself between the two guards. I had told them the moment he did so to at once rise; this they did, and plump went Osmond into the bath. It really succeeded better than I had anticipated. He did not at first realize he was sitting in the water, but when he did he tried to get out of the tub, making an awful splashing; I never heard so much laughter. Poor Osmond stood dripping, a sorry figure and raging; the more he raged, the more we all laughed. When early in the evening I was voted to be the fool, he had said in his horrid sarcastic way, "That *rôle* exactly fits you." I could not refrain from going up to him and saying, "You now have a *rôle* that fits you like a bathing-dress." You see, on the *Jour des Rois* nobody must lose their temper, so he had to grin and bear it. He went in the kitchen to be dried but did not appear again. My cousin, Count Gallatin, tried to look serious and, taking me by the ear, reprimanded me, saying, "That was quite sufficient to cause war between France and America." I answered, "For the evening I am a fool, and it was a fool's prank." Anyhow, no more was said about it, and I think all enjoyed the joke.

JANUARY 9

We had a very large supper-party last night, but extremely dull. It may have been very intellectual, it undoubtedly

* Monsieur d'Osmond, son of the Marquis d'Osmond and brother of the Comtesse de Boigne.

was, but my intellect was not sufficiently cultivated to appreciate it; but I saw how happy father was and that quite resigned me to my fate. Poor mamma did not understand a word of the general conversation, but kept nodding her head and smiling in the most intelligent manner until I feared the feathers would fall out of her turban. Monsieur de Lafayette gave a long harangue on the subject of liberty. I think father was a little uneasy, as it does not do for people to express their opinion too openly at an embassy. Pozzo only laughed at the whole thing. Our silver, which was the service of poor General Moreau, made a very fine show. Mamma has great taste—the flowers and fruit on the table were beautifully arranged. Madame Récamier recited some poems in the most affected and stilted style. I really think she humbugs herself; she loves to hear the sound of her own voice. Count D'Orsay was the only amusing person. He made a violent speech on the political questions of the day, without head or tail, beginning or end; I rather loved him for it. After all the guests had retired I was off to a *bal masqué* at the opera—had lots of adventures, made at least a dozen rendezvous, and by now have forgotten both places and names. *Telle est la vie.*

FEBRUARY 3

A great sensation has been produced by the appearance of a pamphlet printed in London and called "The Manuscript of St. Helena." It is supposed to have been written by the Emperor himself. It is read in all the great *salons*, and many say they recognize the style of the Emperor. Monsieur Naville (father's cousin) brought it to him yesterday from the author, who is Monsieur Lullin de Chateauvieux, also a cousin and a Genevan. We are all sworn to secrecy. This makes it most amusing for me, as I hear of nothing else in all the *salons* I frequent and often have a good laugh to myself. A most extraordinary person who I must here give a place to is the Queen of Sweden, wife of Bernadotte. She was a Mlle Eugénie Désirée Clary.* Her sister Julie married Joseph Bonaparte. They were the daughters of a tallow-chandler in Marseilles. She has left Sweden as she says the climate did not agree with her. Her position here is a curious one. A private note was sent to all the ambassadors and ministers of foreign Powers not to receive her as Queen of Sweden but simply as Madame Bernadotte. She is not received officially at Court, but still the King receives her as Madame Bernadotte in private. I have met her in several different *salons*—a most common-looking person, with a loud voice and coarse manners, and dressed in clothes you expect to see a cook wear. She has a strong Marseilles accent. When I was presented to her she said in horrible French: *"Comment, vous êtes Americain et vous n'êtes pas noir. Ma sœur Julie a été en Amérique."* She would be better if she were black—she has some sort of eruption on her face which is not nice to look at. Another extraordinary female is the Duchesse de Duras; she is quite as ugly as Madame Bernadotte. Since the death of Madame de Staël she seems to think the latter's mantle has fallen on her shoulders. She apes her as much as she dare do. Instead of a small laurel-branch which Madame de Staël always carried in her hand and gesticulated with (I have mentioned this before), she has long bits of paper which she twirls about and tears to pieces; it's most amusing to watch her. Her daughter, the Princesse de Talmont, a widow, has lately married a Monsieur de Rochejacquelin, much against her mother's wishes.

I fear I am drifting into a serious love affair. At several houses I have met a handsome Spanish woman, wife of

* Eugénie-Désirée Clary, wife of Jean Bernadotte, who was elected Prince Royal of Sweden in 1810, succeeded the King Charles XII in 1818; reigned as Charles XIV. He was never recognized by the King of France.

a Secretary of Embassy; she is several years older than
I am and does not live happily with her husband. She
has asked me to meet her at out-of-the-way places; I
have been weak enough to do so, but I must break it off.
It would be a serious matter for me and for father's
position if there were any scandal, particularly in the
diplomatic circle.

Serious talk of the resignation of Monsieur de Richelieu;
father seems worried. Monsieur Decazes is spoken of.
The King has shown him great favour lately. This
means that father will have to begin all over again.
Nothing definite has been settled with Monsieur de
Richelieu. Our Government is pressing and seems to
think it is father's fault.

We are in a very unsettled state on account of the
approaching change in the Government. So many
different rumours. General Dessolles spoken of as the
new leader. Father hardly thinks this possible, but
believes Monsieur Decazes will certainly (if not actually
in name) be the leader. Prince Talleyrand is now in
Paris; he is such an intriguer, so absolutely false, that
nobody trusts him. I heard a good story about him
yesterday and his astuteness. When he was in power
a gentleman, accompanied by a small suite, presented
himself at his house as the Margrave of C., a German
princeling. His credentials were all in order, but Talleyrand suspected there was something wrong from the
man's demeanour. Nevertheless, he invited him to
dinner—putting him, as his rank demanded, on his right
hand at table. When dinner was at an end and olives
were passed with the wine, the Margrave took a fork
to eat his with. At once Talleyrand clapped his hands,
a prearranged signal, saying in a loud voice, "Arrest
this impostor. No gentleman eats olives with a fork."
Several officers disguised as footmen rushed forward and
seized him. His suite immediately rose and tried to
escape from the room, but they were also arrested.

Talleyrand was quite right; he afterwards learned that the Margrave of C. had been waylaid on his way to Paris, stripped of his clothes, baggage and papers, and left with his suite penniless. The fine gentleman and his band took the Margrave's coach and made use of the relays, so arriving in Paris. The poor Margrave wandered about for some time, as nobody would believe his story and thought he was an impostor. Another story is not out of place here. One day Talleyrand, who is very mal-formed, pointing to a particularly tall and handsome footman, said to the lady next to him, "That is the way we make them, and this is the way they make us."

Mamma is in despair, as father hates entertaining. He only cares to see his old friends—Lafayette, La Place, the Humboldts, Pozzo di Borgo, &c. They continually dine and sup with us. I have my own amusements, so it does not affect me. I am beginning to find out that all the Court and official functions are a great bore; they are all the same thing over and over again. The exceptions are the entertainments at the Elysée and the Palais Royale. The Duc and Duchesse de Berri are so gay and cheerful that they instil life into all. At the Palais Royale it is so informal; although very fine entertainments, one is not hedged in by that eternal etiquette as at the Tuileries. The Duke and Duchess d'Angoulême are so formal and sad—Monsieur so repellent in his cold, stiff way, though they say he can be charming if he chooses. The poor old King is far more gracious; he really seems to enjoy father's society, and certainly shows him great favour. He laughingly said to him the other day, "I wish you would give us French lessons and we will give you English ones." Poor father's French accent is so strong in English. I sincerely believe it is one of the reasons he is so disliked in America, and it is a great drawback in political life. He is certainly in his right place here, but I think he longs for a more active life.

JULY

He has accepted a special mission to England; it is a very important one. The terms settled at the Treaty of Ghent expire in 1819, so all has to be reconsidered and settled afresh. He is the only person capable of carrying through these negotiations on account of his intimate knowledge of all details. Mr. Rush is our Minister in England. Father discovered him and had him put in his present position. He has most kindly extended his hospitality to us. Father has availed himself of his kind offer to stop at his house when in London. We expect to leave here in July. I fear London will be very dull after Paris, but I will have plenty of work to do. Father insists upon having a copy of every document and prefers me to make them. Albert dislikes Paris so much he is to go back to America this summer. He only cares about birds, animals, and so forth, and likes a wild solitary life. Frances promises to be pretty, and I hope she will grow up so and make a good marriage either here or in England. Her religion will be a great obstacle to her here, and if she changed it mamma would promptly give up the ghost. I am quite certain she will never be content to live in America, and I am sure I won't.

JULY 24

To-day we received the *faire-part* of the Duc de Guiche, the eldest son of the Duc de Gramont, with Mlle D'Orsay, the daughter of the Count and Countess D'Orsay. Mademoiselle is quite lovely and de Guiche is very handsome; they will make a brave couple. I have seen a great deal of de Guiche but not *dans le grand monde*. I suppose now he will settle down and we will see him no more. The contract of the marriage was on the 10th. Very beautifully done. Masses of flowers everywhere—from the chandelier great wreaths of roses; the wall lights were connected by huge garlands of pink roses. Count

D'Orsay is famous for his taste. The wedding was in the Sainte-Chapelle by special permission of the King. The Duc and Duchesse de Berri were present and signed the register. The *corbeille de mariage* was superb; there were over five hundred presents. I think there is what may be called hot blood in the de Gramont family. There was a Comte de Guiche in the seventeenth century who was a lover of Queen Henrietta Maria, wife of Charles I. He was exiled, and on his return compromised himself with Mlle de la Vallière, the King's mistress; was exiled a second time. Not bad. The sister of the present Duc de Grammont married Lord Tankerville. She was quite lovely.

AUGUST: LONDON

After all, we did not leave Paris until August 10 and arrived in London on the 16th. Mr. Rush is most kind; he has placed the whole second floor of his house at our disposal. Of course London is quite empty and dull. I have plenty of work to do. Father has had several interviews with Lord Castlereagh, who is most conciliatory, but Mr. Frederic Robinson (now President of the Board of Trade) and Mr. Goulburn are the principal Commissioners. The former, as always, is delightful, and father likes dealing with him. The questions to be settled are the Fisheries, the Boundary Question, the West India Trade, and the Captured Slaves. Mr. Robinson begs father to put in writing exactly what his demands are and his reasons for making them; he thinks this will expedite matters. There are daily conferences, and from what I can understand an agreement satisfactory to all parties will soon be come to. Lord Castlereagh is very advanced in his ideas and has no insular prejudices. Mr. Robinson the same. Mr. Goulburn is not quite as enlightened as they are, but all is very amicable and pleasant.

SEPTEMBER 10

I had found it so dull, and not feeling very well, father insisted upon sending me to Brighton for two weeks. I arrived yesterday, and at once went to the Pavilion and paid my respects to the Prince Regent. These were father's orders. He is here with some of his dandies and his last reigning favourite. I am very comfortably lodged not far from the sea, in James Street. The Pavilion is a most extraordinary place—Moorish, I think, in architecture; all sorts of domes and minarets. There is a huge riding-school where the Regent takes exercise in bad weather. They say the cost of the building was something enormous. I only went into the first hall and wrote my name. The decorations are Oriental and dazzling, but, although I am informed to the contrary, I should not think the remainder of the decorations are in good taste.

SEPTEMBER 12

Such perfect weather, I feel much better already; the heat in London was very great. I had so much writing to do that now I want simply to rest. I was out all the morning lying on the shingle basking in the sun. Returned at 2 o'clock to my dinner. The air here gives me a fine appetite, otherwise I should not be able to eat the food they give me; it's like all English food, heavy and greasy. When will they learn what cooking is? In any small inn in France they give you an appetizing meal, well seasoned and well served. For instance, for dinner to-day I had salt boiled beef with carrots and dumplings; the beef was hard, the carrots were harder, and the dumplings I could have thrown against the door without breaking them; but still I was hungry and managed to make a good dinner. This afternoon, when I went for a walk I met the Prince Regent driving in a most gorgeous chariot; it seemed to me every colour of the rainbow. He was accompanied by a lady, but I do not know who she was—in fact, I don't know anybody in England. Several gentlemen accompanied him on horseback. The Prince looked very red as if he had been drinking; they were all very noisy. Mr. Brummell was a great friend of the Prince's; he was called the "mirror of fashion," and although of very humble birth, he managed to work his way to the higher society, and all through his wit and his manner of dressing. He was for a long time the arbiter of fashion. They tell me he often used to destroy a dozen white neckcloths before he tied them to suit him. The Regent used to imitate him though he was most insolent; he was known as "Beau Brummell."

SEPTEMBER 15

Poor Lucien has afforded me great amusement ever since he left Paris. I asked him if he was a good sailor. "*Mais oui, Excellence.*" Now he had never even seen the sea, but I said nothing and awaited events. Full of pluck, he marched on board the packet at Boulogne. We were barely under way when I lost sight of him. On arrival at Dover no Lucien could be found. At last, after a search in the forecastle in one of the sailor's bunks, there was a helpless and limp mass. He was carried on deck, and after having brandy poured down his throat began to revive. His first words were: "*Est-que je suis mort?*" But with the wonderful elasticity of the French nature, before we got to Sevenoaks he was cheerfully chatting with father's man in the rumble. London astonished him; he could not understand the dirty streets or the grimy houses. He was comically miserable —so homesick that at one time father contemplated sending him home, but he would not consent to this, saying, "What would monsieur do without him?" He certainly is devoted to me. Here at Brighton he is much happier. He is a very good-looking lad. Yesterday I actually saw him walking arm-in-arm with a very pretty

girl. As he cannot speak two words of English, I cannot
understand how he managed it. Oh, but the language
of love is not difficult, and I fear he has taken a leaf out
of his master's book.

SEPTEMBER 17

I had a little adventure yesterday which I hope will turn
out well. Nobody knows me here, so I really don't
care what I do. I noticed the day after I arrived a very
pretty woman. There is a certain look that one gives to a
pretty woman and which I have always found a woman
understands. The second time I found her walking
alone she dropped her eyelids, but not till after she had
had a good look at me. After passing her I turned and
followed her, dropping my pocket-handkerchief (I always
carry a lady's handkerchief with me as I have found it
such a help in making acquaintances). I ran after her
saying, "Madame, I think this must be yours?" She
looked at it and said, "Oh, how stupid of me," and with a
pretty curtsy she quietly put it in her reticule; then she
said, "I see you are a stranger here." Of course I poured
out all my woes, telling her I did not know a soul in the
place. She took compassion on me and has promised
to meet me to take a little walk to-morrow evening.

SEPTEMBER 19

My inamorata is charming, she is married to an old man
who is in the city in business—she is down here with a
younger sister, to recoup the latter's health. She has
promised to meet me to-morrow and to take me home to
supper—her sister goes to bed at 7 o'clock.

SEPTEMBER 20

The worst possible luck—this morning I received a command from the Prince Regent to attend a concert at the
Pavilion to-night—what am I to do? I do not know
my fair lady's name or where she is lodged. She will never

forgive me—I cannot tell her the real reason of my not being able to keep the rendezvous. She thinks I am simply a young American travelling for my health.

SEPTEMBER 21

A most gorgeous entertainment at the Pavilion; as I entered rows of lacqueys in Royal liveries and floured heads lined the hall. A most magnificent and important person asked my name with a profound bow—he motioned to two lacqueys who threw open the doors and I was ushered into a gorgeous saloon. A gentleman advanced and said his Royal Highness would receive me in a few minutes, which he did. I was escorted to a smaller saloon, at the far end of which the Prince was half reclining on a divan. He was most gracious and inquired kindly about father—he also asked me some questions about the Royal Family in Paris, particularly about the Duc de Berri. While he was talking to me the doors were thrown open and several ladies and gentlemen came in; the Regent rose and with the aid of two sticks and followed by the Court, in which I joined, proceeded to the Concert Saloon. He was seated in the centre in a large gilt arm-chair with a lady either side of him—I was in the second row. I do not know who the two gentlemen were who were on either side of me, but one knew my name and both of them seeing I was young and feeling a little bashful and a little embarrassed made themselves most agreeable to me and soon put me at my ease. What astonished me very much was when any one of the performers, either male or female, did not please the Prince he expressed his displeasure in a loud voice, much to their mortification—and he is called "The First Gentleman in Europe." When the concert was over, bowing to us all he retired, with several ladies and gentlemen. We were then conducted to the dining-hall, which is very fine. A very lavish buffet supper was served, a fine display of gold plate—some of the gentlemen were half drunk while they were at the concert and when I left after midnight several of them were helplessly so, a disgusting sight and one that is never seen in France, even in Bohemian society. Some of the decorations of the Pavilion are very fine; the chandeliers are huge dragons painted in colours and gilded. What I liked the best were some beautiful wall-hangings of Chinese paper—I have never seen any before like them— but the whole effect of the furniture is vulgar, at least to my eyes, which are so accustomed to the refined taste of the French. Oddly enough I did not see a picture of any kind or description.

SEPTEMBER 22

I have been walking about all day and cannot find a trace of my *belle dame*. I sincerely regret it as I am leaving now in a few days and fear I will never see her again. I went to write my name at the Pavilion. Just as I was leaving the Prince's curricle drove up; of course I had to wait at the door for him to pass—he passed me without a sign of recognition—he was very red in the face, and, may I only breathe it—I fear he was drunk. They told me he had just come from a cock-fight.

SEPTEMBER 23

Not a sign of my fair lady—I so deeply regret it, and of course as I cannot find her, I want to see her all the more. I am leaving the day after to-morrow. Lucien did not come home last night, so my landlady informed me; I must talk to him.

SEPTEMBER 24

Still no sign. It is odd as Brighton is not a large place—it does seem odd. I fancied I knew the direction she lived in and have been haunting that quarter all the morning. We are off to-morrow, in one of the fast coaches—I will enjoy the drive. I am certainly feeling much better.

SEPTEMBER 26: LONDON

We had a splendid journey up, racing another coach the whole way. I am glad to say we arrived first, the other coach had an accident. It's wonderful the rapidity with which they change the horses. We came by Cuckfield, a lovely English village and the Weald of Sussex—lovely views. I thoroughly enjoyed it. Lucien followed with my baggage—these fast coaches do not take any. I found father as usual, calm and unruffled—he was very pleased to see me looking so well. Mr. Rush had a dinner-party, but excused me from appearing as I was fatigued.

SEPTEMBER 28

To-day I was taken to White's Club and Brook's—I had never been into a club before; they say very high gambling takes place at night—as I have never touched a card in my life it does not interest me. Father has a horror of gambling and gamblers. I have been putting some papers in order this evening. London is absolutely empty. Everybody is in the country shooting.

SEPTEMBER 29

I went to-day to Chelsea Marshes with Mr. Compton; we both took guns but there was nothing to shoot—he told me there was very good snipe-shooting later on. To-morrow I am going to the Tower of London. We will be going back to Paris very shortly—another dinner to-night—all men much older than myself. When the wine was put on the table I begged to be excused and went to bed.

OCTOBER 1

Queen Charlotte it is rumoured is very ill—she is suffering from dropsy; it seems she has a violent temper and when she has an outburst it brings on spasms which they fear may cause her death at any moment. The Duchess of Cambridge is devoted to her and hardly ever leaves her.

It is very sad with her poor mad husband. She goes to see him every day but he never recognizes her—he always thinks he is holding a Court and talks incessantly to imaginary people whom he thinks surround him; what a living death! One of the first signs of his coming madness was one day a large pasty of blackbirds was on the Royal table, covered with a thick crust. When it was cut he remarked: "How very extraordinary; how on earth did those blackbirds get in that dish?" He would not allow it to be served and had some clever philosopher sent for to go into the matter.

OCTOBER 2

We dined with Lord Castlereagh last night, only men again; everything fine—we were over three hours at table, the conversation was far above me, although I take a great interest in politics. Father thinks this all does me good and no doubt he is right. We leave on the 10th. I frankly don't like England or English customs and manners.

After many meetings and it seems to me endless discussion the result is as follows:—The articles on impressment and maritime rights are thrown out, a ten years' agreement to cover the Fisheries question, the boundary between the Lake and the Rocky Mountains, also the joint use of the Columbia River; indemnity for the slave owners and the renewal of the commercial treaty of 1815. England has been most generous in every way and father has done his best to conciliate all—Lord Castlereagh has worked in perfect accord with him. The navigation of the Mississippi is settled for ever. With regard to the West India trade, Mr. Robinson made concessions and father met him half-way. On the minor questions in dispute little was settled—Lord Castlereagh wisely said, "Time will do much more than we can"; in this father absolutely agrees. Since the Treaty of Ghent he thinks the American people are a little swelled with pride, which he thinks in time will wear away. We return to Paris very shortly. I shall not be sorry, as it has been desperately dull and very hard work.

OCTOBER 10: DOVER

We left London, I without regret, this morning; we hope to cross to-morrow but it is blowing great guns and the packet did not leave to-day; the French one did as there is a good harbour here. At Boulogne it is sometimes impossible to land. I feel sorry for poor Lucien, he is pea-green in anticipation—I cannot boast much myself, but I am getting used to it.

OCTOBER 11

Still here on account of stress of weather. It does not affect us as we are not in a hurry, as there is nothing for us to do in Paris at present. I visited the Dover Castle—it is on a very high down above the town. It was very interesting—I could hardly keep my feet the wind was so violent.

OCTOBER 12

We embarked this morning, the wind has moderated considerably and the Channel looks quite calm, the sun is shining and we can see Cape Gris Nez distinctly—Lucien is quite cheerful.

OCTOBER 14

We sleep at Amiens to-night.

OCTOBER 18, 1818: PARIS

We returned here on the 16th. Mother is still in the country but returns shortly.

OCTOBER 19

Mamma and Frances returned to-day both looking so well. I have for the last few days been visiting all my old haunts to see if they were still there. We will soon have to return to fashionable life. The Court has returned, and Paris looks very gay.

OCTOBER 22

I even love the smell of Paris. I love the smell of the fruit and vegetables which the market-women hawk about the streets in their push-carts. I love the cry *"Oh, les belles fraises. Oh! les raisins, dix sous la livre,"* and later, *"Oh! la valence, la belle valence."* Dear Albertine de Broglie came to see mamma to-day; they have bought a beautiful hotel, quite close to us. They have a fine boy; she wants us to dine quite *en famille* on Sunday—that is mamma, father, Frances and myself. Mamma could not refuse her, but it is the first time she has dined out on Sunday since we came to Paris.

OCTOBER 25

We had such a pleasant dinner at the de Broglie's. Their hotel is really beautiful. He had superb pictures and furniture, silver, &c.; her mother left her all she possibly could, so it all makes a fine show. The precious baby was brought down before dinner. Of course mamma and Frances made a great fuss over it. I am not an expert in babies, they always look so crumpled and red to me and I never know how to pick them up. We saw a fine portrait of de Broglie's father who was guillotined in the Revolution. She showed it to us. It is covered with a black curtain which she drew aside when he was out of the room, as he cannot bear to look at it. This is the reason I suppose he is so serious.

OCTOBER 29

I am really beginning to vegetate. I will get prematurely old, if I go on at this rate. I am going to-night with Puységur to a ball given by a lady of the "other world." The Duc de Berri protects her and will be there. I have

just come in from a turn in the Bois de Boulogne where
I met many friends whom I had not seen since I had returned from England. The men all wanted to know
about the English fashions as everything is *à l'Anglaise*
now in France. Certainly Englishmen are better dressed
than Frenchmen. I met Count D'Orsay; he is certainly a
fine figure of a man and carries himself so well. His handsome face is rather spoilt by his teeth, which although
very white are very much separated, which gives his
mouth an animal look when he smiles.

NOVEMBER

Very cold and in the mornings we have a thick white fog.
I am fully *lancé dans le monde* again, dancing every
night. The ball at the Duc de Berri's friend was very
enjoyable, but oddly enough up to a certain point the
behaviour was even more dignified than *dans le vrai
monde*. It was not until after supper and the Duc
had retired that things became rather mixed. I know
about 3 A.M. I was sitting on the lap of a lady, who dis-
played ample charms, and she was calling me her " *Bébé,
petit chou,*" &c. I did not stop there long—I prefer
lamb to mutton.

NOVEMBER 1818

Christmas will soon be here. For the first time we are
to dine out at the de Broglie's. She made such a
point of it. We are going to have a New Year's Eve
party.

.   .   .   .   .   .

Of course, I am in another scrape—the same old story.
At Madame Récamier's. She is short, has the most
beautiful auburn hair, is an Austrian by birth, married
to a Frenchman. She swears eternal devotion—I do the
same but do not mean it in the least. It is, I hope, only
a passing fancy. Her husband neglects her, so she says

—but will meet him to-morrow as she has bidden me to
a large dinner-party. We went last night to the opera.
Mamma took Frances for the first time. She was
delighted, it was a pleasure to see her so happy.

NOVEMBER 16

Some most important dispatches have arrived from
America which will keep me busy for a long time. Father
frets a little that he has not more important work to do.
He is writing on finance, which keeps him very busy.
We have a dinner to-night, all Americans. Mamma
is so pleased as she then can join in the general conversation. It must be very hard for her when only French is
spoken.

DECEMBER 1818

There is no doubt that the Duc de Richelieu will resign.
He has been attacked in the most unseemly manner by
the party headed by Monsieur Decazes. The New Cabinet
has been formed led by Decazes.
Mamma came back for Christmas from Fontainebleau;
we were very quiet as one of her sisters has died in America
—which had placed us in mourning.
I am sorry to say I cannot get rid of Madame S. She
will not leave me alone. Something must be done to
bring about a rupture. The New Year may bring me
some luck.

JANUARY 3, 1819

As everybody does, I have made all sorts of good
resolutions for 1819. I do not suppose I'll keep one of
them. The new Government seems very obstinate, *re* the
Indemnity claims—always some excuses, something crop-
ping up to delay the settlement. Poor Monsieur de Richelieu, the most simple of men, has inspired Madame Bernadotte (the Queen of Sweden) with a violent passion; she
follows him like a dog, her carriage waits outside his door
for hours; and the moment he appears from the *porte-*

cochère, her coachman whips up his horses and follows. Madame de Duras also causes much amusement, she cannot conceal her jealousy of Madame Récamier, who has stolen M. de Chateaubriand from her. Really these old ladies and their love affairs are too funny!

JANUARY 10

There is much scandal about the treatment the Duke of Wellington has received at the hands of the Royal Family. I wonder he has stood it so long. Monsieur has at times been most insolent. Father has decided to go to Geneva for three months. He has taken a house called "Bocage," at Pregny. There is really nothing to keep us in Paris. Mr. Sheldon and the staff are quite sufficient. We leave on June 1—Madame S. threatens to follow me there; if so, I will drown myself in the lake. Madame Bonaparte is in Geneva. I think I will ask her advice how I am to get rid of this woman—I must do something. The Chamber voted yesterday the grant of an income of 50,000 francs a year to the Duc de Richelieu—this has given great satisfaction in all quarters; he is not a rich man and has proved his devotion to his country. Father went to congratulate him, I accompanied him. He was much pleased, kissing father on both cheeks. They are in great sympathy, as both are men of the same calibre: simple, honest, without fear of expressing their opinion and holding it, if they think they are right. Since I have been so continually with father, seeing how he attracts people to him—those whose friendship is worth having—I believe in magnetic influence, which he strongly has. When he shakes your hand you feel a thrill go through you. When he looks into your eyes, he seems to absorb your soul. The Duke lives in such a simple manner, only two footmen in the ante-chamber. The *Cabinet de Travail* he received us in was without a carpet, the plainest of chairs and a very long table covered with black cloth. A *carafe* and a *carafon* of *eau de fleurs d'oranger.*

He never touches wine of any description. He engaged
father to dine with him *sans façon* on February 3,
to meet some of his (the Duke's) enemies. He said they
were quite tame.

FEBRUARY 4

We dined yesterday with the Duc de Richelieu—that is
father and myself. It was a curious company composed
of most of his political opponents; as he had said they
certainly were tame, much too tame for me—I was bored
and glad to escape. First for a short time to the opera,
nothing interesting there. I remembered it was Madame
Récamier's reception evening, so hied myself there. Her
salon is very beautiful, very classic, but not quite the
place for me. If I were twenty years older I might take
a mild dose of that sort of entertainment. I flew when I
saw the majestic form of Madame de Boigne approaching—
hid behind a portière to escape Madame de Duras and fell
into the arms of Madame S. Of course then I knew
what was in store for me. Bitter reproaches, why had
I neglected her who had given her soul for me: I didn't
want her soul. Well, it ended as it always does; she
arranged her coach to stop at the corner of the Rue
Bonaparte, which it did, I got in and accompanied her
home. *Bonsoir.*

FEBRUARY 6

Father had a fainting seizure this morning which alarmed
us all very much, as that sort of thing is so unusual with
him—he enjoys such wonderful health. Mamma would
burn feathers; Berthal wanted to drop a key down his
back; this last proposition cured him I think, anyhow
he sent everybody out of the room except mamma. I
went for the leech and he was bled.

FEBRUARY 8

I am glad to say that father has entirely recovered from
his indisposition. He thinks it was caused by a very strong

brand of segars he has smoked lately; he is going to change
them.   He was in one of his happiest moods at *déjeuner*
to-day.   He said that if anything was calculated to
bring a person round who had fainted it was Madame
Berthal.   Poor woman, she is not beautiful; she is very
tall and angular, has a distinct moustache, a very long and
inquisitive nose, a huge mole on her chin which is full of
hair—which I am certain she puts in curl-papers at night
—but a wisp of hair on either side of her head; this is surmounted by a monumental cap; having nothing to fasten
it to she balances it as a mountebank does a ball on his
head at a fair.   I always have my hands ready to catch
it.   Still I do not think we could dispense with her services
—she is invaluable.   Lucien told me in confidence that she
cast her eagle eye on him, but as he did not reciprocate
she transferred her affection to Albert's black Peter.
I think this must be true as I certainly did hear a flutter
and a squeak in the corridor one day.   Berthal disappeared
down one staircase and Peter down the other.   Mamma
thinks her a citadel of virtue, so I have not undeceived
her.   How fortunate we all can find some one to love or
to love us.   What would life be without it?

FEBRUARY 10

There is a great scandal about the Orléans family and
their relationship with the Court.   The King snubs the
Duke publicly on every occasion possible.   At some Court
functions lately he has really refused him his proper
rights as a Bourbon prince.   The Duchesse de Berri was
enceinte but it came to nothing.   After the Duc de
Berri, Orléans is the heir.   I can quite understand the
Duchesse d'Angoulême's dislike for the son of a man who
voted for her parents' death.   Twice lately the Duc de
Berri has invited me to supper.   Not at the Elysées—
ces dames and most cheery they have been.   The truth
is the Court is as dull as can be.   Since the death of

his father, the Prince de Condé, the Duc de Bourbon*
has come to live in Paris. He retains his old name as he
says he cannot live up to that of Condé. His whole life
is a scandal, worse here than in London.

FEBRUARY 12

I have neglected to write for two days. It is really so
difficult to find time. I make up my mind to write every
night before going to bed, but as lately I have not been
home until 3 or 4 A.M., it is the next day. This is a
problem that my brain is too addled to probe. There was
a grand *défilé* at Court on Sunday; always the same
thing—very magnificent no doubt to anybody who has
never seen it, but as we have to stand for such a long time
it is most fatiguing. I don't see how father bears it.
Mamma escapes it as she has been excused from attending
any Court function on account of her religious principles.
Monday the Carnival commenced; a lot of us made
egregious apes of ourselves, but it amused us. We had
pierrot costumes and each one a musical instrument.
We supped with some of our operatic friends at the *Maison Dorée;* we did everything that was foolish. Puységur
had much too much to drink and would pour all the coffee
into the piano. We heated francs and sous in the fire
and threw them out of the window and watched the poor
devils scramble for them, only to burn their fingers.
It may have been funny for us, but it was not for them—
on calm reflection I think it was very cruel. Tuesday
a small ball at the Palais Royal, which was very amusing.
A great many English were present, one very handsome
woman, Lady Westmoreland.† Her husband is in the
Diplomatic Service. She is a very great friend of the
Duke of Wellington's, also of Pozzo di Borgo. As there

* Louis Jean Joseph de Bourbon-Condé, son of the Prince de Condé.
† Priscilla Ann Willesley Pole, born 1793, Countess of Westmoreland,
an intimate friend of the Duke of Wellington and Pozzo di Borgo, the
Russian Ambassador.

are young people at the Elysée, Frances was allowed to go. She enjoyed it immensely. She is so fresh and pretty, has a lovely neck and shoulders. I was very proud of her. Mamma has great taste and dresses her to perfection, but with great simplicity. My diary is really very frivolous. I must try to record more interesting matter.

FEBRUARY 14

We are now having difficulties with the Spanish-American Colonies which are in revolt. Father thinks it of the greatest importance that no European Power should interfere in the quarrel. He feels he must be continually on the alert and keep himself informed on all matters concerning the subject. He also feels it of great importance that the United States should recognize the South American Republics. On this subject he has sent a private note to all the European Powers to prepare them for the action to be taken by his Government so that it will not come as a surprise to them. The Congress of Aix la Chapelle is now sitting. Its policy with regard to the United States is very favourable. Spain finds herself isolated by the Powers and is treating with father, or at least through him for the sale of Florida. I have to give up all gaieties at present as it is a serious matter, and all private notes are drafted by me before being dispatched to the Secretary of State. Spain has refused to ratify the treaty.

FEBRUARY 15

There has been a new revolution in Spain and a complete change in the Government. They have ratified the treaty, much to father's satisfaction. He said to me to-day that he felt more contented in doing something really of importance, as for some time he had been idling his time. Complications have also arisen with regard to the Treaty of Commerce with France which has lain dormant for some time. Father has now taken up the matter with great vigour. M. Hyde de Neuville is the French Minister in Washington and father is in close correspondence with him.

FEBRUARY 16

As I am now pretty free from work, I have again started my *vie de polichinelle*, as mamma insists on calling it. Father always smiles when she says this as her pronunciation of the words is so funny.

FEBRUARY 17

The last days of the Carnival—a *bal-masqué* at the opera to-night.

FEBRUARY 19

I have really been too tired even to open my diary. I make such good resolutions, but once I get in the swim with my friends, off I go, like a champagne cork. I love amusing myself. I know very shortly I will have to settle down to some steady work. To-night we have arranged a very original car for the Carnival. We, the men of course, are carefully disguised, for it would never do for us to be recognized, particularly in the company we so much prefer. I am to be an apple, P. a pear, R. a peach, D. a carrot, G. a bunch of grapes, L. a fig. The ladies are each a different flower and the car is in the shape of a large gilt basket with a high handle hung with paper lanterns all in the shapes of fruits and flowers. We hope it will be a success.

FEBRUARY 21

Indeed we did have a success; we were cheered the whole length of the boulevards, but one unfortunate incident. Célestine of the honourable *corps de ballet* in her eagerness fell out of the basket; fortunately she fell on a fat woman or she might have been seriously injured. But I hold my breath when I recall the scene: she was dressed as a poppy, but I suppose by sheer forgetfulness she had forgotten to put on anything but the dress; or she may have wished it to be very realistic, and as poppies do not wear underclothes, she did not. The fat woman was so incensed that seizing her opportunity as Célestine was completely turned up, began to belabour her with her reticule on that portion of the body on which generally we receive punishment in our early childhood. We dragged poor C. more dead than alive back into the car. The reticule was of sharp steel beads. Célestine stood up for the remainder of the evening. The usual supper, &c. &c.

FEBRUARY 23

Ball at the Elysée last night—very brilliant as usual. The beautiful Lady Westmoreland came escorted by Pozzo di Borgo; she was much admired. The Duchesse de Berri was full of animation; she has an unfortunate way of moving, which is totally devoid of elegance or grace. She is more like a child. She will suddenly run up to the Duke and hang on his arm, no matter whom he may be in conversation with. The Orléans family is in full force, but oddly enough no other members of the Royal Family. I think it really made it more informal and far more enjoyable. I begged hard for mamma to allow Frances to go. I even enlisted father, but he said he left such matters to mamma, that they were far too grave for him to decide. I know all the same he would have wished Frances to enjoy herself. She is really too young.

MARCH

Now that Lent is here there will be more rest for me and I intend doing some serious reading. I have asked father to make a list of books that he thinks will be of benefit to me. He had a long letter from Madame Patterson Bonaparte to-day. She is in Rome, is evidently very well

MADAME PATTERSON BONAPARTE (THREE VIEWS)

By Gilbert Stuart

By kind permission of the Countess Moltke-Huitfeldt, née Bonaparte

received, particularly by all the members of the Bonaparte family. In most of her letters is asking his advice about investments for her savings. Her one god seems to be money. Father has the highest opinion of her intelligence—particularly on financial matters—she is so shrewd. He often has said had she met the Emperor Napoleon, and had joined forces with him, the fate of Europe might be quite different from what it is to-day. Mamma does not like her, but like the sensible woman she is, never commits herself; in fact she always refrains from expressing any opinion that may annoy father. They really are a model husband and wife. I do not see such another happy and contented couple anywhere. Among our relatives in Geneva I find them, but their lives are so simple, they are so unworldly, living only for their families. I suppose it is rather a selfish one, but still it has always struck me that it is the right life to lead. Moralizing now. Well it is Lent. What could I do better?

MARCH 1819

So little of interest to record. I have been trying to do my duty, and have been taking Frances to see all the fine churches, to the Luxembourg and various places of interest. I think it as well she should have something to talk about when she comes out in the world next year. Mamma has no idea of keeping her always at her side and not allowing her to talk to young men. It is really quite absurd the way French girls are brought up. How can they learn anything about the man they are to marry if they are never allowed even to see them without a duenna is present. Madame de Staël was so sensible on this matter. She allowed Albertine at Coppet to go for long walks with de Broglie, so that they would know each other before marriage. It certainly in this case is a success as I have never seen a happier couple in my life; they are a model to all young married people.

APRIL

Such lovely weather. The trees are all breaking into leaf, all is so fresh. Really I think the spring is the best season. It has the same bloom of freshness like a young child. I must really marry. I am sick of the thraldom of Madame S. I have begun to dislike her. Of course, I blame myself, but still she was older than me. I am quite sick of this liaison. I have tried to break it on several occasions but she makes such scenes, and as I am rather weak where women are concerned I always give in.

APRIL 8

There is much entertaining at present, but I am keeping very quiet. I really have not felt at all well for some time. My teeth have been giving me a great deal of trouble. The dentist says it is from the fever I had in Russia and the intense cold there. I will be glad when we get to the quiet of Geneva; I love going on the lake. Father has a horror of my sailing. Two of his cousins on the twenty-first birthday of the eldest went for a sail in a new boat that had been given to the latter for his birthday. Their house is actually on the lake on the way by the lower road to Pregny. The wind is very treacherous on the lake on account of the surrounding mountains. The boat capsized in full view of both their father and mother and both of the lads were drowned before help could be obtained to rescue them. By their death, father was left the last male of the Gallatin family.

APRIL 20

I was told such an interesting story to-day about Robert Fulton.* It seems during the Terror he was in Paris; wishing to go to England on business he obtained a permit

* Robert Fulton (inventor), first steamboat on the Seine, Paris, August 9, 1803. At New York, 1807, started a steamboat, the *Clermont*, on the Hudson River.

and passport. By accident it was made out for Mr. and Mrs. Fulton. Arriving at Calais he was detained as there was no packet crossing. In the evening at the *auberge* where he was lodged, he noticed a young woman who seemed in agony of mind—this was rather a common thing in those days. At last she summoned up courage to speak to him, saying, "I throw myself on your mercy. I see you are a foreigner. I escaped from Paris where I had foolishly gone to try and save some important documents. My husband would have gone but he is very ill in England and I persuaded him to allow me to do so. I am without a passport, and hardly dare to embark as there is a price on my head, and I am certain to be arrested and sent back to Paris. Can you help me?" Fulton said, "I will do my best. I have my American passport, oddly enough by error it was made out for myself and wife, but she is in America. If you are willing to pass as Mrs. Fulton, my wife, you are welcome to the little protection I can give you." As the lady in question was disguised and very simply dressed the plan succeeded and with the deepest gratitude she parted with him at Dover, without revealing her name to him. Some years later when Fulton was in Paris trying to raise money to put his inventions into practice, he strolled one night into the Théâtre Français. Looking around the auditorium he spied, much to his astonishment, in one of the boxes the lady of his adventure splendidly dressed and covered with jewels; at the same time she recognized him and waved her fan to him, sending her husband at once to escort him to her box. It was through her all the money was found for him to carry out his great work. One rarely hears of such gratitude. It was the Duchesse de L.

APRIL

Mamma is in her element. We are most uncomfortable. Everything in the house is turned upside down, nothing but cleaning. There is but one room sacred and that is father's, where I take refuge. Every window is open, we might as well live in the street; fortunately we are *entre Cour et Jardin*. The *concierge* at the gate has orders to refuse admittance to all carriages. It is mamma's and Berthal's carnival as we have taken a house near Geneva for several months. We are taking some of the servants, the others we will procure there. The servants leave shortly as they go by *diligence*. We have hired a roomy travelling carriage and will only take our body servants with us—that is, two maids, father's man and Lucien. They will be stowed away in the rumble. It will take us over a week. I am not looking forward to it.

MAY
We leave for Geneva to-morrow. I will be glad of the rest. The life of a young man is a very gay one, burning the candle both ends.

MAY 12
After all when everything was packed, the travelling carriages engaged, father has some very important dispatches which will keep us here another two months. I was sorry for mamma and the servants who were going to take their holidays. The house was all done up for the summer, now everything has to be uncovered and put straight. The best part of it is, Madame S. had started to Aix en Savoi en route for Geneva. She will be furious. She is quite capable of coming back. Still, I will have a short breathing time of freedom. We had excused ourselves to so many people who had sent us invitations that we will look very stupid. To console Frances, who was looking forward to our visit, I took her to Suresnes; drove her in my curricle, hired a canoe and we went on the river. It was a glorious day, with that delicious smell of spring in the air. We started early and

I took something to eat, landed on an island and had a picnic. We had chicken and hard-boiled eggs, but we had forgotten the salt—it was stupid of Madame Berthal. She had put in some splendid peaches that we were going to take on the journey, they were good: it quite restored Frances to her usual gaiety. She and I are such good friends but she has got a temper of her own. I have none, I often wish I had. We did not get home until after sunset. I lost an oar, which delayed us. I think it must have been the peach juice which went to my head as we had nothing to drink stronger than barley-water with lemon. We were as happy as two children. I think I was the younger of the two.

NOVEMBER 1

We are now settled down at home, glad to get back. Father still doing his best to effect a settlement of the Indemnity claims, but it is an uphill task. Monsieur Decazes is far more difficult to deal with than the Duc de Richelieu. Paris very gay—balls every night. The King is far from well; we have no Court functions as yet. The Duchesse d'Orléans gave a splendid ball on the 4th; all the gardens illuminated—a fine sight. It seems the poor old King was really made ill by the discovery of a plot to make him abdicate in favour of Monsieur; although Monsieur denied all knowledge of it, he nevertheless was the instigator of it. We are having a large Christmas dinner—Americans, French, and English. Christmas is little kept by the French; New Year's Day is the great festival. The Carnival is very early this year, so the gaieties will go on. Both the Duc de Berri and the Duc d'Orléans have made great innovations. They said the Court was much too dull, so have invited all sorts and conditions, not only to parties but to dinners—savants, wits, deputies of all shades and colour.

DECEMBER 8

The famous Abbé Grégoire* was turned out of the
Chamber of Deputies yesterday. He certainly is an
extraordinary mixture. It was he who proposed the
abolition of royalty; he also demanded of the Assembly
the condemnation to death of Louis XVI. It was he
who made the Assembly accord civil rights to the Jews
and coloured people. He tried to oppose the great
Napoleon in every way, but with little success.

We dined yesterday with the Comte and Comtesse
D'Orsay. He is a wonderful fop but very witty. Some
of his stories would make even a man blush, but he
seems to be a privileged person. Sosthène de la Rochefoucauld was one of the guests—a person very full of
his own importance. Also that terrible Madame de Boigne
and her brother were among the guests; she tackled
father after dinner, asking him all sorts of questions
about manners and customs in America. I think he was
a little wearied by her, as I heard him say to her, "Madame,
when we have a social revolution in America we may
have better manners, as you have." She exclaimed,
"You are not an American, you are one of us." He
answered, "Pardon me, I represent a young and great
country of which I am justly proud." She is really a
firebrand.

DECEMBER 8

Mamma is preparing for Christmas: plum-puddings are
being made. Madame Berthal looks utterly disgusted
when she goes down to the kitchen to stir the puddings;
I do the same and so does Frances. Father only laughed
when we told him about it, and says, "Why not?"
Madame Récamier has invited me to dinner for the 17th.
I consider it a great honour as I am so young. Four notes
to-day from Madame S.—the first in despair, the second

* The Abbé Grégoire, born December 4, 1750, died April 28, 1831.

apologizing for being in despair, the third gay and frivolous, the fourth apologizing for being gay and frivolous. Why will women write so much?—a dangerous habit. All four went immediately into the fire. Hysterical shrieks from the housekeeper's room. I rushed out to see what was the matter. I met Berthal supporting Frances and trying to balance her head-dress. Frances was peeling some apples and had cut her finger; like the silly little goose that she is, she fainted at the sight of her own blood. I looked at her hand and said, "What nonsense, it's nothing!" As she passed she gave me a good kick. She has inherited something from mamma. Off to a supper. No time to write any more.

DECEMBER 18

A most amusing dinner at Madame Récamier's, followed by a very funny little lampoon on the Queen of Sweden; it was called *Trouvez-moi, mon Homme*. It was really very clever and well acted. Madame de J. represented the unfortunate queen, and I really thought at first it must be the Bernadotte in person. Some music followed. One fat lady with ample and bulging charms—in fact, bulging everywhere—played the harp. Her arms were like legs of mutton; both arms were covered with jingling bracelets. This, perhaps, was fortunate, as it sounded like sleigh-bells with the occasional breaking of a string or the snapping of a whip. When she had finished there was not a string left on the harp.

DECEMBER 19

The Duc de Coigny has invited me to Fontainebleau for a *chasse* for two days. He is the governor of the château and has a beautiful house. I am certain to enjoy myself.

DECEMBER 20

We are a very large party, all men—Mathieu de Montmorency, the Duc de Serent, the Prince de Poix, the

Marquis de Champonet, and a host of others. I drove down with the Prince de Poix, who kindly offered to take me. We hunt to-morrow morning. The duke has placed two horses at my disposal. To-night he presented me with the badge of the *chasse*, which was a great honour.

DECEMBER 22

We had a perfect day, but I was too tired to write last night. It was very late when I was able to retire, as I cannot leave until my elders and superiors go. The fine air made me so sleepy. We killed seven fine *sangliers*— one fell to me, of which I was very proud; also two fine deer. It is a wonderful pretty sight the *curée* in front of a château by torchlight at night; all the spoils of the chase are laid out in front of the famous horseshoe staircase, then a sort of fanfare of *cors de chasse* is blown for each head of game—in fact, a sort of funeral hymn.

I go back to Paris to-morrow in Mathieu de Montmorency's coach; he is Governor of Compiègne. Such funny posts they have at Court. The Comte de Cossé Brissac is *Premier panetier du Roi*.

DECEMBER 24

I have managed to save a little money, and with the legacy which I had from my aunt, which was five hundred francs, I have bought Frances a small string of pearls with a nice diamond clasp. As we were not able to dine with the de Broglies last Christmas we are dining with them to-morrow. Mamma sent the Duchesse a plum-pudding, a huge one. Our cousins Naville and Jules de Budé arrived to-night from Geneva to pay us a visit. Jules is a kindred spirit of mine. Adrien Naville's mother was an heiress, Mlle de Gallatin, the only daughter of the Count Paul Michael, the head of the family and father's guardian. Her mother was *née* de Bugnac and niece of the Duc de Biron; so Adrien has a host of relatives in Paris. Father is very fond of him as he is very clever

and studious.   Jules is quite the opposite; his studies
are devoted to that of the female form divine.

DECEMBER 26

We had such a cheerful Christmas Eve.   Some Americans
who have no relatives here; father insisted on inviting
them and made mamma prepare a present for each.   For
supper we had one of the famous plum-puddings, which
was carried in all ablaze.   Frances has been hugging me
ever since I gave her the necklace.   I tell her to pay
attention to all the pearls that fall from my lips.   Oh,
woman, woman!   Dear mamma gave me a large pair of
worsted mittens which she had knitted herself; she
intended them for a great surprise, but every time for
the last fortnight I went into her room there was a
scuffle.   One day they were lying in her chair; she
suddenly sat down on them, needles and all.   They are
orange and brown, absolutely hideous, but I will wear
them as I cannot wound her feelings.   Father gave me
five hundred francs—it was good of him; Frances, a
satin shaving-paper holder which she had worked with
our coat-of-arms, which was quite crooked.
The dinner at the de Broglie's was quite delightful, without
any ceremony.   Both Adrien and Jules are cousins of
Albertine's.   We were twenty in all—mostly family.
First we had some silly charades and then we ended by
dancing.   Jules drank much too much.   Mamma said
to me, "How could you?"   I said, "It's Jules; I'm
not drunk."   We all had presents: mine was a beautiful
whip for my curricle with an ivory handle and gold end
engraved with my initials.   To Frances they gave a
lovely brooch formed of a large aquamarine surrounded
by small diamonds.

DECEMBER 30

I have been literally burning the candle at both ends.
I do not think Jules and I have slept in our own beds

since Christmas night. He looks a wreck. I am sorry to say that both he and Adrien leave on New Year's Day; they are going on a tour to Germany and Italy. They are great friends, although so absolutely different in character.

DECEMBER 31

Jules and I have made all sorts of engagements. I am going to have a nap this afternoon as I am certain we shall be up until the small hours of to-morrow morning. Good-bye 1819; I part with you with regret. What a pity I cannot say *"Au revoir"*!

JANUARY 1, 1820

"A Happy New Year." New resolutions, only to be broken. Such a night! Last night I did not get home until 7 o'clock this morning. This is rather Irish!

We have just come from paying our respects to the King—the same New Year's Court; also to the Palais Royale and to the Elysée. It is such weary waiting, standing all the time. I wonder father bears it so well; he never seems tired.

JANUARY 24

A magnificent ball at the Elysée last night. In the morning news had come to us of the death of the Duke of Kent, but it was not to be made public until to-day, so the ball would take place. The Duc de Berri looked very much out of temper. The Orléans family did not appear, and it at once became whispered about that the Duke of Kent* was dead. Of course it had a very bad effect. Had the Allies still been here there would have been no ball. It seems a great relief to the Royal Family that the Allies have been withdrawn. I am not surprised—but that they do not show much gratitude.

* Duke of Kent, son of George III, and father of the late Queen Victoria.

FEBRUARY 8

We had a fine time yesterday. Some of our ladies of
the opera were going to have a fine car for the Carnival.
Several of us wanted to join them, but they were not
allowed to have men in their car. We got over the
difficulty by getting women's costumes. There were
six of us all dressed in full ballet dress, fleshing tights,
and full ballet-skirts; bare arms and necks, wigs and
masks. I was nearly frozen. We had a lot of champagne, which helped to keep us warm. We had supper
at the *Maison Dorée* and such a supper! About 2
o'clock in the morning there was a loud knocking at the
door: "*Ouvrez, au nom du Roi.*" You can imagine
our feelings—particularly mine, as I was the only one
belonging to an embassy—to be found in ballet-skirts
by the police! The door was opened and in walked
three of the heads of the police. "*Vos noms, messieurs
et dames.*" We had taken off our wigs and masks, so
were easily recognized. Suddenly there was a shout
from Rochefoucauld, who jumped on the leading man,
dragging off his hat and wig, discovering Puységur. To
all three he did the same thing. With roars of laughter
they told us they had disguised themselves and had been
to every room in the café and had taken the names of
all the occupants. We were the first to find them out.
As they were all friends of ours, we made them join us,
and the fun became fast and furious. De la Rochefoucauld had suddenly remembered that during the Carnival
no descents of the police were made, so he risked pulling
off Puységur's wig. It took me a long time to recover
from the shock. It would have been a serious matter
for me, particularly if it had been made public. I would
have been obliged to leave Paris. I do not know what
father would have done. Oh, my head to-day! We
are planning some more mischief to come off before the
end of the Carnival. Puységur had a list of several well-
known people, whose names he took. We are going to
make them dance before we have finished.

FEBRUARY 10

We put our heads together and have sent the most official-looking documents to all whose names were taken to appear at the Hotel de Ville to-morrow. We intend going to some vantage-point to see them arrive.

FEBRUARY 11

Our joke came off splendidly. Coach after coach drove up, but when the occupants asked for a certain room, which number we put on the document, they were informed there was no such room. Then one of the documents was shown to an official, who said, "It is Carnival; you have been duped." I wish you could have seen their faces. Some of the ones of high rank had written to the Duc de Berri to intercede for them and did not appear. He had been informed that it was a joke and joined in it. We won't hear anything about it. There is not one dare make any trouble. It seems the Duke was very much amused, and has made many sallies about it to the unfortunate ones, particularly the married ones.

FEBRUARY 13

On Saturday there was a magnificent ball given by Monsieur de Greffuhle. He had lately been made a peer. The Duc and Duchesse de Berri were present. There had been rumours that there was a plot to assassinate the Duke; all noticed that Monsieur de Greffuhle never left him, and seemed much relieved when the Berris retired. The Princesse de Galitzin bade me come to her box at the opera on Sunday. We had the box adjoining the Royal one. The Duc and Duchesse de Berri were very well received. At the conclusion of the opera, before the ballet commenced, the Duchess rose and, bowing to the audience, retired with the Duke. As I was not feeling well, I begged Madame de Galitzin to excuse me and immediately followed. In the corridor

I heard a commotion, and, opening a door, I found myself by the Royal exit. Monsieur de Brissac rushed up to me saying, "Shut the door and stand by it; do not let any one pass in or out. There has been an attack on the life of the Duc de Berri." At that moment the Duke appeared, supported on one side by the Duchess and on the other by Madame de Béthisy.* I could see a dagger sticking in his breast, but he was talking in a low voice to his wife. She was wonderfully calm, but tears were running down her cheeks. She is *enceinte.* I fear this may kill her. I heard orders being given to send at once for Monsieur and the Duc d'Angoulême. Monsieur arrived first, accompanied by the Duc de Fitz James, and immediately went into the Royal *salon,* which is behind the King's *loge.* They were closely followed by the Duc d'Angoulême and the Duc de Maille; then came Monsieur Decazes and a host of others. It was all the more tragic as I could hear the music of the ballet which was still going on. The audience had no knowledge of what had happened. I forgot to mention that before anybody arrived I heard a sharp cry from the Royal *salon.* I was told afterwards that the Duke tried to pull the knife out of his breast but was unable to do so—that Madame de Béthisy, with great presence of mind, pulled it out. Both she and the Duchess were deluged in blood. I heard somebody say, "Does anybody know if the knife was poisoned?" Monsieur Decazes passed me hurriedly with Fitz-James. When they returned (it seems they had been to question the assassin) I heard Monsieur Decazes say in a loud voice, "The knife is not poisoned." By this time several doctors arrived and were doing all they could to staunch the flow of blood. I could see into the *salon,* as the door was left open as there were so many people. Monsieur Rohan-Châbot† came up to me and begged me to still stop by

* Lady in waiting to the Duchess.
† Son of the Duc de Rohan.

the door I was guarding. At that moment the Duc d'Orléans, with the Duchesse and Mlle d'Orléans, passed into the *salon;* they were all in tears. The next thing I heard was an order given to send for the King. The Duc de Maille went to fetch him. I felt then there could not be much hope. To my horror, I heard the Duchesse de Berri in loud tones denouncing Monsieur Decazes, saying, " *C'est lui, le vrai assassin.*" They tried to stop her. A sudden hush and the poor old King arrived, leaning heavily on the Duchesse d'Angoulême and the Duc de Maille.* His Majesty was composed and looking very stern. It was an extraordinary sight. The Duchesse d'Angoulême hurriedly passed me and met poor little Mademoiselle, who had been sent for and came carried in the arms of Mlle de Gontaut.† Then two priests passed. I knew then the end was near. Suddenly all knelt. As the sacrament was being given to the dying man I think everybody was in tears; I know I cried. Then in silence we all rose to our feet and waited. It seemed hours to me, as I was ready to drop with fatigue. Then the priest began intoning a prayer. Again all sank on to their knees. The end had come. Then a horrible thing happened. The Duchesse de Berri again commenced to scream, calling Monsieur Decazes " *Assassin! Assassin!*" It was really too horrible. After they had quieted her, in absolute silence—with the exception of the Grand Chamberlain announcing "Le Roi, le Roi"—a mournful procession passed me. First, the King supporting the Duchesse de Berri, who had the hand of Mademoiselle, the Duchesse d'Angoulême on the other side of her; they were followed by all the rest of the Royal Family. I could hear the orders given by the officers to the soldiers who by now were keeping the streets.

Monsieur de Brissac came to me, shook my hands and

* Grand Chamberlain of Louis XVIII.

† The MS. here is illegible and I have had to guess at the meaning.—ED.

simply said "Merci." He asked me if I would like to
go into the *salon*. I followed him. He motioned me
to kneel and, handing the brush from the holy-water bowl,
motioned me to sprinkle the corpse, which I did. I
would not believe the Duke was dead. He was still sitting
up in a large gilt arm-chair, his head supported by a
cushion, and surrounded by the officers of his household.
The priest knelt in front of him praying. It was a
sight I will never forget. In silence Monsieur de Maille
shook my hand, and I retired. On gaining the street,
which was packed with people and troops, I had great
difficulty in getting through the crowd, had it not
happened that I was recognized by one of the officers,
Monsieur de Puységur, who sent an escort of soldiers to
make way for me. Although more dead than alive when
arriving at home, I at once went up to father's room and
awakened him. When I told him the news he exclaimed,
"What a catastrophe!—the unfortunate Bourbons—a
blow for France indeed!" He made me go at once to
bed as I was hardly able to stand.

FEBRUARY 16

At 10 o'clock this morning a note was sent that all the
Diplomatic Corps were to go to the Tuilleries at 1 o'clock.
I accompanied father. The large *salle* was in total darkness
with the exception of about twenty large candles (*cierges*) in
great silver candlesticks. In order of seniority, first the
Ambassadors and their suites, then the Ministers, passed
before the throne, in front of which was standing the
Duc d'Angoulême surrounded by the high Court officials
in the deepest mourning. Absolute silence with the
exception of the announcement by the Grand Chamberlain as the representative of each country passed—La
Russie, l'Espagne, &c. &c.—followed by the dropping on
the floor of the halberds with a ringing sound. It was
most solemn and impressionable. The Duke bowed to
each one. Not a word was spoken. So we passed out.

The assassin's name is Louvel, a saddler. It seems he has been following the poor Duke for a long time waiting his opportunity. He must have had many chances as the Duke went about in the most open manner, often quite alone. Rumours of all sorts. Some say it was a conspiracy. The Duchesse de Berri still accuses Monsieur Decazes of being the head of it. Others that it was a personal revenge. *"Cherchez la femme,"* others say; the Duke's *amours* were so well known—he not taking the slightest care to hide them.

FEBRUARY 17

This morning father went to the Palais Royal and was received by Mlle d'Orléans. She was in great grief; she was devoted to the Duc de Berri. She said, when dying he was the most collected and calm of them all, that he thought of everybody—of two children, girls, who were in England; they are the daughters of a "Miss Brown" whom he married in London under a false name before the Restoration. He begged his wife to take them and to bring them up as if they were her own daughters. She promised to do so. He tried to comfort one and all.

FEBRUARY 18

So great is the outcry against Monsieur Decazes that he will have to leave the Ministry. Father is much incensed about it; I will not for one moment believe that he was in any way implicated. Decazes' life has been threatened and he has to go about guarded. The people insult him as he passes in his carriage; they are incensed against him. It is a strange thing that the populace always have affection for a Royalty who is a little wild. It was exactly the same with Henri IV, whom the late Duke much resembled in the life he led.

FEBRUARY 19

A Monsieur Claude de Coursergues, a deputy, denounced Monsieur Decazes in the Chamber yesterday as insti-

VOLTAIRE   Mme. DENISE

From an Original Drawing by the Marquise de la Vilette

gator of the assassination. I am glad to say he was indignantly howled down.

The King sent this morning for the Duc de Richelieu, who was on the eve of starting for England to compliment George IV on his accession. The King requested him to take Monsieur Decazes' place, but he absolutely refused to do so. When pressed for his reasons he said "the King was so old" and that "Monsieur" (the heir to the Crown) was absolutely opposed to him.

FEBRUARY 21

It seems that Monsieur had given his word that if he became king he would support Monsieur de Richelieu. Still nothing decided.

FEBRUARY 22

Monsieur Decazes has begged the King to accept his resignation. After some time, it seems, the King, with great grief, accepted it. He created him "Duc" and he goes to London as ambassador. Monsieur de Richelieu at last has consented to accept office. Monsieur has given him every promise of support in every way. Father has no faith in Monsieur's promises. He thinks him false in everything.

The lying-in-state and funeral of the Duc de Berri was very fine. The actual funeral was not on so grand a scale as that of the Prince de Condé, which I have mentioned before.

MARCH 1820

The Duchesse de Berri is more violent than ever against the Duc de Decazes and his party; it is all very painful. Of course all gaiety and entertaining is at an end. For myself, I have no heart for it. I can scarcely realize that the poor Duke is dead—always so gay and cheerful, so full of life and spirits. He will be more and more missed as time goes on; there is nobody to fill his place. The Queen of Sweden is getting madder and madder, she does not let poor Monsieur de Richelieu alone for a moment; she is the laughing-stock of Paris. He will not even speak to her, but that seems to egg her on all the more. Louvel was questioned in private, but his trial will not take place as yet. Some say he is a lunatic.

APRIL

I only go to the Français now. Mlle George is very fine. Poor old Talma one can hardly hear. It is really sad to see the wreck of such a once fine actor; still at times he has fine bursts of passion, revealing some of his old powers. The opera has been closed since the assassination of the Duke.

APRIL

A bomb exploded yesterday at the Louvre. Rumour says that several bombs have been discovered in the gardens and under the windows of the Duchesse de Berri. The poor old King is much disturbed. He, as well as everybody else, fears that if a bomb did explode near to the apartment occupied by the Duchesse de Berri it might bring on a premature confinement. Since the death of the Duke the Duchess has moved to the Tuilleries. The eyes of the whole of France are fixed on the palace, hoping for an heir. Louvel's trial commenced on the 5th. I applied for permission to attend, which was granted.

It seems he is now thought to be a lunatic and there will be a further trial. All this must be most painful to the Royal Family. There are strange rumours afloat about the bombs; even the Duchesse de Berri's name is mentioned—it is too monstrous.

MAY 1820

An officer of bad character has been arrested in connexion with the bomb explosions. He is to be tried at once.

Madame Patterson Bonaparte has intimated her intention of paying a visit to Paris; she is now in Geneva.
The Duchesse de Courland (Talleyrand's niece) has
been troubling father very much lately. She has interest
in property in America and seems to think it is his place
to attend to it for her. This has given us all a chance,
mamma in particular, as the Duchess comes to see him
nearly daily; we all say it is a second case of the Queen
of Sweden and Monsieur de Richelieu. I really think
it is beginning to trouble him, as he has a horror of any
scandal being attached to his name. Pozzo di Borgo
strongly advised him to get rid of her. He thinks
anybody who has any connexion with Monsieur de Talleyrand dangerous. He has, like father, supreme contempt
for the latter—calls him a turncoat, a liar, libertine, &c. &c.
He certainly is a man without a vestige of principle.

JUNE

Frances is now seventeen and remarkably pretty. Had
the Court not been in mourning she would have made
her début, but will now have to wait until next year.
I think mamma is very glad, as she dreads having to
sit up so late. We tell her she is very lucky only to have
one daughter—that most Englishwomen have eight or
ten.

JUNE 6

To-day was Louvel's trial. I was present. There were
no revelations of any kind. He is a poor lunatic. He
had nursed the idea he must kill somebody for years.
He is to be executed to-morrow.

JUNE 8

I now deeply regret I went to the execution. There
was a large body of troops as there had been serious
disturbance in the night. It was at 3 o'clock in
bright June sunshine, which made it all the more horrible.

I never could imagine human beings could turn into beasts; a French mob is horrible. One now realizes what the Terror was. The wretched assassin was half dead before he was dragged up the steps of the guillotine. It was all over in a moment. I had to go and drink some brandy—a thing I have never done in my life before. It took me two hours to get out of the howling crowd, more like wild animals than anything else—the women far worse than the men.

JULY

We again go to Geneva for two months. I will be very glad of the rest and quiet. Of course father has had nothing to do. The affairs of the Court, with all the plots and counter-plots, have occupied all the time of the Ministry.

Madame de Courland has been got rid of. Father has a very pale face and white hands; Pozzo di Borgo hinted to her that he had leprosy. She wrote begging father not even to write to her, that she feared she had troubled him too much, &c. &c. Poor Pozzo passed a bad quarter of an hour with mamma, who will never forgive him. Father was much amused.

Monsieur de Chateaubriand is deeply hurt that he is not in the Ministry; neither the King nor Monsieur de Richelieu like him. We leave to-morrow for Geneva. . . .

PART IV

THE MINISTRY IN FRANCE

FROM THE ASSASSINATION OF THE DUC DE BERRI
TO THE RETURN OF ALBERT GALLATIN TO AMERICA

SEPTEMBER 1820—*JUNE* 1823

SEPTEMBER 1820: GENEVA

Father has just had news of a great conspiracy. Unfortunately Monsieur de Lafayette is mixed up in it—in fact, one of the leaders; others are the Duc de Rovigo, Monsieur Lafitte, General Pajol, and a host of others. There is to be a trial before the Court of Peers. I am glad we are here, as if we had been in Paris it would have caused father great worry. He has a very deep affection for Monsieur de Lafayette.

Madame Patterson Bonaparte is here. She is much sought after; her wit and beauty seem to open all doors to her. She is very bitter at the present moment against Mrs. Caton, one of whose daughters married Madame B.'s brother Robert and is now a widow. There is great scandal about her and the Duke of Wellington. He follows her everywhere; in fact, it is an open secret that she is his mistress. Mrs. Caton has married another of her daughters to a Mr. Harvey. The third one is very beautiful, and the mother has great hopes of making a fine marriage for her. Madame Bonaparte talks of nothing else but "Bo" her son, and his marriage. As he is now only a fat boy it is a little premature.

SEPTEMBER 28

We arrived in Paris this morning to find the city in a ferment of enthusiasm on account of the birth of a son

to the Duchesse de Berri yesterday. It was really
wonderful to see the change in everybody. When we
left in May all was dull and black; now everybody,
even the streets, are radiant. Cannon are booming;
fireworks at night, *feu de joie*, and goodness knows what.
We had at once to go to the palace *pour nous inscrire*.
They say the King is delighted.

SEPTEMBER 29

The child is called the Duc de Bordeaux.* He was
privately christened at once, but there is to be a great
public christening later on.
We went to-day to the Palais Royal. It did not strike
me that the Orléans family looked or seemed particularly
pleased. The two daughters of "Mrs. Brown" were
there; they are treated with great kindness and have
been given titles. "Mrs. Brown" has been given a
château in Brittany. She certainly behaved wonderfully
well. Her marriage in England was quite *en règle*.
Oddly enough, there is a boy as well, but no notice has
been taken of him; he is simply called "Thomas Brown."

OCTOBER

It has been the most extraordinary trial of the leaders
of the conspiracy of August. All the leaders have
escaped free and only some most unimportant persons
have been punished. The Duc de Bassano has been
allowed to return to France. He is so old and considered
quite harmless now.

NOVEMBER

We have some work to do, as Monsieur de Richelieu has
intimated to father that he is willing to open negotiations
re the Indemnity. That anything will really be done

* Henri-Charles-Ferdinand-Marie-Dieudonné d'Artois, Duc de Bordeaux, born September 28, 1820, afterwards known as the Comte de
Chambord.

I strongly doubt. Mr. Sheldon has gone on a holiday, so all the important work falls on my shoulders. Paris still dull as far as Society goes. I was pointed out the Marquise de Guiccioli yesterday, Lord Byron's mistress; she is very charming to look at, gentle and sweet.

Of course the one topic of conversation is the Duchesse de Berri and her son, the Duc de Bordeaux—"*Espérance de la France*," as he is called. The King looks much better, is far more cheerful. There are some unpleasant rumours of the Duc d'Orléans having thrown doubts on the legitimacy of the Duc de Bordeaux, but I believe it is without question of a doubt that he is the son of the Duc de Berri. When the latter was dying he said to the King, "*Soigne ma femme; elle est enceinte.*"

I am going to fêtes every night as Paris is again plunged into wild gaiety. The people are too glad of an excuse to throw off the mourning and gloom. Frances makes her début at the first Court. I have been telling her how to behave. She has a dancing mistress to teach her how to curtsy and to back without tumbling over.

The christening of the Duc de Bordeaux was a splendid sight. He was held up at an open window to be shown to the populace and was received with roars of cheers. The old Duke of Gordon was present; I was so glad to see him. I had a little love affair with Katinka Galitzin. Her father is not very rich, and as I have nothing, it soon came to an end. We remain the best of friends.

Really Mr. Astor is dreadful. Father has to be civil to him, as in 1812–13 he rendered great services to the Treasury. He came to *déjeuner* to-day; we were simply *en famille*, he sitting next to Frances. He actually wiped his fingers on the sleeves of her fresh white spencer. Mamma in discreet tones said, "Oh, Mr. Astor, I must apologize; they have forgotten to give you a serviette." I think he felt foolish.

A splendid Court ball last night; the dresses and jewels

of the ladies and the superb uniforms of the men
made a fine show. Father looks like a blot of ink
amongst all this finery. Of course I dress as I like;
we have no official diplomatic uniform in America.
Some near-sighted Hungarian officer, not seeing he
was in front of the Duchesse d'Angoulême, caught
his spur in the lace of her dress and tore yards of
splendid lace. He was covered with confusion, but she
was so gracious; she is so womanly. I do not think I
have ever seen so sad a face, but she is the most royal-
looking person I have ever seen; the "descendant of a
hundred kings" certainly applies to her. I noticed her
expression of intense scorn when Prince de Talleyrand
passed; he is horrible.

With the change of Ministry after the disgrace, or at
least removal, of the Duc de Decazes, Monsieur de
Richelieu is again in power. Monsieur de Serre, Minister
of Justice; Pasquier, Affaires Étrangères (which father
much regrets); Latour Maubourg, Ministre de la Guerre;
Portal Marine and Roy, Ministre des Finances; Baron
Meunier, Directeur of Police; and Monsieur Siméon,
Ministre de l'Intérieur. Father thinks it a very weak
Government—that it will not last long. . . .

NOVEMBER

The Marquis de Lauriston, a descendant of Law, the
South Sea Bubble adventurer, is appointed Ministre de la
Maison du Roi. We had a small *sauterie* for Frances
and her young friend. She's now seventeen. It was
very pretty; all the young girls were so fresh and enjoyed
everything so much it was a pleasure to watch them.
Dear mamma had arranged a surprise in the shape of a
gift hunt. We all were given numbers and then we went
into the gallery, where all the presents were hidden in
all sorts of the most out-of-the-way places. I helped her
to arrange it with the invaluable Berthal. Each had a
number corresponding with tickets. It was really good

and quite delightful—such laughter and little suppressed shrieks of delight when the parcel with the corresponding number was discovered. The presents were so pretty— a donkey with a wobbley head for me and a goose full of bon-bons for Frances. We both agreed it was too personal; mamma has more wit than we gave her credit for. Father came in with dear Pozzo di Borgo and looked on at the "hunt," and was much amused. Then a delightful little supper. It was all over by 11 o'clock. Of course there is little entertaining on a large scale on account of the Duc de Berri's death; we of the *corps diplomatique* entertain in a small way. The English Ambassadress has sent out invitations for a party for very young people for Thursday; it is to be *costumé*. Frances is going as "Titania" and I as the ass. I have had a wonderful head made by the costumier of the opera; it is all of silk and is very light— not at all hot.

The little *bal costumé* was a great success; some of the dresses were beautiful. Frances was as pretty as anybody; she has that lovely skin and such beautiful eyes. Her dress was all clinging white silver material, and she had a wreath of light blue cornflowers in her hair, which was flowing down her back. Her wand was a huge sunflower. Sosthène de la Rochefoucauld, with his usual cynical manner, came up to me and said: "*Tout le monde te reconnait; tu n'as pas pu choisir un costume qui t'ira mieux.*" I will be even with him yet. I never knew a man who fancied himself so much; he is a male Madame de Boigne.

We had a Maypole dance; there was a beautiful "maypole" decorated with flowers and ribbons. After this was finished we all (the young people) filed before the Ambassador and Ambassadress dancing a polonaise. We arrived home at midnight, but I went out again. Father has enjoined mamma never to ask me any questions—very wise, I think, as if I told her the truth she would soon be in her grave, with her strict ideas. Will I ever reform? Paris is waking up. Pozzo di Borgo is giving a *sauterie* for Frances. He sent to Russia for all sorts of beautiful presents; he has consulted mamma about some original way of distributing them.

NOVEMBER 20

It was delightful at the Russian Embassy—all very young people. After supper the doors of the ballroom were thrown open; half-way across the room a great rope of flowers about three feet from the ground, at the far end a row of targets. Silver arrows were presented to the ladies and gold ones to the gentlemen; we had to throw them at the targets. If we hit (I am sorry to say the girls often missed), Pozzo, assisted by several ambassadors, presented us with the most beautiful Russian bibelots, much too fine. I had a beautiful inlaid snuff-box; Frances a complete Russian peasant costume —the head-dress had seed-pearls and turquoises on it. We danced all sorts of pretty dances, ending with a Russian mazurka which twelve of us had learnt. I led off with Katinka Galitzin. It was really extremely pretty and very well done. We had straps covered with gilt bells on our ankles—that is, the men; the girls had the same on their wrists. The orchestra as a finale played all the different national airs. "Yankee Doodle" sounded rather tame and vulgar after the grand Russian Hymn and "God save the King." Oddly enough, "God save the King" is the national Hymn of Geneva; it was played after the "Escalade" in 1602. The name of the composer is not known; both Lulli and Handel claimed it, but that is absurd, as the original manuscript music is in the Arsenal at Geneva. After a Russian *punch chaud*, which Pozzo insisted upon our drinking, home we went. I was very tired.

SUNDAY

Frances came down to breakfast this morning in her
Russian costume. Poor mamma's face was a study in
religion. She could not utter at first, so father stepped
in the breach, saying, "How lovely you look, and where
did all this finery come from?" He knew nothing of it
as he has not been at the Embassy. By this time mamma
had recovered her speech. I saw the storm coming.
"Frances, have you forgotten that it is the Lord's Day?
Go to your room and pray for forgiveness." I left the
room; so did father.

NOVEMBER 1820

Dined at the Spanish Embassy. The Papal nuncio was
present. All ladies in high waists. It seems it is not
etiquette for ladies to be *décolleté* when he is present,
excepting at Court. Madame S. embarrasses me at times;
I feel hot all over, as I am quite certain people must see
how she looks at me. Mamma was very fine in red
velvet. Her skin is so deadly white and fine that she
would be noticed anywhere; I was very proud of her.
After the nuncio retired some Spanish dances were danced
beautifully. Such a strange custom! When the nuncio
arrived he was preceded by two footmen walking back-
wards holding silver candelabra with lighted candles;
the same thing was repeated when he retired. I noticed
he looked astonished when mamma did not kiss his ring.
It was afterwards explained to him that she was a
Protestant. Driving home, father laughingly teased her
about it, saying she should have done so. "No such
flummery for me," she said. We found Frances had
high fever. A doctor was sent for and fears it is scarlet
fever; he says he cannot be certain until to-morrow,
as there is no rash as yet.

DECEMBER 2

Poor Frances has scarlet fever and is isolated in the châlet in the garden. Mamma will not leave her. Father had some news from America which has rather annoyed him. It seems some ignorant Yankee called attention to the way he was living in Paris—that his house was too large, that his servants wore showy liveries, &c. &c. Father is simplicity itself, but he feels he ought to keep up a certain style in a country where such things are so much thought of; he feels it is due to the prestige of the country he represents. They might just as well resent his going to Court—it is quite ridiculous. Monsieur de Lafayette has just called; he consulted him on the matter. The former is certainly republican enough in all his ideas. Father has penned a very dignified answer, which I have just drafted. He requests to be recalled if his way of living is not considered proper, but that he will not change it in any way. He and I are dining with the Barings to-day. Of course mamma had to excuse herself on account of Frances.

DECEMBER 4

We had a charming dinner at the Barings'. The old Duc de Bassano was present. He is really about the only respectable person that Napoleon created a duke, although he was a lawyer or *hommes d'affaires*, or something of that sort, but of low origin. Poor Frances is better as it is a mild attack. In any case it will prevent her from going to any of the Christmas festivities. Mamma feared her complexion might be injured, but the doctor assures her it will not be in any way affected. . . .

DECEMBER

I have refused all invitations for the present as, although Frances is still isolated, I have never had scarlet fever myself. The doctor thinks I had better remain quiet for a few days. . . .

DECEMBER 10

I had a piece of very bad luck to-day. A certain lady of the *grand monde* had smiled upon me. I had a rendez-vous with her at the old Palais Royal in the Marais in the afternoon. It is the most unlikely place in the world to meet anybody. I know of a very quiet little café there with *cabinet particulier;* as we walked toward it I spied a lady approaching with a footman behind her. Horror of horrors!—mamma! Now if it had been the moon arm-in-arm with the sun taking a walk I would not have been more flabbergasted, but it was mamma in the flesh. Nothing was to be done but to brazen it out. With a sickly smile and a grand *coup de chapeau* I approached her, instantly saying, "Allow me to present you to the Comtesse de C." Mamma stared, mamma curtsied; Madame de C. did the same. Mamma curtsied again, Madame de C. ditto; but not a word did mamma utter. I own I was rather proud of her, but the situation was becoming rather strained. I said to Madame de C., "Comtesse, will you allow me to conduct you to your coach?" This really meant a *fiacre*, as Madame de C. had left her coach in the Rue de Rivoli. Mamma glared, curtsied again; finding her voice, said, "James, return when you have found the comtesse's coach," with an accent *grave* on the coach. I could not do anything else. When I did return mamma took my arm and walked ten times around the Palais Royal. I suppose it will mean some more tracts when we get home. It seems the poor old dear, on account of fear of infection to others, had come to this isolated place to take a little exercise. My luck is on the wane.

DECEMBER 12

Not a word have I heard since of my little peccadillo. I think father must have said something, for I am certain she told him. She really thinks I am still a child, for-getting I am three-and-twenty.

DECEMBER 17

Madame de C. will never forgive me; she is furious.

DECEMBER 20

The boulevards are so brilliant for Noël, I walk there every evening.

DECEMBER 26

The usual Christmas festivities, but I have become very *rangé*, so remained at home. All my friends seem to be getting married, and I am only semi-attached.

JANUARY 1, 1821

Another year gone, and still we stop on here practically doing nothing. Father is getting old, and I doubt if he will ever return to America. Mr. Astor has written to him again making new offers, all of which he has refused. He says he must not die rich after holding the posts he has. I have never known of anybody, with the exception of the Duc de Richelieu, who is so absolutely honest and disinterested; both on his mission to the Hague and to England he only charged his absolute out-of-pocket expenses. Would that there were more politicians in America of his calibre! I fear there are few, if any. It is not astonishing he has so many firm friends such as Alexander Baring, Pozzo di Borgo, Lafayette, and the Humboldts—men whose friendship is worth having. I only wish I were more like him.

MONDAY

I had a bad accident skating at Vincennes on Saturday and broke my arm—fortunately the left one. Had it been my right arm I do not know what I should have done. It caused me great pain; the bone-setter was very rough. To add to my troubles, my hair is beginning to fall out. This was caused by the fever I contracted

that horrible winter at St. Petersburg. One consolation—
I can always wear a wig.

FEBRUARY 2

I had a horrid accident on Saturday. I was driving a
new horse in my cabriolet with Lucien up behind. Coming
down the Elysées I spied the King's coach driven at the
usual high speed, which makes a rumbling. As etiquette
requires, I drew up at the side, and was holding my hat
off when my horse shied and over we went. Of course,
I fell on my injured arm, which has always given me
trouble; it was badly set at first—in fact, it had to be
broken again and set, causing me great uneasiness. The
Comtesse de Brissac was passing in her coach; she
stopped and most kindly insisted on conveying me to
her hotel in the Faubourg St.-Honoré, which is quite
close. She sent for a surgeon, and, much to my chagrin,
he announced another slight fracture. After attending
to me, Madame de B. most graciously put her coach at
my disposal to take me home. She is forty but still
very handsome. She held my right hand while the
surgeon was binding my arm; I think she squeezed it.
Nous verrons. Lucien and the horse were not injured
but the cabriolet was damaged.

This morning I was sitting in mamma's boudoir reading,
as my arm was so painful I could not write. Frances
was embroidering and mamma going through her religious
devotions, which consists of reading a sermon of Jeremy
Taylor's, her daily allowance. A footman hurriedly
entered without knocking—a venial offence. He looked
white and scared, and mumbled, "Would Madame
l'Ambassadress permit Madame Berthal to speak to her?"
Enter Madame Berthal, very red and flurried, her very
cap quivering with excitement. Approaching mamma,
in a low tone she said, "Madame l'Ambassadress, there
has been an accident. Louise (one of the kitchen wenches)
has tripped over the cat on the lower stairs, and there are

two." "Two what?" asked mamma. "Twins," replied Madame Berthal. "What nonsense!" said mamma. "Is the girl injured? It does not matter about the kittens; drown them." "Not kittens, Madame l'Ambassadress, babies." Never will I forget mamma's face. Down went Jeremy Bentham bang on the floor. Up rose mamma, her cap literally standing on end. She thundered, "Frances, leave the room." I could no longer contain myself and burst into roars of laughter. This was too much for mamma. "James, I am ashamed of you. Leave the room at once." I really expected to receive Jeremy on my head before reaching the door. Only too glad to escape, I sought refuge in father's room. When I succeeded in suppressing my laughter I commenced telling him what had happened. I had only commenced my story when he was summoned to mamma's room. When he returned he tried to look serious, but I saw the corners of his mouth twitching. Poor Berthal mamma has dismissed for her want of discretion. Father sent to the Convent of the Sacré Cœur, which is quite close to us, and obtained permission to send the poor girl and her twins to the hospital there. He sent for a coach and had her conveyed there. What passed between him and mamma I do not know, but she locked herself in the room for the remainder of the day. Frances asked me this evening if I thought she could have one of the kittens. I told her they were drowned! ! !

The twins died last night. . . .

My arm is so painful I cannot write any more. . . .

Mamma has forgiven me. Jean, such a nice-looking groom, is the cause of all the trouble. He is going to marry the girl as soon as she is well. Father insists on retaining them both in his service. Mamma looks injured and draws deep sighs. Poor Berthal has been reinstated; father insisted upon it.

FEBRUARY 12

There have been more bomb explosions and the police have not the slightest clue. On January 27 a bomb in the Tuilleries—nobody injured. On the 31st another at the Treasury, several near the palace windows; still not the faintest clue. Scenes every day in the Chamber, one party accusing the other. Then a lull for a time.

FEBRUARY 15

I do not feel well enough to join in the Carnival this year. The fact is, I have had enough of it all. I am now nearly four-and-twenty, and it is high time to settle down. Frances is to make her début this year but not until the spring.

FEBRUARY 17

Such a magnificent ball at the Tuilleries last night. The Duchesse d'Angoulême was superbly regal: her train of white velvet thickly embroidered with gold fleurs-de-lis with a broad gold border, lined and faced with ermine; her dress entirely of superb lace, which they told me had belonged to her mother; the highest diadem of emeralds and diamonds that I have ever seen, it was quite four inches. A veil of superb lace hung down below her shoulders; a belt and stomacher of diamonds and one enormous emerald in the centre; from the shoulders hung great strings of diamonds. The Duchess d'Orléans in rose-coloured velvet; Mlle d'Orléans in blue; the Duchesse de Berri in white with a train bordered with sable (this was her first appearance since her husband's assassination). They made a truly royal group. The poor King was in a chair with wheels, as he suffers from swollen legs.

FEBRUARY 20

At last I have had a bilious attack. Mamma is in her element; she loves to say "I told you so." Now, when one is bilious one is not in the best of tempers; I do so long to throw a boot at her.

FEBRUARY 22

All right again and taking Frances to some small evening parties. She has not been brought up in the French way; mamma allows her much more liberty. Frances can take care of herself; she has great dignity combined with sweetness, and under it all—what shall I call it?—a will of her own. She is very lovely to look at.

FEBRUARY 24

Now Lent has come—a respite for which I am very grateful. I am going to do some serious reading and improve myself; I fear I have been very frivolous up to the present. Mathieu de Montmorency has invited me to hunt at Compiègne, of which he is governor; I shall certainly avail myself of his kindness. If it were not that the King's horses were at his disposal and he offered to mount me, I would not be able to do so on account of the expense.

MARCH 2

I took Frances to the Palais Royal yesterday afternoon to see a little religious play acted by the children of the Duc d'Orléans. The Duc de Chartres* is now nearly twelve years old, and Mlle d'Orléans is nine. Some of the younger children also took part. The other actors were children of the Duc d'Escar and the Montmorency children. It was really very pretty. After the little play all the children sat down to a simple dinner; we waited on them. Their aunt, Mlle d'Orléans, is so charming, so simple and unaffected. She is very fond of father; I think it is that attracts me to her.

* Duc de Chartres, son of the Duc d'Orleans, born at Palermo September 3, 1810.

MARCH 4

Father has had some disquieting letters from America about Albert. He has not shown them to me, nor has he told me of their contents, but I fear there is some trouble; Albert is so odd. I am very sorry, as I dislike to see father troubled.

MARCH 7

Madame Patterson Bonaparte has been much disappointed that she has not been able to arrange a marriage for her "Bo," whom she considers a prince of the House of the now fallen Bonapartes. Mr. Astor, in whom she has great confidence, and who has been in Rome, has informed her that she must not put any reliance in any members of the Bonaparte family. Madame *mère* is the most sincere and the Princesse Pauline Borghesi is absolutely unreliable. Her friend, Lady Morgan, is also in Rome, and told her the same thing. She has written volumes to father asking his advice. She is really too bad, as she is certain not to act by it. He has a great dislike for the Bonaparte family; of course the great brains and pluck of the first emperor he cannot but have admiration for.

MARCH 9: COMPIEGNE

I have been here since yesterday, and finely lodged in the château. All are most civil and nice to me. We hunted all day to-day and I am tired out. Just going to bed.

MARCH 12

I came back to Paris yesterday after a most enjoyable visit. I am a little sorry I went for so long. I find father has been doing the copying of his own private letters and dispatches, which he will not allow any one to do with the exception of myself. We dine with the Duc and Duchesse de Lavalle. I have never seen their hotel, but father tells me it is the finest in Paris.

MARCH 14

A most painful disclosure has been made. It seems
the Duchesse de Berri told her Father-confessor that
she was the instigator of all the bomb explosions, which
were placed by her own people. He made her tell all
this to the King. All the King said was, "Stop all
further inquiry and try to forgive her." She is an
Italian and a lover of intrigue. All this has made a most
painful impression.

MARCH 16, 1821

I really do not know how it will end. Yesterday I was
dining *tête-a-tête* with Madame S.—her husband being
away, as she thought. Fortunately, she has a most
discreet maid. She, hearing Monsieur S.'s carriage in
the courtyard, rushed and warned us. I was just able
to escape down the *escalier de service*. I went to the
opera, and I suppose after the fright I had had nothing
amused me, so I returned home. I am glad I did, as
I found the house in an uproar. Poor Berthal had fallen
down the whole flight of marble stairs. Frances says
she is broken to bits. All I could see of her was her
cap, which had at last fallen off and was sitting quietly
on a hall chair. There is a surgeon and two doctors
with her now. Of course mamma is very much worried;
but this did not prevent her forbidding a priest to enter
whom one of the servants had sent for.

MARCH 19

I forgot to write about the Lavalle dinner. It was absolutely superb—on a scale of magnificence quite equal to
a Court entertainment. We sat down eighty at table,
and the banquet lasted for four mortal hours. I counted
thirty footmen. The Duchess was a very great heiress
and the Duke was also very rich.

MARCH 21

I drove to St.-Cloud to-day in my curricle. It is beginning to rattle a bit. If we stop here much longer I
must have a new one. Poor Mrs. P., of "Bologny"
fame, died to-day. Mr. Livingstone returns from a very
extensive tour and leaves for America at once.

MARCH 25

There is every prospect now of father either going home
or going to London. The latter mamma would prefer,
as she has now become quite reconciled to living abroad;
in fact, I do not think she would care to return home at
present. Father does not like London. He had a long
conference with Pozzo di Borgo to-day. They are such
close friends, and he thinks very highly of Pozzo's opinion.
Lafayette dined here yesterday; he has aged considerably, but is always delightful. Father fears as he
gets older he will be even more indiscreet than in his
youth, or indeed more impulsive.

MARCH 29

Some very disagreeable communications from Mr. Adams
to-day. I really think he, being now Secretary of State,
is paying father up for imaginary wrongs when at Ghent.
When I look back upon that time I am amazed that
father bore so well with him and Mr. Clay; they were
quarrelling like two spoiled children all the time. Father
did all he could to restore peace between them, but it
was of daily occurrence and most trying. I sometimes
think we may return to live in Geneva and abandon
America altogether. I, personally, would be delighted,
but I fear we are not rich enough to do this. I must
make some money; I cannot always be a drag on father.

APRIL 1

There is a smell of spring in the air to-day. Frances
tried to fool me to-day, sending me a letter challenging

me to a duel. I recognized her handwriting at once.
I did not say a word about it. She has been worrying
mamma for a long time to buy her a spencer at Madame
Le Vestris' in the Rue de la Paix; I have heard of
nothing else for weeks. So off to Madame L. I went.
Made her do me up a box with large gold letters with
her address on it. I bought a murderous-looking fish
and wrapped it in many papers. Imitating mamma's
handwriting, I put a little note on top of the silk paper
that she would see the moment the cover was lifted.
I timed the box to arrive while we were at dinner. Great
success. Frances opened the box. Only seeing the note,
she rushed and hugged mamma, who I must say looked
rather astonished. Rushing back to unpack her coveted
spencer, as she thought, the smell of fish met her nose.
With a squeak (women always squeak) she seized the
fish and made a dash for me, but was too late. I was
out of the window into the garden, the fish after me.
A long list of diplomatic dinners to be got through. We
are engaged for every day for two weeks. Father hates
all this but is forced to accept. Mamma now, I think,
loves these entertainments. She, like all women, loves
dress. This gives her an opportunity to show off her
finery.

APRIL 6

There were serious disturbances last evening at the
Ecole de Droit de Paris; some rioting. The troops
had to be called out. What a mistake it is to be dragged
into a liaison, particularly with a married woman! If
something does not happen I shall not have a hair on
my head.

APRIL 9

Since the death of the Duc de Berri a great change has
certainly come over the *jeunesse dorée* of Paris; not
half so much *entrain*. I think he really gave the impetus

to us all. I dined yesterday at the Trois Frères Proven-
ceaux* in the Palais Royal with some boon companions.
I do not know how it was, the dinner was excellent, the
wine as well, but we all seemed dull and depressed. I
hardly dare own it, but I fear we are all blasé. I commenced a little too young to enjoy life. I have had a
good seven years of it; and what I used to look on then
as the height of enjoyment I now find tiresome. I try
to take interest in the political questions of the day.
I read most carefully all the English as well as American
papers that we receive and try to keep myself *au courant*
of everything of importance. I believe one can train
one's mind to serious matters. I certainly have wasted
a lot of time.

APRIL 10

Have been taking Frances to see all the fine churches;
I don't think she cares much about it.

APRIL 12

Father has presented me with a new curricle; it is
painted yellow, which is much the vogue at present. . . .

APRIL 15

We are eating through our dinners. Oh, the bore of it
all!

APRIL 20

A fine entertainment at Versailles with some Russian
Grand Dukes. The King was not able to be present
and Monsieur did the honours. The fountains were all
playing. A splendid banquet. Looking out of one of
the windows looking on the Cours d'Honneur, the whole
scene seemed to be conjured up before me: the *dames
de la halle* more like wild beasts, then women shouting
and screaming, then dragging the coach with the unfor-

* A restaurant only recently demolished.

tunate King and Queen in it. As I was meditating on all this I felt a hand on my shoulder; it was the dear old Duke of Gordon. He said, "A penny for your thoughts." I blurted out exactly what had been passing through my mind. He then, really with much emotion, described the whole scene most vividly to me; pointed out exactly where he stood, the immense scorn and dignity of Marie Antoinette as she entered the coach, the horrible drive back to Paris. He said he did all he could, but he was absolutely powerless in the hands of the frenzied mob. He slipped his arm through mine saying, "It is better to try and bury unpleasant memories." We joined the Court in the Salle des Glaces.

APRIL 21

Father took me to-day to see Madame Condorcet, the widow of the Marquis Condorcet, the friend of Voltaire. She is only fifty-three but looks much older—one of the saddest faces I have ever seen. She welcomed us with effusion, taking both father's hands, holding them, and saying, "You knew my husband." She was a Mlle de Grouchy. It seems they were an ideal couple. Her perfect character made Condorcet a believer in equal rights for women. Her only child is Madame O'Connor, the wife of General O'Connor.

MAY 3

Mr. Adams has been playing more of what I call "Yankee tricks"; he certainly is an impossible person. He is not a man of great force or intelligence, but his own opinion of himself is immense. I really think father, in a covert way, pulls his leg. I know he thinks little of his talents and less of his manners.

MAY 21

Frances is greatly excited as the time approaches for her to make her début at Court. She came to me in rather a mysterious manner to-day and began to make much of me. I suspected there was something at the bottom of it, so said to her, "Out with it; what is it you want?" She is a little afraid of mamma. She wants me to persuade the latter to let her have a more elegant frock for Court. I promised to do my best.

MAY 22

Mamma is adamant. Frances is to wear what she decrees. Simplicity above all things. For a wonder, I quite agree with mamma. Frances is quite pretty enough and she needs but a very simple setting. I told her this and consoled her with a little judicious flattery about her skin, eyes, hair, &c. &c. She is but a woman.

MAY 24

The brothers Humboldt were at *déjeuner* to-day. Formerly I did not take any interest in their conversation, but it was quite different to-day. I was sorry when they retired. Father delights in their society. They certainly seem to appreciate him; for this I love them.

JUNE 2

Frances made her début at Court last night. She certainly did look very lovely. All I know of her dress—she was in white, a great big wreath of pink roses round her head. She was quite self-possessed and bore herself with much dignity. All the members of the Royal Family smiled on her. Driving home she burst into sobs. Poor child, I suppose it was the pent-up excitement.

JUNE 10

I have suffered a great deal lately with my arm; I fear it will be permanently stiff—I can hardly raise it now. I hope father will decide on Aix-en-Savoi, as I will then be able to go in for the cure. I am afraid rheumatism has settled in my arm.

JUNE 15

So little of interest to record in my journal at present. I seem now to think that the everyday occurrences of "the *monde*" are not worth recording. Of course, anything of importance that I want to remember I make notes of. If father should ever get hold of this diary I wonder what he will think of it. Mamma asked me to-day if I thought he was worrying about Albert. She does not think he at all approves of the life the latter is leading. He does not seem to care for people of his own class—only farmers and their families.

JUNE 30

There have been rumours that the Emperor is ill at St. Helena. Nothing confirmed.

JULY 10

The news has just arrived of the death of Napoleon. He died on May 5. I was much astonished at the way the news was received. The hero which the whole French nation had worshipped, whom all Europe had trembled before, it might have been an ordinary actor who had died. Really one could feel great disgust. A mighty man indeed he was with all his faults. The first I heard of it was cried about the streets: "La Mort de Napoléon à St. Helena, deux sous." Oh, the irony of it!

JULY 15

The Bonapartists here show the greatest respect to the Emperor. They have petitioned the King to allow the body to be brought to France and buried, but he will not hear of it. Father says it would be most unwise—that France is beginning to settle down after all the troubles she has gone through; that even the Emperor's body will excite enthusiasm in many and might lead to very serious results. Father received several letters asking if he thought America would join in petitioning the King. It is really too absurd. What has America to do with it? Madame Patterson Bonaparte, wonderful to relate, has written to father full of praise of the dead Emperor.

JULY 18

An extraordinary thing has happened. Father wished for a document, and applied for it to the Duc de Bassano; the latter has all the copies of the archives of the Emperor. A document was sent, but not the one applied for; it was a copy of a Trianon Decree of August 5, 1810. This decree was entirely withheld from the American Minister. Had it been known there would not have been any war between England and America. It bears the same date of the Berlin and Milan decrees, which were to be revoked on November 1. Never before have I seen my father so angry; he absolutely lost control of himself and used the strongest language. The underhand meanness, the perfidy, injustice, so low and despicable. It was the Emperor's wish, evidently, to do all in his power to crush a young and rising nation. Father went at once to see the Duc de Bassano, but on arriving there he could hardly say anything, he found the poor old Duke utterly crushed by the death of the Emperor. He evidently knew nothing of his mistake, so father did not undeceive him. He sent a copy of the decree to Mr. Adams with very strong remarks on the subject.

GALLATIN to J. Q. ADAMS

Paris, September 15, 1821

Sir,

[First part of letter omitted.]

But the Trianon Decree was intended for the St. Sebastian, Amsterdam, and other cases of the same period. It is not a condemnation either in form or in substance, but it certainly announces the intention to condemn. It bears date the same day on which it was officially communicated to our Minister that the Berlin and Milan decrees would be revoked on the first day of the ensuing November; and no one can suppose that if it had been communicated or published at the same time the United States would, with respect to the promised revocation of the Berlin and Milan decrees, have taken that ground which ultimately led to the war with Great Britain. It is indeed unnecessary to comment on such a glaring act of combined injustice, bad faith, and meanness as the enacting and concealment of that decree exhibits; and I cannot suppose that it will ever be brought forward by this Government for the purpose of repelling our claims to indemnity, especially as the grounds assumed for the measure are evidently mere pretences and altogether untenable. Yet when I first conversed, in 1816, with the Duc de Richelieu on the subject of our claims, he alluded to a statement prepared in his bureau for him, in which the Act of Congress of March 1809 was mentioned as having afforded cause for reprisals.

The copy of the Trianon Decree was given to a friend of Mr. Parish by the Duke of Bassano, then Secretary of the Council.

I enclose a Greek copy and a French translation of an appeal of the Greeks to the citizens of the United States.

I have the honour, &c.,

ALBERT GALLATIN

DÉCISION DU 5 AOÛT 1810*

Vu le rapport ci-dessus fait au conseil de commerce et des manufactures, d'où il résulte:

(1) *Que le Gouvernement de Etats-Unis ne s'est pas borné par son acte du 1er mars, 1809, à ordonner qu'à dater du 20 mai suivant les bâtiments et marchandises françaises qui entreraient dans les ports seraient mis*

* For translation see Appendix III.

sous le séquestre, mais qu'il a ordonné la confiscation des dits bâtiments et marchandises:

(2) Qu'il a établi par le même acte que lorsque les communications avec le France viendraient à se rétablir, les confiscations continueraient à avoir leur effet:

(3) Que l'acte du 1er mars, 1809, a été mis en exécution toutes les fois que l'occasion s'en est présentée, nonseulement contre les marchandises, mais aussi contre les bâtiments français:

Nous avons ordonné et ordonnons ce qui suit

(1) Les fonds provenants des ventes des marchandises américaines qui ont été effectuées jusqu'à ce jour, et dont le montant avait été mis en dépôt à la caisse d'amortissement, seront transportés au trésor public.

(2) Les marchandises américaines qui sont mis sous le séquestre seront misés en vente, et les fonds en provenants versés au trésor public.

(3) Les bâtiments américains sur le soit desquels il n'avait point été statué jusqu'à ce jour, seront également mis en vente et les fonds en provenants versés au trésor public.

(4) Attendu que l'acte des Etats-Unis du 1er mars, 1809, ne contient aucune disposition contre les équipages de nos bâtiments, voulant toujours traiter les Etats-Unis aussi favorablement qu'il est possible, et n'usant qu'à regret du droit de représaille à leur égard, nous entendons que les équipages des bâtiments américains entrés dans nos ports ne soient point considérés comme prisonniers, mais soient envoyés dans leur patrie.

(5) Les dispositions ci-dessus seront executées à l'égard de tous les bâtiments américains entrés et séquestrés dans nos ports depuis le 20 mars 1809, jusqu'au 1er mai de la présente année 1810, date de l'acte par lequel les Etats-Unis ont revoqué celui du 1er mars, 1809.

(6) A l'avenir et jusqu'au 1er novembre prochain, époque fixée par la lettre de notre ministre des rélations

extérieures au plenipotentiaire des Etats-Unis pour la révocation de nos décrets de Berlin et de Milan (dans le cas où les conditions établies dans la dite lettre seraient remplies), les navires américains pourront entrer dans nos ports; mais leur déchargement ne pourra avoir lieu, à moins qu'ils ne soient munis d'une licence signée de notre main, que sur un rapport fait en conseil de commerce, constatant qu'ils n'ont pas été dénationalisés par leur soumission aux arrêts du conseil Britannique, et qu'ils n'ont point contrevenu à nos décrets de Berlin et de Milan.

En notre palais de Trianon, le 5 août, 1810.

(Signé) Napoléon

JULY

Madame Récamier has closed her *salon* for the present. Most of the adherents of the Bonapartists are in the deepest mourning. Surely it is the least they can do, considering the Emperor picked most of them out of the mud and made them rich and noble. Joseph Bonaparte seems to have saved an immense fortune; he is living in luxury in America. Some of those wretched Murats are also there.

JULY

As Frances has been presented at Court, mamma now takes her to balls, &c. It is very trying for her. I am glad to say Frances is far prettier than I thought she would be, and I am very proud to have such a pretty sister. I do hope she will make a good marriage and not have to go back to America. We have to go to some waters for mamma's rheumatism. I think Aix-en-Savoi will be the place decided on. The baths are good but primitive. It is near Geneva. Also we have relations in the neighbourhood.

AUGUST 1: AIX-EN-SAVOI

We are comfortably installed here in a little villa they supply us with. Both mamma and myself are taking a cure for rheumatism. Father only remained a few days to see us settled and then went to Geneva; it is so close. He is staying with the Navilles. This is a beautiful country but very hot. The Lac du Bourget is about a mile from here. I have hired a boat and take Frances out fishing with me. It is such a rest after Paris. We have some friends from Geneva; the de Sellons from Allaman are also here. The Monastery of Hautecombe is on the other side of the lake. It is the burial-place of the Dukes of Savoy and their families; and they also used to live in a part of the monastery. There is a long terrace on it about ten to twenty feet above the lake. The story is that the ladies of the House of Savoy used to fish from this terrace, that there were men in boats below who placed live fish on their hooks and then gave a little jerk—much to the delight of the ladies, who thought they were fine fisherwomen. My arm is much better; I can raise it quite high already. Very much troubled by flies, which sting. The grapes are ripe, and we pay fifty centimes to go into a vineyard and eat as many as we like.

OCTOBER

Aix did mamma good, and now we are installed for the winter. Father fears there will be poor results *re* Indemnity from France. He says the Ministry play with him and are continually changing their tactics. He really thinks he ought to return to America and enter into more active life. He likes his life here; it all suits him, but he feels he is wasting time. He is continually being urged to enter public life again in America; he will not, I think. The whole system of political life in America has undergone a change, and he feels it will be most distasteful to him.

NOVEMBER 10

Poor Albertine de Broglie is in great trouble as she has lost her baby—fortunately, the youngest one. I have to relieve mamma, taking Frances to balls, &c.   Madame S. returns to-day.

NOVEMBER 12

Ball at the Palais Royale.   Frances looked lovely and was very much admired; she danced every dance.   I love to see her enjoying herself.   Of course, Madame de Boigne had to say something disagreeable to mamma. Looking at Frances, who was dancing with La Roche-foucauld, she said, " I see you have brought your daughter up *à l'Anglaise*."   "No, *à l'Américaine*," said mamma, with a strong stare at the opposite wall.   Bravo, mamma ! I told father when we arrived home; he laughed, which is rare for him.   Frances says she will not marry any man who does not propose to her personally and not to her parents.   She says she is not an object of barter. I consider her a most advanced young woman.   A serious row with Madame S.   May it be the end, but I doubt it.

NOVEMBER 26

Father has been much vexed by some letters from Mr. Adams, who is now Secretary of State.   It is all on account of the seizure of a French ship called the *Apollon* in the St. Mary's River on the Spanish side, for evading the navigation laws.   Father thinks it is a high-handed action and unjustifiable.   He has taken his own line with the French Government in entire opposition to Mr. Adams.   What amazed Mr. Adams was that father wrote to him that he considered his argument of the case, as well as his own, not worth a straw.   At times he certainly is an extraordinary contradiction.   Undoubtedly father has far superior talent to Mr. Adams, and likes playing the latter as a cat does a mouse. Father, although he never admits it, I am certain feels very deeply the gross injustice and prejudice that shuts the door of the Presidency to him simply because he was not born in America.   Although he tries to disguise it, he has a strong belief in the superiority of European intellect. He looks upon the American-born politicians as a lot of rough colts who want breaking in. Not one of them has had the early training that he has—brought up, as he was, among the flower of intellectual men. The Americans have great intellect and brains but they are untrained. What can be expected of them?

DECEMBER 25

Christmas again. We are having a large party for Frances. Already three fathers have appeared in orthodox costume to formally demand her hand for their respective sons. She will have none of them. The Duchesse de Broglie has pressed one suit, but Frances is obstinate. I tell her she must not be too particular.

DECEMBER 26

Everything went off very well. Now that Frances has grown up we have put aside fooling, but really it is not half as amusing. Our cousins the Gallatins are giving a Twelfth-Night party for Frances.

DECEMBER 31

I have been counting up my money for my *étrennes* to-morrow. I will have exactly 150 left after all the servants are tipped. It is a bad custom. Mamma always has a nest-egg, so I will have to draw on her. Good-bye, Old Year. Off to an old-fashioned *réveillon*. Dear old diary! Much as I have confidence in your discretion, I will not record where I am going or who my companions are to be.

JANUARY 1, 1822

We are quite worn out with all the duties we have had to perform. The long time we are kept standing at Court is most trying. The King paid marked attention to father yesterday, so did Monsieur. The Duchesse d'Angoulême, who on many occasions has noticed Frances, asked if it was true that she was *fiancée*.

To-night a ball at the Palais Royale.

Monsieur de Richelieu looks very ill. He is still pursued by the Queen of Sweden, it is really too absurd; she makes him as well as herself the laughing-stock of Paris. We are bidden to a reception at Madame Récamier's for the 10th. Madame Bonaparte arrives in a few days.

JANUARY 11

A delightful evening at Madame Récamier's. The funniest sight was the Queen of Sweden; she was dressed in a most extraordinary manner—I never saw a person so absolutely out of place; she looks more fit to be behind the counter of a tallow-chandler's than in a *salon*. We have had some very nice Americans here lately. A Mr. Ogle-Taylor and Mr. Livingstone, both men of education and polished manners; the latter was very anxious for me to go to Italy with him, but I could not be spared.

JANUARY 12

Madame Bonaparte dined with us yesterday, she is really more brilliant than ever, a little embittered perhaps, particularly against the Catons, they are her *bête noire* for the moment. Her sister-in-law, Mrs. Robert Patterson, *née* Caton, came in for her full share. It seems that the Duke of Wellington writes to her every week, and there is much scandal about their relationship.

Father has told Madame Bonaparte there will always be a *couvert* for her at our table. We were all rather astonished at this, for he does not often show such marked hospitality, particularly to Americans. He feels very sorry for her, and thinks she has been badly treated; that she is a woman of brilliant intellect, but that her troubles have quite ruined what might have been a most delightful personage, as well as a power.

JANUARY 13

Fine skating in the Bois de Boulogne to-day. I took
Frances; she got on wonderfully well as she had learned
to skate in America when she was a child. She looked
very lovely, mamma dresses her so well. With the exercise of skating she had the most brilliant colour in her
cheeks. One horrible old woman went up to her and
rubbed her cheeks with her pocket-handkerchief, saying,
"*Tiens, ce n'est pas du rouge.*" I think some of the
French ladies were shocked that mamma was not with us.
Princesse Galitzin had kindly offered to chaperone Frances.
It is really too absurd that now she is grown up she is
not allowed to drive alone with me; it is not that either
mamma or father object, but it would be considered
quite wrong, the argument being that everybody did
not know that I was her brother. In fact, I cannot walk
with her alone, without one of our footmen following.
A very fine ball at the Carillion-Latours. I very much
pitied poor mamma, she had to sit waiting for Frances
until the early hours of the morning.

JANUARY 14

The King has been failing very fast; they say for the
moment he is very much better. A ball at Court on the
16th. In fact, I do not think there is a single night that we
are not engaged till Lent. Madame Bonaparte takes
great interest in Frances, and says with her beauty she
ought to make a great marriage. I fear the latter has
but little ambition.

JANUARY 15

Mr. Crawford is urging father to return to America, as he
wants him to use his influence for the vote of the State
of Pennsylvania for the Presidency. Father has not the
slightest intention of doing so, and does not think Crawford has the slightest chance. The President wishes
father to remain in Paris, and he willingly agrees to this.

In fact, I think he wants to hold himself aloof from politics in America. He often talks of building a fine house in New Geneva; he already has a small brick one there. I cannot understand this new idea of his: to wish to bury himself in the wilds of Western Virginia; to take poor mamma there after the life she has led in Paris. She detests the country; of course we never disagree with him or contradict anything he says. I think it may be sentiment. He pictures New Geneva as a new Eldorado. Of course Frances will marry. So will I. He cannot expect me to live in idleness in the backwoods of America. Practically he and mamma are to be quite alone. Albert may stop with them, but I doubt it. I had an odd letter from him yesterday. He evidently is in some entanglement with a farmer's daughter; he begs me not to mention it to anybody. It is so strange that he always liked low company. It is a great pity, I think, that father did not send him to Geneva to be educated. The people he mixes with are of the lowest class, totally without education or manners. I cannot understand where he inherits his low tastes from, certainly not from father's family; nor have I ever heard of a Nicholson who was not a gentleman. Albert has a brain, in fact in his way is very clever. I fear now it's too late to make any change in him.

JANUARY 16

I took Madame de R. into supper last night at the Russian Embassy. She is very witty and does not hesitate to express her opinion in the most clear terms *à mauvaise langue*. I am rather afraid of her. During our conversation I asked her if she knew the reason why Madame X. had such success: the very best people fighting for invitations to her entertainments, although she had neither beauty nor wit, was really dull and vulgar. "There you are wrong," she answered. "She has much more than wit or beauty, tact. When I dine or sup with her, she puts my reigning *amani* on my right and the one

I hope to succeed him on my left. What does a woman
want more? Now do you wonder at her success?"

FRIDAY

Mrs. Robert Patterson dined with us on Thursday; she is
really beautiful and has a wonderful charm of manner.
Her one topic of conversation is the Duke of Wellington.
They say he allows her 100,000 francs a year; at least
so says Madame Bonaparte. Her jewels are very fine.
Madame B. says they are mostly imitation, but I think
it is a case of sour grapes.

JANUARY 18

Father has refused the office of President of the Bank of
the United States, which was kindly offered to him.
He has the fixed idea in his head to lead an absolutely
retired life when he returns to America. I can hardly
credit it and think it is but a passing fancy. Monsieur
de Lafayette, Pozzo di Borgo, all beg him to remain in
Paris.

JANUARY 20

I took Frances to a ball at the Gay de Lussacs' last night,
mamma was not well. She had written to the Comtesse
de Gallatin if she would chaperone Frances. On our
arrival I could not find any of the Gallatin family, and
really did not know what to do—at 12 o'clock the
Countess appeared. It seems that they had a bad
accident, one of the horses having fallen, dragging the
other one with it and overturning the coach; one of her
daughters was badly cut on the neck and face. She made
all haste, after her daughter had been attended to, to come
to the ball, on account of Frances—it was most kind of her.
I would not allow her to stop late as I know she must be
anxious to get home, so we retired at 1 o'clock.

JANUARY 21

Skating all day; it is an exercise I love. Had a bad fall with Katinka Galitzin, and am sorry to say that the blade of my skate tore her coat and cut her arm. After her mother had bound it up, she insisted on returning to the ice and skated until dark. If the frost holds we are going to have a grand *fête de nuit* on the ice in a couple of days; the Duc and Duchesse d'Orléans have promised to be present; a *quête* will be made for charity.

JANUARY 22

Louise, of kitten fame, gave birth to a fine boy yesterday. I am the *parrain* and Frances the *marraine*. Mamma does not approve but father does. Of course we asked him first and mamma never goes against his will.

JANUARY 24, 1822

The frost held; in fact it is freezing still. The *fête de nuit* was a grand success. It was beautifully arranged on the Petit Lac. Wreaths and wreaths of lanterns made it quite light enough to see everything and everybody. Sledges in every shape and form hung with lanterns. Some with most grotesque heads. The Duc and Duchesse d'Orléans and the Duc de Chartres arrived at 9 o'clock. They were conducted to a raised platform on which was a species of divan covered with fine fur rugs. All fashionable Paris was there as it was a novelty. I was on the committee of arrangement. We had hired some Swedish skaters to give a performance in costume, which they did at 10.30. We had a *retraite aux lanternes*, over six hundred joined in it; everybody had a stick with a Chinese lantern on it. Some of the men had poles of wood about two feet from each shoulder with lanterns on each end. There were fifty men two by two holding bentwood frames with lanthorns, two fine military bands played, and, for the *retraite*, we had the Corps de Chasse from Compiegne and Fontainebleau. The

198

royalties retired at 11.30. A most successful fête. The proceeds collected amounted to about 7000 francs. I forgot to mention we had coloured fires burning at intervals: red, green and yellow. All the way from the Petit Lac, at an interval of four feet apart, were stationed soldiers holding blazing torches to light the way, this extended as far as the Champs Elysées.

JANUARY 25

I was so tired this morning, and stiff from skating. Father had some writing for me to do. I took it over to a table in a window in his room. I made a brave start but I suppose I was overcome with fatigue and the warmth of the room combined. I was awakened by the sound of the gong for *déjeuner*. I found a cushion had been placed under my head. Father stood by me smiling, and said, "I hope you had a good sleep, my petit *vaurien*." I made every excuse, but he only laughingly said, "Come to breakfast, and finish your writing this afternoon."

JANUARY 27

Mamma called me into her boudoir this morning; she said she wished to have a serious conversation with me. She began by asking why I had not written to my aunt, Mrs. Montgomery, in America; that I had neglected her terribly, &c. &c. Now as I had never written to this respected lady in my life, I was at a loss for an answer. By degrees it all came out. It seems that Mrs. Montgomery is rich, has no heir; mamma thought I might stand a chance. I at once consented to do so. I wrote a letter in a burlesque style. Knowing Mrs. M. to be a violent republican, I abused and ridiculed everything that had to do with a republic; that I hoped Americans would come to their senses and have a king; that I hoped that I never would be obliged to return to the land of the free. I showed the letter to mamma. After reading it she stamped her foot, a bad sign, and threw the letter

I had taken so much pains with into the fire. I don't think she will ever ask me to write another. I hate humbug and don't want anybody's money.

JANUARY 29

Madame Patterson Bonaparte dined with us yesterday, as well as her sister, Mrs. Robert Patterson. Mathieu de la Rochefoucauld, the Alfieris and several others. Madame B. was as usual brilliant, and kept the whole table alive with her witticisms. Pozzo di Borgo, who was also one of the guests, said, "Really, Madame Bonaparte, you should have been a man: you would have been a diplomatist."

FEBRUARY 1

Very serious trouble I fear is brewing for me with Madame S. If this diary falls into the hands of any young man beginning his career, may I warn him never to have an intrigue with a married woman.
Off to Fontainebleau to hunt to-morrow.

FEBRUARY 3

We had a poor day, as it had frozen hard in the night. I stuck one pig, quite a youngster, who squealed like a baby. A very large party. The usual "curée." Nothing very much to record. I had to leave early this morning, as I knew there would be business for me to attend to for father.

FEBRUARY 5

The King is now entirely in the power of Madame du Cayla;* he does nothing without asking her advice. There has been a great deal of intriguing about the post of Archbishop of Paris. Monsieur du Quellon, I believe, will be appointed, he is very young for such a post.

* Zoë Talon, Comtesse du Cayla, born 1784, died 1850, daughter of a secret agent employed before the Restoration. Mistress of Louis XVIII, whom she dominated.

ALBERT GALLATIN

PAINTED BY MADAME MEUNIER-ROMILLY, GENEVA, JANUARY, 1815

FEBRUARY 7

Mr. Astor has been pressing father to accept the Presidency of the United States Bank, but he will not hear of it. He had rather a disagreeable experience to-day. Some most extraordinary Americans called. The rule is for them simply to write their names and addresses, but they insisted upon seeing father. He received them with great civility, but the moment they commenced to speak I gauged what sort of people they were. They did not request father to present them at Court, but absolutely demanded it as a right. Now he has made it a rule not to present anybody unless they hold some distinguished position in their own country. These people were absolutely impossible. Father quietly but firmly said, "I regret not being able to present you." They demanded the reason why in the most insolent manner. Father rang the bell, and when the footman appeared simply said, "Show these gentlemen to the door." They commenced to use the most disgraceful language. I with the help of Mr. Sheldon insisted upon their leaving. Father with a bow left the room by another door. It is really dreadful he should be subjected to such indignity. He has now given an order that in future nobody is to be ushered into his presence without first being interviewed by Mr. Sheldon or myself.

FEBRUARY 12

There seem to be internal troubles all over France. Monsieur is suspected of starting the agitation. They say the Duc d'Orléans is also stirring up discontent.

I do not even intend looking at the Carnival this year, much less taking part in it. I suppose I have sown about one-half or, say, three-quarters of my wild oats. I am glad that father and I are on the best of terms, and I am quite convinced we always will be. Madame Bonaparte dines here continually; she is certainly a most delightful and entertaining person. I rarely hear her say an ill-

word of anybody, with the exception of the Catons and
of her husband; she certainly has reason in that quarter
after the treatment she has received at his hands.

FEBRUARY 13

Father had a private audience of the King to-day. I
accompanied him as I always do. To our amazement
when we were ushered into the presence, Madame du
Cayla was present and did not retire; she seems to hold
absolute sway over him. He actually appealed to her
for her opinion on matters political which she certainly
had no knowledge of.

Driving home father expressed his disgust, and said
it was high time he abdicated if he was governed by a
woman. It has always been the same thing with the
Bourbons; in their old age some intriguing woman has
governed them.

Very cold: if the frost holds we will have skating to-
morrow.

FEBRUARY 15

I have been skating the last two days on the Petit Lac. ...

FEBRUARY 17

Katinka Galitzin was married to-day to Caumont la
Force. The contract for the marriage was signed last
night. A great crush, splendid *corbeille de mariage*.
The family jewels, which are those of the Duc de la Force,
magnificent. There were two ceremonies, a Russian
one in the Chapel of the Embassy, and the Catholic one
at St. Pierre de Challiot. I was present at both. I will
miss her very much as we were really such good friends.
I will always have a soft spot in my heart for her.

FEBRUARY 20

There are extraordinary accounts, about his Most
Gracious Majesty King George the Fourth, from England,

all the scandal about Queen Caroline, it is certainly very disgraceful. He moves under the absolute sway of Lady Conyngham. I was weak enough last night to allow myself to be dragged off to a supper. I am glad to say I was bored and returned home early. I think father was rather shocked when he was told that Pozzo di Borgo was on the Committee of "Crockfords," but Russians are all born gamblers. It seems that immense fortunes change hands nightly at this establishment, which is in St. James's Street, opposite Mr. White's. The man who started it has already realized a large fortune. Some of the heavy gamblers wear large straw hats, pulled well over their eyes: this is to conceal their features so that no one can see their expression when they are winning or losing. Thank God, I have not the slightest temptation to gamble— about my one and only virtue. Here in Paris play is not so very high, and is not indulged in by the higher classes to any very great extent. Lent is here, which means quiet and plenty of leisure. I am now studying banking systems, both English, American and French. The Alexander Barings come to us to-morrow for a week. They are both so charming. It is a great pleasure for mamma to have Mrs. Baring as she is an American and so sympathetic. He and father are always engaged in financial questions in which they are both absorbed.

MAY 18 *

The Duc de Richelieu has been looking very ill, he died suddenly yesterday. He had come from Versailles to Paris the day before. His sister was with him. Several doctors were called in, but without avail. He died gently in his sleep. Father is much distressed as he had the highest opinion of him, of his wonderful honesty, and of his devotion to France.

*From February 20 until May 18 the diary has been destroyed. —EDITOR.

MAY 25

The Queen of Sweden is making herself quite ridiculous. The Duc only spoke to her twice in his life. She has even been to the King with her lamentations.

MAY 30

The Duc d'Angoulême is the only member of the Royal Family who seems to show any regret. It is disgusting, as he gave his life to his country.

I have had my own troubles lately—result, a boy which father in his large-minded manner has provided for. Madame S. is to live in Switzerland, her husband has repudiated her. Was there ever such a father as mine? He has never mentioned the matter to me but, after he had arranged everything, last night on retiring to my room, I found a letter on my table. It was couched in the kindest terms. He informed me he had settled everything, and that the subject would never be mentioned by him, that mamma was in total ignorance of it. God bless him!

The question of the navigation with the United States has been discussed in the Chamber. Father is not quite satisfied. Monsieur de Chateaubriand seems to ignore everything. He has not even answered our notes lately; it is really very exasperating. Nearly six years wasted.

JUNE 2

We have organized a new form of amusement; at least the Gay de Lussacs promulgated the idea. We drive out to St. Germain leaving Paris about 5 o'clock. A picnic dinner at the Pavilion Henri Quatre, then dancing, singing, &c., until 10.30, then a drive home by moonlight. Several of Frances' friends. Mamma took two very nice American girls, Misses Thorne, the Gallatins, and their daughters. The English Ambassadress brought four very nice English girls, about ten married couples going and a host of men. It was a great success and we have agreed to

repeat it every week. Each pays his own share. I
feel now as free as the air, since I have got rid of Madame
S.: it may be ingratitude, but I always feel so ashamed
of myself. I believe most of the French mammas
refused at first to join the St. Germain parties, but I
believe before long we will have many more joining
us. My miniature is very good and I have given it
to mamma.

JUNE 3

Just after *déjeuner* to-day we heard a great noise in the
servants' quarters. As it continued mamma rang and
Monsieur Caron the *maître d'hôtel* appeared, crimson in
face. He begged that I would be allowed to come down
and see what had happened: the spectacle that met my
eyes when I reached the kitchen is indescribable. Poor
Mamie Kitty, the nigger cook, had made some waffles
for *déjeuner;* one of the footmen, out of sheer mischief,
had taken the remainder of the paste, and with the aid of
two of the kitchen wenches, who had held Mamie, they
had smeared her head and face with the white hominy
paste and had sprinkled flour over it, turning her into a
white woman. She lost her temper and when she was free
made a dash for him and literally had torn his clothes
off. There he was, clothed as he came into the world,
standing behind a large table, while Mamie was trying
to belabour him with a rolling-pin. The moment I spoke
to her she dropped the pin and went on her knees and
began saying, "Oh Jesus forgive a poor nigger." If it
had not been so pathetic I would have laughed. It
seemed to sober all the servants who were assembled.
I told her to get up, and taking her by the hand took her
straight upstairs to mamma. The poor old dear was
trembling and wailing. Mamma made her tell her story:
although she did not at all approve she told Mamie
that it was only meant in fun. Frances took her up to

her maid to be cleansed; the poor old soul sat moaning all the rest of the day. Father will interview all those who took part to-morrow and will see that the delinquents are punished. I felt so sorry for her as she kept repeating, "I am only a poor old nigger and God made me black. I am a miserable old sinner."

JUNE 4

Much to our surprise Monsieur and Madame d'Osmond have bidden us to dinner for the 10th. Mamma is quite flurried, as she says she has worn all her frocks out and she has no time to have one arranged. Father gave her five hundred francs and said, "Get yourself and Frances the finest 'war paint' that that can purchase." The young footman was very contrite and begged not to be dismissed. Father told him he must apologize to Mamie Kitty and beg her pardon before all the servants, and that he would be present—the footman, George by name, did so, and the poor old woman threw her arms around his neck and gave him two ringing kisses: I think he was sufficiently punished.

JUNE 5

At the opera last night I spied a charming and mysterious-looking lady in a frilled *peignoir*. Every time I looked at her she put up her fan, but I saw her peeping between the sticks. I waited at the finish close to the exit of her *loge;* she made the slightest sign to me, the very slightest, for me to follow her. In the crowd I saw her put her hand behind her back. I edged near to her and saw there was a piece of paper in it; watched my opportunity, and covering her hand took it. As soon as I got the chance I opened the little three-cornered note, only a few lines—"28 *rue Boissy d'Anglas—minuit demain.*" I am sorely puzzled—I thought I knew *toutes ces dames* by sight. A splendid footman met her and put her into a fine coach—*à demain,* but I am intrigued.

JUNE 5

I had a batch of letters to copy this morning which kept me very busy. Mr. Crawford is still writing to father begging him to come home, on account of the elections: the latter says if he does so he will be again drawn into political life, which is undesirable. I am thinking of to-night and wondering. I met some of my *intimes* this afternoon, but thought it wiser not to mention my adventure to them. I am dining at the Café Anglais with Guy de Montesquieu and the lady he protects. Will look in at the opera to while away the time till midnight.

JUNE 6

I am disgusted with myself. On the tiptoe of expectation I arrived at No. 28. All was darkness. I waited for a few moments, when the small door of the *porte-cochère* opened and a hand beckoned me in. The moment the door closed there was a brilliant light, two footmen in the hall, and I saw several other cloaks and hats: the mystery was soon solved, *tout bonnement*—a gambling house. I was ushered into a superb salon, the rattle of dice assailed my ear and my charmer stepped forward to greet me. I might have known, as the police are so down on *maisons de jeu* at present. Not a soul I had ever seen before: that struck me as quite extraordinary. I must be getting old! No more *aventures galantes* seem to come in my way. I did not play and soon retired, evidently much to the disgust of my hostess.

JUNE 10

We have been very quiet for the last few days. To-day is the dinner at the Osmonds'. Albertine de Broglie came to *déjeuner* to-day to eat American food. I do not think she really cared for it, but was too polite to say so. Albert has written that the house is getting on famously. We certainly must be returning soon.

JUNE 11

I must acknowledge the dinner at the Osmonds' was superb. We were forty and the *fine fleur* of society. Madame de Boigne in her own house is an excellent hostess. I escorted a very pretty woman to dinner—a Comtesse Chabot: she had passed much of her life in England and longed to go back there to live, which is rare for a Frenchwoman. Lady Westmoreland, a handsome Lady Fane, the English Ambassador, a son of the Countess of Sutherland, whom I met at Coppet, I think it was in 1815. After dinner, which lasted three mortal hours, we retired to the ball-room. There was a raised *estrade*, and Malibran sang. I went rather late to the Spanish Embassy. Father was too tired to go. A great crowd— the "Nuncio" as usual.

JUNE 14

We had one of our jaunts to St. Cloud yesterday, a much larger company and most enjoyable.

JUNE 15

Very hot, I sat at Tortoni's until supper-time eating ice-creams, which I really think made me hotter.

JUNE 20

A catastrophe this morning: poor mamma sprained her ankle and will not be able to move for at least a month. Her feet are very small, and as she is short she wears very high heels—not being quite as light as she was her ankles easily turn. Countess de Gallatin called to-day. She is getting up some little plays and wants to enlist Frances and myself in her company. Father gave his permission for Frances. I have never acted, but am going to see what I can do. I am cast for a little play called "Un Mari en 1815." I am to be a soldier bold, six women in the cast. I am the only man. Like a rooster in a farmyard.

JUNE 22

Our first rehearsal to-day. I fear we all laughed so much
that little progress was made. I have to kiss two of the
girls—my daughters. This we did not rehearse.

JUNE 24

Second rehearsal to-day. It went much better as now
we have some idea of our rôles. There is no doubt
father intends going home soon. I will be glad in one
way, but very sorry to leave my beloved Paris. Puységur
and Montesquieu misbehaved so much to-day at rehearsal
that Madame de Gallatin threatened to get substitutes
for them—they both are very funny.

JUNE 25

A reception at the Palais Royal to-night and a Court
ball on the 29th. How sick I am of these entertainments.
We have a dinner-party to-morrow. Mamma has a
wheeled chair, so can be present. The invitations were
launched before her accident.
Mormornsen had six more kittens to-day, father unknown. Glorious weather. I drove father for the first
time in my curricle to-day. He enjoyed it very much.
He and I dine at the English Embassy on Wednesday.
Mamma has begged to be excused.

JUNE 26

The reception at the Palais Royal was far more amusing
than I thought it would be: a great many English
friends that the Orléans family had made in England. It
ended in a dance.

JUNE 28

Our dinner was a great success. It was for the Osmonds.
Father insisted that Monsieur de Lafayette should
be invited. He made himself most agreeable. The
Osmonds have always kept up their relations with him.

JUNE 30

A very grand ball at the Tuilleries. I enjoyed it although I was very fatigued, having rehearsed for four mortal hours.

JULY 2

A very long and stately dinner at the English Embassy. Mr. and Mrs. Baring were of the guests. Neapolitan singers in the garden, sang during dinner. Sometimes I feel I never want to dine out again. Why do people want to meet together to eat?

JULY 4

Father received as usual all the Americans in Paris to-day, all sorts and all kinds—a motley crew. Buffet in the garden. I will go to bed early.

JULY 6

Our last rehearsal to-night—some people are coming so as to give us confidence. Very warm—Frances very excited. Mamma is a little nervous about her acting when she cannot be present. Father has promised to take her not only to-night but to-morrow as well. I am afraid he will be bored.

JULY 8

All went off capitally. In the first play Frances looked lovely and really acted so well. I saw father laughing. I was indeed a warrior bold. My six young ladies were one more charming than the other, unfortunately I was made up as an old man—that seemed to put them quite at their ease. Puységur drank too much champagne and forgot every word of his rôle, but I don't think the audience noticed it. We were all very merry: the great drawback was the heat and the smell of the oil lamps on the *rampe*.

JULY 10

Most people are leaving Paris now. Mamma's so much better that she drives out to St. Cloud and St. Germain. Hardly any entertaining. The Court is at St. Cloud. The Duchesse d'Angoulême loves it, but nothing will induce her to go to Versailles. I am not surprised—the memories would be terrible for her. The King is worse. Madame du Cayla absolutely rules him with a rod of iron. Albert has had measles, but is well again. My aunt Few went and fetched him to her home in Baltimore and nursed him. Mamma is still a little anxious about him. It takes so long to get an answer to a letter.

JULY 14

Intolerably hot. I have been to the baths in the Seine all day trying to keep cool. Our garden is nice with some shady trees.

JULY 16

Have been trying to read in the garden, but the combination of flies and the heat was too much for me, so darkened my room and went to sleep. After supper mamma allowed me to take Frances for a drive—we had to return post-haste as there was every indication of a violent thunderstorm. We only just got in in time. It is an extraordinary thing but the only fear I have ever seen father show is that of lightning. He was waiting anxiously on the *perron* for our return. He had had some feather beds brought into the centre drawing-room, all windows were closed and the shutters shut. He insisted on mamma going in and there we sat for three mortal hours, stifling. It certainly was one of the worst storms I have ever seen. After it was over it was deliciously fresh and I went for a good walk, not getting home until 1.30.

JULY 19

Mamma and Frances leave to-day for Fontainebleau, then they go to the de Lussacs' (she was an American and an old friend of mamma's), afterwards to pay some visits on the Loire. I stop with father. My arm has been very painful lately. I must have it examined again.

JULY 20

Our old nigger, Mamie, is quite well again, the chef is going for a holiday and she is going to cook for us—as we will be quite alone she will not have too much work to do.

JULY 23

Still this horrible heat; I can do nothing. I feel like a wrung out dish-cloth. . . .

JULY 25

A little cooler. Have been putting all father's proofs of his pamphlet in order and correcting them for him. I do not know how he manages it. He is always cool and calm and serene. His is indeed a blessed nature.

JULY 26

To our astonishment Monsieur de Lafayette appeared last evening, full of mystery. He asked for hospitality, which father was only too pleased to extend to him. His baggage consisted of a large roll of green canvas tied with a thick cord. He is very funny.

JULY 30

Great heat again. Monsieur Lafayette still here. He only goes out at night. He is plotting something. Not a soul in Paris, and those who are here do not show themselves. I sat outside at Tortoni's until midnight: with the exception of Carrillon Latour I did not see a soul I knew.

AUGUST 1

Some annoying news from America: I sincerely hope father is not going to be dragged into politics again. He is not so strong as he was, but his brain seems to be even more active.

AUGUST 6

Nothing to record. Absolute monotony. Everything at a standstill. I am getting so fat. Mamie Kitty feeds us on all sorts of fattening things.

AUGUST 8

Monsieur de Lafayette left hurriedly to-day. About 10.30 this evening two mysterious noisy men sent in a note to father. He received them alone: what transpired I do not know, but he seemed greatly annoyed. . . .

AUGUST 9

Father sent this morning his confidential servant to Mr. Parker's to try and get Monsieur de Lafayette's address. He evidently wishes to warn him of some impending danger.

AUGUST 11

I could have had an *aventure galante,* but it is too hot.

AUGUST 13

I had a bad attack of indigestion, am dieting on peaches— they are so plentiful now after the abnormal hot weather.

AUGUST 17

Horrible nettlerash. I cannot get any sleep, sent for the physician; he says it was caused by the peaches. He has put me on milk and barley-water.

AUGUST 19

Two inches less around the waist. Must go and see Alfred, he will be overjoyed.

AUGUST 20

Ordered some new *surtouts* for the autumn, four pairs
pantaloons and three silk vests—one striped the others
with flowers.

AUGUST

Another shock, Lord Castlereagh that was, now Lord
Londonderry, committed suicide on the 12th at North
Cray. He seemed perfectly well: dressing for breakfast,
he cut an artery in his arm; there was no reason for
such an act, political or otherwise. They say there is
hereditary madness in the family. Father had the greatest respect for him. He had always been just in all his
dealings, so large-minded, and his word was to be depended
upon.

We remain in Paris all the summer, mamma and Frances
are paying visits in the country. . . .

SEPTEMBER 15: CHATEAU DU ROSEY ROLE

Father insists upon my coming here. He put it on the
plea that he wanted me to attend to some business in
Geneva for him, but I know he thought I was dull alone
with him. I did not like leaving him, but as he has Monsieur de Lafayette and several other friends I consented.
It is lovely here and I am very glad to be with my cousins.
They make me feel more like a dwarf than ever, they are
so colossal. They have planned a trip to Chamounix
for me. Adrian Naville is to be of the party—we are
going in a few days.

SEPTEMBER 17

We went yesterday to Allaman and slept at the château.
My cousins the de Sellons were so glad to see us; they
have one whole side of the château covered with a vine
of American grapes: they are not quite ripe yet. A sister
of the Comte de Sellon married a Count Cavour from

Turin. They were on a visit at the château. They have a son* with an enormous head, and one daughter who is very handsome. Another sister of Monsieur de Sellon's is the Duchesse de Clermont-Tonnerre, whom we see so much of in Paris.

SEPTEMBER 19: CHAMOUNIX

We started early yesterday morning, a glorious day. Mules met us and we reached here by the Tête Noire Pass. A most beautiful road. Only one guide. A very famous one who has made the ascent of Mont Blanc eleven times. His name is Jacques Balmat. To-day we have been to the Mer de Glace, a rather fine but dirty glacier. We remain here till Friday.

SEPTEMBER 20

We have made several more ascents of moderate mountains. My cousins are far more keen on finding some chamoix to shoot. We saw several; they are very difficult to approach and I only secured two. I am going to have one of the heads stuffed as a trophy. The inn is very modest, good beds, and the food very eatable but simple; in fact, we are always ravenous, the air gives such splendid appetite. Very few tourists. Some English, who seem to be doing the ascents more as a task than a pleasure. A French honeymoon couple who are most amusing. They seem to imagine they are quite alone here.

SEPTEMBER 22: GENEVA

I left Chamounix with great regret. The Navilles insisted on our paying them a visit of a few days. I have been to see my cousins the Diodatis. Lord Byron occupied the villa for several years and wrote several of his poems there. They tell many funny stories and some very odd ones about him, not quite fit for my diary.

---

* This boy was the famous Count Cavour who helped to make united Italy.

SEPTEMBER 24: COPPET

We posted here to-day from Geneva and are stopping the night. Such a truly hearty welcome from the de Broglies and Auguste de Staël. The Duchesse de Luynes and Monsieur Rocca* are here. It seems so strange to be in this house and no Madame de Staël. Every time a door opens I expect to see her enter. We leave to-morrow for Du Rosey.

SEPTEMBER 26

A large shooting party arranged in the Jura to-morrow. Blackcock is the principal game. We start at daylight, which is about 3 o'clock.

SEPTEMBER 28

A delightful day and really quite a large bag. Twenty-eight blackcock, sixteen miscellaneous birds, four foxes, seventeen hares, two rats. A picnic-luncheon and more champagne than was good for us; this was in my honour.

SEPTEMBER 29

I leave to-morrow for Saconnex to pay a visit to the Budés; my friend Jules writes to me to be discreet, that he is like a bird in a cage when at home. I will leave here with regret, but I must be making my way back to Paris. I feel it is my duty.

SEPTEMBER 30

Monsieur Du Rosey and his sons accompanied me part of the way and Eugène and Jules de Budé met me and drove me here. Jules confided in me that they were going to have a *soirée* in my honour, adding "*Mais les jeunes filles ne sont pas même décolletées.*" He is incorrigible. After an excellent supper and a most genuinely hearty welcome I retired early. I am now writing between the most deliciously lavender-smelling sheets.

* Second husband of Madame de Staël.

OCTOBER 2: SACONNEX

The *soirée* after all was very amusing. Notwithstanding the *jeunès filles* wore bright spencers they were so perfectly natural and so thoroughly enjoyed themselves. They have far more liberty than French girls. I think I must take to myself a Swiss wife!

OCTOBER 7: DIJON

After a really charming visit I left Saconnex, slept one night in Geneva. What delicious Burgundy is obtainable here! It is such a delicate wine that transport changes the flavour. I have a very pleasant travelling companion who is on his way to the Embassy in Paris; he has been at Berne and has risen a step—his name is Cornwallis. He has not borrowed any money from me as yet, so I believe he is genuine.

OCTOBER 14: PARIS

After several halts, arrived last night. Father very well. He was pleased to see me back. I found plenty of work to do, and have been hard at it all day. Matters political in America are anything but satisfactory. Unless there is some radical change, I hope we will not return. Albert has written that the new house is in process of building. As there is no architect to superintend it I fear it will be a strange building. Father has sent out marble mantel-pieces, &c. I dare not say so, but rather out of place in Western Virginia. I told how in Geneva all his relations hoped he would return there and settle down. When I told him this there was a wistful look in his eyes.

OCTOBER 16

We can do so little now as the Government is entirely taken up with the war with Spain. At first it was thought it would be disastrous to France, but opinion has now changed. England has remained absolutely neutral.

OCTOBER 17

Absolutely no work to do, always the same life here. I can hardly realize we have been here for six years. I have quite made up my mind not to remain with another Minister. I feel I ought to be "up and doing" and make a career for myself.

OCTOBER 19

I have persuaded father to take a good rest, and he has consented. Having remained in Paris all summer he is looking very white and tired. To my great pleasure he proposed that we (he and I) should go to Bourg and see the fine Palace of Jacques Cœur—this has been a pleasure long postponed.

OCTOBER 20

We are going in our own coach. I have to-day seen about the relays of horses. Father takes his man Carden, and I take Lucien. It is a good four days' journey.

OCTOBER 25

It has indeed repaid us to come here. I never realized what Renaissance architecture was, and what a wonderful man was Cœur—almost a magician. His origin is hardly known—but at one time the richest man in France, until Charles VII stripped him of his fortune to carry on his wars against the English, then by way of gratitude threw him into a prison on a trumped-up charge of poisoning Agnes Sorel, the former's mistress. He was absolved of this charge. Went to the East and made another fortune. One of his daughters married a Lenthène, their daughter Agnes a Tudert, and Sarah Tudert a Gallatin, our direct ancestor.

OCTOBER 26

We have been all day roaming about the château which is a marvel of carving and decoration. Father has also been studying the archives of Bourg and has found much of interest. The *auberge* is very clean—good beds and food. The place is absolutely a city of the dead. I go to bed at 10 o'clock.

OCTOBER 27

We have made a few excursions in the environs to-day— it is not a very pretty country. I have not seen a single pretty woman—how do the men exist?

OCTOBER 28

We are leaving for Paris to-morrow by an entirely different route which he has mapped out. I have thoroughly enjoyed this quiet time with him, he is always interesting and I know that I can always learn something from him which improves me. For the first time, he has mentioned his first wife to me. She evidently was the real love of his life. They were only married a few months when she died. Now I understand why he wishes to return to Western Virginia: she died and was buried there. I do not think he has ever mentioned her name to mamma. Her memory is a sort of sacred cult to him. It seems there was no doctor within reach; he dared not leave her, and she died in great suffering in his arms.

NOVEMBER 4

Back again and settled down to work. Mamma and Frances returned this morning. They have been all the summer on the Loire paying visits. Frances looks so well. Mamma's temper is slightly uncertain—her first remark to me was: "How your hair has fallen out." "Let me look at your teeth; they're going too." I replied with a Chesterfieldian bow, "We all cannot look as young as you do." She snapped, "You should show more respect for your mother." She is now absorbed, looking over all the new autumn fashion-plates which have been sent to her by her *couturière*. That will put her in a good humour. It is wonderful what a soothing effect the prospect of a new frock has upon the female mind. They will sell their very soul for a new bonnet.

NOVEMBER 6

We were much surprised this morning in receiving an invitation from the Duchesse de Berri for a *soirée intime* in her apartments in the Tuilleries on the 8th. This is the first invitation she has honoured us with since the death of the Duke.

NOVEMBER 8

We dined at the English Embassy yesterday—a very large company. The Marquis and Marquise d'Osmond— they have just returned from London where he has held the post of French Ambassador for a long time. There were some rather odd stories about Madame d'Osmond. Madame de Boigne, their daughter, has taken a large Hôtel in the Rue Bonaparte. Her mother and father are to live with her, not that she needs a chaperone. The Duchesse de Courland was another of the guests; she renewed her attentions to father; I suppose that she must now know that Pozzo di Borgo hoaxed her. I sat next such a pretty English girl; she was so bright and cheerful. I believe she is a niece or daughter of Lord Clanricarde. Another charming girl was a Miss Edwards, daughter of Lord Somebody, whose name I did not catch. She took a great fancy to Frances and asked to be allowed to call to see her. Mamma told her she would be delighted to receive her.

The gardens of the embassy are beautiful. The Hôtel* is in the Faubourg St. Honoré, and the gardens run to the Champs Elysées. I believe the English

* The Hotel Borghése, bought by the Duke of Wellington for the English Government for £36,000.

Government bought it for some absurdly small sum after the Revolution. Why is it so many English women have those rabbit teeth? it quite spoils their beauty.

NOVEMBER 9

The *soirée* at the Duchesse de Berri's was very gay. She had a band of Neapolitan singers and dancers in costume, a great novelty for Paris. The Duchesse d'Angoulême was present and was more unbending than I have ever seen her before. I do not think she quite approved of the *sans façon* style of the entertainment. Neither the Duc nor Monsieur were present. The Duchesse de Berri has grown fat, but has improved in her looks. She is very loud, was dressed abominably and has lost her figure. Many lovers are assigned to her, but I never believe half I hear. The Duc and Duchesse d'Orléans were both present, all was over at 1 o'clock. We danced until midnight, when supper was served. The Palace is so very dirty, it has not been cleaned for years. I hear the Royal Family are all moving to St. Cloud and the Tuilleries is to be entirely cleansed. I am sure it is not healthy.

NOVEMBER 10

I am seriously thinking of going in for the Diplomatic Service. Commencing as I have at such an early age, I have already acquired some useful knowledge. Father hopes that a regular Diplomatic Service will be organized in America the same as in other countries. In any case I believe I would always be employed by the Government. Some relations sent mamma some live terrapin from Baltimore. Frances and I took out two into the garden and tried to make them race—Frances's won. It seemed to cheer them up after their long sea voyage.

NOVEMBER 12

I was to shoot at Fontainebleau but the rain has not ceased for two days. Monsieur de Lafayette has been here for a few days, and he does not seem to care to go out of the house—he is very mysterious and father is convinced that he has some new plot. He was closeted with Mr. Baring for several hours this afternoon. A report has just come that the King is very ill at St. Cloud. The Court was to have returned to Paris to-day but it is now postponed.

NOVEMBER 13

A fine day at last, bright sunshine. Father has mapped out a regular course of reading for me. Books on diplomacy. I shut myself up in my room this morning from 9 until 12. I hope to keep this up every day. I gave the first sitting for my miniature this afternoon. Had two teeth drawn—great pain. We heard to-day that Mrs. Robert Patterson is going to marry the Marquis of Wellesley, the Duke of Wellington's brother; he is Lord-Lieutenant of Ireland. Madame Bonaparte will burst with envy.

NOVEMBER 16

Miss Edwards and Cornwallis dined with us to-day, the former is a daughter of Lord Kensington, she and Frances have struck up a great friendship. Unfortunately she is leaving shortly for England, and returning after the Christmas holidays. She has invited Frances to go back with her, and Lady Kensington has written to mamma requesting her to allow Frances to accompany her daughter. Mamma will not give her consent. When father heard of it he said, "All women have unreasonable reasons."

NOVEMBER 17

The Duchesse de Courland called this morning, absolutely forced her way in. Father was greatly annoyed and had great difficulty in getting rid of her. I have been all the afternoon at Alfred's, my tailor's.

He is making me some coats and pantaloons of the latest fashion. I must either eat less or wear a whalebone belt. Alfred is in despair; he says my figure takes all the soul out of his creations. Lucien is in trouble and has confessed to me—this time it is a married woman and the husband has found everything out. Mamma has discovered an old nigger cook, an escaped slave, and has promptly engaged her. Simply to cook hominy, Maryland chicken, buckwheat cakes and waffles. If I eat much of this fare, no whalebone belt will keep me in bounds and the great Alfred will commit suicide.

NOVEMBER 20

There are extraordinary stories, more or less true, of the immense sums that Madame du Cayla has obtained from the poor King. Sosthène de la Rochefoucauld was, and some say is still, her lover; he has carried through all her disgraceful intrigues against the Government. The Duc de Richelieu had the greatest contempt for her and did not disguise it. The last scandal of Madame Bernadotte, Queen of Sweden, is that when poor Monsieur de Richelieu went into the country she followed him, stopping at all the *auberges* that he did. What is incomprehensible is that Bernadotte allowed her to behave as she did. But it seems he is only too delighted to get rid of her. Father says when he first saw him he was a coarse, vulgar creature, without manners and totally without education. I believe the only descendant of the last King of Sweden is the Queen of Würtemberg. I must ask Comte de Gallatin about him. I suppose some day the descendants of Bernadotte will rank with the other Royal Families of Europe.

NOVEMBER 22

We dined yesterday with the Duc and Duchesse de Montmorency. They have not lived together for many years. He was seized with a religious mania. She has now fallen violently in love with him; it is absurd to see her behaviour in public. It makes it far worse as she is an extremely ugly woman. He on the contrary is known as the handsomest man in France.

NOVEMBER 30, 1822

This I fear will be our last Christmas and New Year in Paris; as far as I can look ahead we will be in Western Virginia this time next year. What an extraordinary change it will be. I often ask myself, was it right to bring me, at the age of sixteen, abroad? To lead a life absolutely different from that at home. To accustom me to luxury and excitement. I never like to question what he does, but sometimes I fear he made a mistake. Here I am at the age of twenty-five, without any future mapped out for me, accustomed to simply wasting my time in an everlasting routine of enjoyment. He is wise and may be perfectly right—that I will tire of this life and will be only too glad to settle down to a quiet and rational existence. Naturally with his influence he can always place me in some good position. Last year Alexander Baring offered to take me into his banking house in London, but father seems to cling to me and if I once went to London in all probability we would be separated for years. It would never enter my heart to do anything to displease him or cause him a moment's pain.

DECEMBER 2

Frances has begged to have a *soirée* on Christmas Eve. So that is settled. We are going to act a little fairy-tale, which I think will be very pretty.

DECEMBER 4

More and more invitations—the trouble is that most of them are from the Corps Diplomatique and we cannot refuse.

Several pages entirely ruined by dampness.—EDITOR.

Tried on four pairs pantaloons and two coats to-day. Alfred is pleased that I am thinner.

Father seems much disgusted by news from America. He has not told me what it is, but I believe it has to do with the Presidential Election.   Mr. Adams has written me a very friendly letter, asking me what my opinion is with regard to father, and hinting that a place in the new Cabinet would be found for him if Mr. Crawford is returned.   I do not think this is quite right as they are both opposed in political opinions and belong to opposite parties.   I cannot gauge his reason for writing.   I know in his heart of hearts he has a very strong opinion of father's ability.   I have not mentioned the receipt of the letter to father and will answer it without committing myself in any way.   I fully recognize the fact that it is quite useless to remain here.   Father is simply wasted.   Any one can fill the post as there is absolutely nothing to do.   Father is deeply occupied in writing some pamphlet, and so absorbed is he that at times I really believe he forgets he is in France.

DECEMBER 6

Our poor old nigger, Mamie, had a stroke to-day, her lower limbs are paralysed.   The doctors think she will recover.   I went up to see her in her room.   As I approached I heard her singing and waited to hear the words; they were repeated over and over again, always the same. "Nobody pity me, nobody pity me, but Jesus, she came riding by and said, 'Nigger foller me.'"   Poor old soul. I asked her how old she was.   She said, "Perhaps twenty, perhaps a hundred."

DECEMBER 7

I find I can only write every two days in my dear old diary.   Our little fairy-play will, I think, be very pretty. It is from an old one father found in his grandmother's papers, and was acted at Cassell.   Of course there is a

Princess (this is Frances), a good fairy and a bad one, a naughty boy (myself), a Prince and a host of fairies of all sizes. I have borrowed all sorts of scenery, &c. &c., from the property man at the opera. Mamma is in her element with the dresses.

DECEMBER 8

First rehearsal to-day. Mamie Kitty has recovered the use of one leg—the guilty footman I met on the stairs with a large bunch of violets. The French are so good-hearted. He said to me, *"Excellence, ce n'est ma faute, n'est-ce-pas?"*
Skating again, but I have not been out as yet.

DECEMBER 9

Father had a long talk with me this morning. He has quite decided to return in the spring to America. The new house will be completed and we will bury ourselves. I will not remain there long.

DECEMBER 10

Have been skating all day. Bright sunshine, but very cold. Katinka Caumont la Force as energetic as ever. She seems very happy.

DECEMBER 12

No time now except for rehearsal—the girls will chatter, so I have offered a prize to the one who keeps her tongue quiet for ten minutes at a time. No one has won it yet.

DECEMBER 15

Between rehearsals and skating I don't seem to have time for anything else. If it were summer we could have had our play in the garden, still the ball-room is quite large enough. We have invited four hundred guests. Before the play the two de Lussac girls, a Clermont-Tonnerre, Mlle de Montesquieu and two Gallatins are going to dance such a pretty *pavane*. The dancing mistress of the opera is teaching them. They are to be *poudrées*. It will be all "milk and water," but pretty. Many of my suggestions have been scouted with horror. The only person who backs me up at all is Pozzo di Borgo. He says: "*Mais pourquoi pas?*" He does not know mamma.

DECEMBER 16

Skating all the morning. A thaw has set in. A venturesome Frenchman was boldly pushing one of the sledges with his fiancée in it, when crack went the ice and in they went, only about two feet of water. Both shrieked "*sauvez-nous.*" We sensibly answered "walk to the bank." When they did manage to climb up, they were received by their respective mammas and papas, hugged and embraced as if they had escaped a great danger.

DECEMBER 16

Obliged to go to a reception at the Spanish Embassy. Father insisted upon my accompanying him. A great crowd. The Orléans family were present. Talleyrand looked like an old rat. I hate the sight of him.

DECEMBER 21

Father has just had an official note that Monsieur de Montmorency has resigned from his post of Minister of Foreign Affairs and that Monsieur de Villèle is to keep the place warm for Monsieur de Chateaubriand. This has amazed him exceedingly. The continual changing of the Minister of Foreign Affairs absolutely places the negotiations *re* the Indemnity claims at a standstill; after Monsieur de Montmorency's pledges given to father in July it is not just or straightforward. Father has sent a very strong note couched in these terms to Monsieur de Villèle.

DECEMBER 23

All is now ready and our last rehearsal will take place to-night. This morning Madame de Boigne called. The Duchesse d'Orléans had intimated to her that they would like to see our little play. Of course father went at once in person and apologized on the score that he did not think the little entertainment worthy of their Royal Highnesses. Begged they would honour him with their presence. They are all coming.

CHRISTMAS DAY

The *pavane* and fairy-tale were really charming and far surpassed what I had expected. The moving trees in the play were a great novelty. They were worked by small fairies, which I had trained. When Frances appeared riding a wee white donkey led by fairies the Duc led off the applause, which was very hearty. Frances did look lovely and acted so well. After all was over the Duc and Duchesse and Mademoiselle stood by the fire-place and we (the actors) all *défiled* before them. Their congratulations were very hearty.

DECEMBER 26

We had a quiet Christmas dinner—some waifs and strays that mamma had invited.

DECEMBER 28

I have promised to go to a supper to see the New Year in, as I am nearly certain this will be our last New Year in Paris—Paris that I adore, Paris that has at last taught me that there is more in life than frivolity and amusement. Father is wise. I know he wished both Albert and myself away from any town in America. Paris has taught me much and I think now I will profit by the lesson.

DECEMBER 30

I went with mamma to-day in a common coach. To-day
she took all her New Year offerings to some poor Americans. She is so truly kind. Hampers of food, clothes,
&c. &c. She did not even forget the children, and had
toys for them all. Frances has a cold or would have gone
with us. I dread a tedious dinner at the de la Roche-
foucaulds'. All of us are bidden.

JANUARY 2, 1823

I have been too busy to write a line in my diary.
The usual Court *défilé* on New Year's Day. The King
looking very ill and did not seem to take any interest
in anything. Madame du Cayla triumphant by his side.
It seemed such a strange thing, as if she were his wife.
We dined with Pozzo di Borgo at the Embassy; nearly all
Russians, a Monsieur Narishkin, the greatest noble in
Russia, but who bears no title, his card is simply "Narishkin." It is very strange, but Russians are only semi-
civilized. Perfect manners, external polish—the moment
they have just a little too much to drink, the savage
comes out. Very true the saying is, "Scratch the Russian
and find the Tartar." Such a round of calls for the New
Year commencing at the Palais Royale, all the Diplomatic Corps, &c.—it took us the whole day.

JANUARY 5

I have had a sore throat and not able to go out for the last
three days. Disquieting letters from Albert in America.
Father has quite decided to return to America and give
up his post here. Mr. Astor, with great courage, has written begging him to remain. Rather amusing as it is
evidently for his own interests, as he is shortly coming to
Paris.
Miss Edwards comes to stay with us for a month on
Friday. I am pleased for Frances's sake as I fear she is
a little dull being so hemmed in by *les convenances*.

JANUARY 6

Katinka Galitzin (Caumont la Force) had a baby last night.   Oddly enough the sex is not yet decided.

JANUARY 8

My throat all right again.   Miss Edwards has postponed her arrival until the 12th.   I go to Fontainebleau for four days for the chase.

JANUARY 10: FONTAINEBLEAU

Perfect weather.   We are a large party, several ladies for the first time.   The rage is now to gamble—the tables are set out directly after dinner, which is over at 8 o'clock.   They play until 11.30 and then supper is announced.   The moment it is over back again to the tables.   The favourite game is "Boston"; it was invented I believe by the officers on the French ship of war in Boston Harbour.   I, without being noticed, steal off to bed after supper as I do not gamble, so find it very tedious.

JANUARY 12

Madame Carillon la Tour lost the skirt of her riding dress to-day, it caught in a low bough of a tree and was literally torn off.   There fortunately was a coach close at hand, as we were near to the *Grand Pharamond*.   She did not appear at dinner.   The daughter-in-law of the Prince de Poix had an altercation at the gambling table and slapped Madame de Montesquieu's face—the Comtesse de Maille lost very highly and burst into tears, saying she was ruined.   How gambling debases people.   The gentlest of women becomes a virago when she is gambling. A noisy supper—soon after I was off to bed.

JANUARY 13

Horrid adventure last night.   I have had just the ghost of an intrigue with a certain lady who is here with her sister.

She had made an appointment for me to come to her room after all was quiet in the house. I arrayed myself in a large flowered damask dressing-gown (made of an old frock of mamma's) and sallied forth *à l'aventure*. All went well. I found the room; the door was slightly ajar. Entering I locked it, the key snapped off short in the lock. Horror of horrors! No other means of exit. Too high for me to jump out of the window. We were at our wits' end; *quoi faire?* After much thought I decided on a plan—Madame de L. was to knock loudly on the door the moment she heard the servants moving in the morning. I was to lie *perdu*. She, after the door was opened, to go to her sister's room which was on the floor above, taking the servant with her. All went well until I emerged from the room. I saw four distinct heads looking out of four doors, nothing to be done but to make a bolt for it, which I did; I do not think they recognized me. As soon as I reached my room I kindled the fire and burnt my dressing-gown as that could easily be identified. I am now waiting events. We are just off to the chase.

JANUARY 15

Last evening at dinner Monsieur de Champeau suddenly asked, " Who has a red and green damask dressing-gown? " nobody responded. Tour du Pain said, " How odd, I certainly have seen one," still no answer. Madame de Castries turned to me and said, " What colour is your dressing-gown? " I blandly answered " rose ": the old cat, she must have been looking out of her door. Madame de Cossé Brissac exclaimed, " I certainly saw a figure in a most gorgeous red and green damask gown in the corridor."

I had confided my adventure to George Caraman. He had two dressing-gowns with him and had lent me his " rose " one so I feel perfectly safe. Madame de Castries said, " The only way to decide this was for all the gentlemen to retire and to put on their dressing-gowns and to defile before the ladies." This we did—and returned to the *salon*. Shouts of laughter when old Comte de Laval appeared in a dressing-gown of broad green and red stripes. He is the brother of Madame de Brissac; she instantly said, "That is not the one, it was large flowers of red, green and gold." Madame de Castries instantly said, "You know more about the pattern than anybody else, so it must have been from your room that I saw the gentleman emerge at 6 o'clock this morning." Madame de B. answered, "At least respect my age." This was received with shouts of laughter.

JANUARY 16
Paris, arrived home late this afternoon and had to dress with all haste to take mamma and Frances to a concert at the Palais Royale. Father had intended to accompany them, but he has had a cold. Katinka's baby has declared itself—it is a boy.

JANUARY 18
The concert very fine. *Grande toilette*. All the Corps Diplomatique; a host of English; the Countess of Stafford whom I had met at Coppet in 1815. She recognized me at once and was most gracious saying, "I can no longer call you Cupid." Father has bidden mother to invite her to dinner for the 26th. Also the Duc and Duchesse d'Orléans and Mademoiselle. He has told me to make out a list of the people whom I think will best suit, and to submit it to him, so that he can forward it to the Palais Royale for their approval.

JANUARY 19
A hard frost. Skated this afternoon. Opera in the evening. Frances ate too many candies and had indigestion, so could not go. Mamma had her put to bed

before we started. Letters from Albert not satisfactory. I am going to-morrow to consult Alfred about my costume for the 26th. It is very late and I have just finished drafting some dispatches to Mr. Rush. They were laid out on my table where I found them on my return from the opera. Mlle Favier looked with favour upon me. I will send her some flowers to-morrow.

JANUARY 20

Sent Mlle Favier some flowers, cost me 20 francs; hidden in them a little "could I would she" *billet-doux*. I will await results.

JANUARY 21

No answer as yet. I will go to the opera to-night; she is dancing. Father is disgusted with the childish behaviour of the French Ministry. If they would only give a decided answer one way or the other, he would then know the position he stood in. Still no answer to my note. Last night she did not even look at me. A louis thrown away.

JANUARY 22

All our guests have accepted for the 26th. The Duc approved the list. In fact, I believe he never alters one sent by an Ambassador or Minister of a foreign Power. We are having a tented room built over the garden, for the music.

JANUARY 23

An extraordinary note from Madame de Boigne saying she supposed her invitation must have miscarried, but that she accepted with pleasure; *quoi faire?* We now have to find another man to balance the table. A note has just been brought to me from Mlle F., would I sup with her on the 26th—was there ever such luck? I will try to see her to explain. We do not dine until

8 o'clock and the Orléans always stop very late.   Albertine de Broglie has just offered the loan of her fine plate.

JANUARY 24

Father has just put his veto on our using the de Broglie's plate so kindly offered.   He dislikes anything like show or pretence in any way.   Mamma is sad and silent.   I went this afternoon and parted with another louis d'or and literally laid some flowers at the Favier's feet. She was at home and received me most graciously.   I explained how I was situated and with great grace she begged me not to apologize but to come to supper the next night.   The louis was well spent after all.   I cannot but feel sorry for the Bonapartists.   They are barely recognized.   Even their showy titles are not given to them.   There is a son of the Emperor, a Count Walewski, his mother was a Pole.   He is quite young, a handsome lad, and is being well brought up.   One of our guests on the 26th is the Countess de Flahaut, she is very old. Her son was the lover of Queen Hortense, the wife of Louis Bonaparte, King of Holland.   She has a son by Flahaut.   The old Madame de Flahaut was born Souza-Bothelo, and is a very grand dame.   Her coach is the finest in Paris after the King's—four footmen standing up behind.   She looks like a mummy. Very cold. Father sent for me this afternoon to copy some dispatches for him in post-haste.   I do hope he is not going to be drawn into political life again.   I said quite innocently to mamma, "So Katinka's child is a boy after all." Mamma answered, "The Princess wrote to me it was a girl."   I replied, "The Prince told me yesterday it was a boy."   Seeing mamma was beginning to show unmistakable signs of strong character I cried, "A truce, she must have had twins."

JANUARY 26

Everything is in a bustle and a hustle.   It is not an easy matter to entertain at dinner sixty people when the house-

hold is not a very large one. Chevet is doing the main
part of the cooking. Our Russian glass is very fine; it was
a present to father from the Tsar Alexander. Mlle
Favier was more than gracious. I will see more of her.

JANUARY 27

The banquet was very fine, and marked by great simplicity
in comparison with those at the Russian, Spanish, and
English Embassies. The Orléans did not leave until
after midnight.

All the heads of the Corps Diplomatique were present with
their ladies. The Marchioness of Stafford wore very magnificent, superb jewels. She is so absolutely simple and
unaffected, but such a great lady. The dinner was
excellent. Music just loud enough. Mamma radiant.
The Duc d'Orléans speaks such perfect English and as she
had the English Ambassador on her left she was quite
at her ease. Monsieur de Lafayette, who is well received
at the Palais Royale, was present. The Duc d'Orléans
expressed great regret to both father and to mamma that
we were returning to America. Father has only applied
for six months' leave and will await the turn of events.
Albert is most anxious for him to see the new home, which
has cost far more than father had estimated.

JANUARY 29

As this is our last Carnival I am going to try to amuse
myself, but I have not much heart for it. I frankly own
I dread returning to America. I have no friends of my own
age there, nothing in common with the young American
men. They are all absorbed in making money. The
idea of being tied down to a counting-house stool after
my life here is most repugnant to me. Father cannot
expect me to settle down in a wild country without
neighbours—absolutely thrown on our own resources.
Madame de Duras and Madame de Béthisy called on
mamma to-day, the former to express the regret of her

Royal mistress, the Duchesse d'Angoulême, and the latter that of the Duchesse de Berri, at our approaching departure. Madame de Duras said her Royal mistress expressed a desire to receive mamma and Frances absolutely privately—not officially. The interview is to be on February 4. It is certainly most gracious of her. Father wishes to pay a short visit to Geneva, but the weather is much too severe at present for him to undertake the journey. Frances is rather elated at the idea of returning to America. She wants the freedom which young girls enjoy there. I can quite understand that. Monsieur de Lafayette has informed father that he intends paying his last visit to America. This will be at least something to look forward to.

JANUARY 30

Easter is late this year. The Carnival does not begin until the middle of next month. Rumours that the King had a stroke to-day, but not yet verified. Madame Bonaparte very much annoyed with father for leaving France without having married Frances into some great family.

FEBRUARY 2

Always some petty and annoying dispatches from America framed by Mr. Adams. I really think he spends his idle moments in writing them, simply to vent his spleen on father for his imaginary grievances at Ghent. A delightful letter from Mr. Rufus King* in an entirely different strain. Madame Patterson Bonaparte was most amusing to-day at dinner relating all her experiences at Rome and Florence with the Bonaparte family. Madame Mère she prefers to them all, saying she is a simple Corsican country woman with common sense. The others, she says, cannot get over the position they

---

* Rufus King, grandfather of Madame Waddington, late French ambassadress at the Court of St. James.

once held, and in everything they do, show their bad
breeding. She says that there is not one of the Emperor's sisters who has not one or more illegitimate children and that they seem to glory in it instead of thinking
it a disgrace. It seems last evening she was at the
Russian Embassy when the Duc d'Orléans was announced. She at once tried to withdraw, but he met her at
the door and made her a low bow saying, "*Bon soir,
Princesse.*" I am certain she was flattered or she would not
have repeated it. A dear old American woman called
to-day; she has a great desire to see the King at close
quarters. Father was so impressed by her simplicity
and sincerity that he is going to arrange for her to be in
one of the rooms his Majesty passes through. She is
from the West and told father she had actually seen
the Dauphin there (Louis XVII), that he had been brought
up by some Indians who had turned Christian. Father
was much interested as she described the clothes he had
worn when he came to America. All of the finest quality;
that he himself could not remember anything beyond
a prison, a mob and a very beautiful mother—also great
grief. If he is not the Dauphin (which father doubts)
he must be the child of some great noble who was guillotined during the French revolution. Still it is interesting.
The Duchesse d'Angoulême is convinced that her brother
is still alive. Father thought perhaps of introducing
this woman to her presence, but on maturer thought
thinks it would perhaps be unwise to open fresh wounds.
His belief is that this child may be the son of the Duc
de Bourbon, or some other Bourbon.

FEBRUARY 3

Very cold again. Skating on the Petit Lac. I miss
Katinka, who was always such a cheerful companion.
Madame Bonaparte has been extolling the beauty of a
Mlle Joséphine Pascault, the daughter of the Marquis
de Poléon, who lives in Baltimore. She says to see her

is to fall in love with her. She is the youngest sister of Madame Reubel, who was the great friend of Madame Bonaparte when she was a girl. There is twenty-two years' difference in their ages, as Mlle Pascault was born when her mother was fifty-two years of age. I have something to look forward to as I worship beauty.

FEBRUARY 5

All the Corps Diplomatique have called upon us to express their regret at our departure. I really believe they are all sincere. Father with his great simplicity of manner, his sincerity, has won all hearts. I do not think he ever has an evil thought.

Mamma and Frances had a most delightful interview with the Duchesse d'Angoulême yesterday afternoon. She received them in her boudoir absolutely without ceremony; expressed her regret that mamma was leaving and said many flattering things. When they retired she drew Frances to her and kissed her on both cheeks. Poor woman, she has always longed for a child of her own.

FEBRUARY 7

I am going to make an ass of myself at the Carnival—have been drawn into going with some boon companions in a car. I go to-morrow to Compiègne to hunt, but for one night only.

FEBRUARY 9

Enjoyed Compiègne very much: a fine day, and we killed several head of deer. The party was entirely made up of men—so was devoid of interest.

FEBRUARY 10

Showers of invitations for farewell dinners before Lent. Father will go to Geneva as soon as Lent commences.

He goes alone. That Comtesse de Boigne is irrepressible;
she had the audacity to ask mamma at the Spanish
Embassy last night if her jewels were real. I cannot
understand a woman of her birth and education being so
absolutely tactless. I think mamma must have given
her a decided answer.

FEBRUARY 15

Full Carnival. I am beginning to enjoy it. We have
arranged a car—also various suppers. A masked ball
to-night at the opera. I am going to escort Mlle F.
Supper at the Maison Dorée.

FEBRUARY 17

Car a great success. Representing a "Horn of Plenty,"
we were all most carefully disguised, *ces dames* as well. A
boisterous supper. *Enfin*—the last for me, so I will
enjoy it though I have not got quite the zest and *entrain*
of a couple of years since.

FEBRUARY 19

A dinner of farewell to-night at the Duc de Fernan
Nunez, the Spanish Ambassador's. To-morrow the Baron
Vincent entertains us. I will have to manage to get off
early as there is a ball at the opera and we have a supper—
this time *des dames du monde*.

FEBRUARY 22

To-night, Shrove Tuesday—our last supper, our last
ball, my last time in the half-world as we leave, I
believe, in April—*finis !*

FEBRUARY 24

Bad news from America about Albert, both father and
mother much troubled. I am sorry. Serious work now;
all entertaining at a standstill until Easter. It is freezing
again, I am glad to say—prospects of skating.

Frances had an excellent proposal for her hand to-day, a man of good family, well off, &c., but she has only seen him twice. Father would not think of such a marriage for her.

MARCH 4

I think we all begin now to realize what a wrench it will be to leave Paris. Mamma was trying to make plans for our arrival in America. Her sister, Mrs. Montgomery, has very kindly placed her country house near New York at our disposal. Father will have to go both to Washington and to Geneva. Baltimore will be our ultimate end until that wretched house is finished. Mamma actually burst into tears when talking over plans for the future. She has now acknowledged that it will be hard for her to leave Paris. Of course none of this is said before father; we never distress him if it can be avoided.

MARCH 12

As soon as Lent is over we begin our round of *adieus*. I am making out the list so that we will not offend anybody by forgetting them. Mamma says it is useless for her to order any more frocks for either herself or Frances as they will have no opportunity of wearing them.

APRIL 16

Easter being over we are beginning to strike our tents and packing has already commenced. The Government has placed the *Peacock* at father's disposal. As the King is leaving for St. Cloud we take an informal leave of him on the 19th. As father has only applied for leave for six months this does not necessitate a formal leave-taking. Madame Bonaparte has been most kind. She has done everything to cheer mamma and Frances. She told us to-day that she had written to her father to do all in his power for us in Baltimore. We really will be home-less. No use regretting, it cannot be mended.

APRIL 20

At 11.30 we were received privately by the King.
Wonderful to relate, Madame du Cayla was not present.
Both Monsieur and the Duc d'Angoulême were. The
King seemed overcome, expressed deep regret at parting
with father. Mamma and Frances were then admitted
and took a formal farewell of him. Both Monsieur
and the Duc d'Angoulême accompanied father and
mamma to the door of the ante-chamber and expressed
a wish that they would return to Paris. The Duc
d'Aumont then escorted us to the apartments of the
Duchesse d'Angoulême. Half-way he handed us over
to the care of the Duchesse de Serent and the Vicomte
de Montmorency. Mamma and Frances were received
first—after they retired, father and myself were introduced. The Duchesse was most unbending and expressed
regret, but the hope of seeing father again. She handed
him a sealed packet, begging him to take great care of it.
We then retired and to our amazement found a Royal
carriage had been ordered to take us home; a second
one followed with a gentleman and a lady of the Court.
This was a very great compliment—as it was only an
informal leave-taking. To-morrow we go to the Palais
Royale to take leave. To-night I am going to the opera
with a heavy heart, there to take a loving farewell of all
the ladies who have shown me much kindness. I cannot
afford to offer them a supper, I only wish I could.

APRIL 21, 1823

We had a most charming reception at the Palais Royale.
They one and all expressed their regret at our departure,
and I believe it was sincere; certainly on the part of
the Duchesse and Mademoiselle. All the elder children
were present and each one in English wished us a pleasant
and speedy voyage and hoped we would soon return.
They had been taught their little lesson very well.
Father opened the package that the Duchesse d'An-

goulême handed to him. It contains several copies
of letters addressed to her from America from people
who imagine they are the Dauphin (Louis XVII) and
from others who state that the poor child was given into
their care. A note from her begging father to investigate
the matter if he possibly can, as it is the great wish of
her life if her brother is alive to be able to find him.
Of course father will do all he can, but he is very sceptical
on the matter and fears that wicked people are trying
to prey on her feelings with a view of making money.

APRIL 22

Count Pozzo di Borgo has been kindness itself. He
breakfasted with us to-day. He brought Frances such
a pretty bracelet. Alexander Humboldt and Lafayette
come to dinner to-morrow for a last farewell. Monsieur
la Place* sent his regrets, but he is confined to the house
with rheumatism. He sent mamma some beautiful
flowers.

All is quite settled and we sail for America in May.
Father is much vexed that he has wasted all these years
on so futile a mission. He has in plain words informed
Monsieur de Chateaubriand that France must change
her policy if she wishes to retain the friendship of America.

MAY 10

We leave on the 14th. I regret parting with so many
kind friends—the de Broglies in particular. I have
made nearly all my *adieus*. One and all have expressed
a wish that we will return. Some I know to be sincere,
the others are not worth a thought. I will always look
back upon these seven years spent in my beloved Paris.
Father has had that stone house built at New Geneva,
an absolutely wild place. I doubt if he ever inhabits it.
I deeply regret for Frances's sake that we could not remain
a few years longer. Mamma, who has that impassive

* A well-known writer on finance.

242

nature that nothing upsets, is quite serene and happy now. Madame Bonaparte has really shown deep feeling at parting with us. I think she is very grateful but she does not allow herself to show too much of her true nature.

LE HAVRE, ON BOARD "THE PEACOCK"

I am glad that it is over and that the great wrench is made. I am writing in my cabin. We sail early to-morrow morning. Mamma has brought her maid, who will do for Frances and herself. Father has his man. Lucien begged so hard to come with me that father consented. He is a very good lad, and I feel he is a sort of link between me and the last seven years of my happy life. I shut my eyes sometimes hoping when I open them to find I am still in the Rue de l'Université, and that it has all been a horrible dream. The very smell of the ship makes me feel ill. The cackling of the chickens and the squealing of the pigs adds to the horrors I know I will have to undergo. Lucien is now pea-green. The weather very fine. Captain Rogers says we will probably have fair winds and that we will make a quick passage—I hope so. Frances has just come to me in despair, her two canaries have been forgotten. We have sent a man on shore to see if they can be found. Every-thing is in such terrible confusion. A couple of the King's couriers have just arrived with letters from his Majesty, Monsieur and the Duc d'Angoulême—a more than gracious act. Canaries found, Frances delighted.

JUNE 26: NEW YORK

We arrived here yesterday after a fast passage. The heat is intolerable.

PART V

THE SPECIAL MISSION TO ENGLAND

JULY 1823—OCTOBER 1827

JULY 4: NEW YORK

A horrible day here; the noise of the July 4 celebration intolerable. I have to rub my eyes to see if I am awake, that it is true I am not in the Rue de l'Université. How I regret it. Father is going alone to see the new house in Western Virginia—also to Washington. I take mamma and Frances to Baltimore to-morrow. We are stopping right in the country at a nice old house which belongs to the Montgomery family. But the difference in everything; only about three private coaches in New York— no means of getting about. The streets absolutely filthy and the heat horrible. I have been nearly every night for a long walk. No roads—no paths. I never realized the absolutely unfinished state of the American cities until I returned. The horrible chewing of tobacco— the spitting; all too awful. We have had a charming and hospitable reception, but all is so crude.

JULY 8

We are now in Baltimore. Not quite so dirty as New York. We are with mamma's relations—the Nicholsons. They are kindness itself, but I even see that mamma feels the change most keenly. The young men of Baltimore stare at me as if they thought I were a wild beast let loose. Everybody knows everybody else, and all

244

call each other by their christian names. If I am offered a post, no matter how humble, abroad, I will accept it with joy.

JULY 12: BALTIMORE

The heat is something I did not ever realize. We go in a few days to some place by the sea. Frances has lost all her colour. Albert has written me the most distressing letter. It seems he compromised himself with a farmer's daughter. They threatened him with exposure and he was weak enough to marry her on May 23, when we were at sea. He is afraid to tell father and begs me not to do so. The girl is living with her family. I do not know what to do. Troubles do not come singly. It seems this girl is without education.

SEPTEMBER 10

Back again in Baltimore and most thankful. A horrible place on the Eastern shore of Maryland called Sennox, a wooden shanty to live in, food not so bad but we have to eat like pigs. When we arrived and saw what it was going to be like we commenced to laugh and we could not stop ourselves. The poor people thought we must be lunatics. Father has gone to his beloved Western Virginia alone. Albert is there. He is going to report to us how the beautiful new residence is progressing. They tell me Baltimore is very cheerful in the winter. It does not look much like it now. Mr. Patterson, Madame Bonaparte's father, has kindly invited us to dinner, fortunately the weather is much cooler. General Reubel and his wife have just called. They are living with Monsieur Pascault who has the beautiful daughter.

SEPTEMBER 22

I have seen Miss Pascault; Madame Bonaparte was right. I have never seen anything more lovely. As Madame Reubel has invited me to call I will certainly take advantage of her invitation.

SEPTEMBER 24

I went this afternoon to Monsieur Pascault's* house, it is the oldest house in Baltimore. Most beautiful iron gates that he had sent from France, an air of refinement about the interior that I have never seen out of France. I was received by Madame Reubel, who is very handsome. She has a daughter and two sons; the youngest, Frederic, is the handsomest young man I have ever seen. He must be about seventeen. Mlle Pascault was charming. I am without doubt in love with her. Her father has lost most of his money. Madame Reubel begged me to sup with them to-morrow evening; quite *sans façon*. She wishes to present me to her father—he is very old. Madame Pascault never appears.

SEPTEMBER 26

I am quite off my head. Monsieur Pascault, who is the Marquis de Poléon, is a gentleman of the old *régime*. No wonder his daughter is so well bred. He received me with the most wonderful courtesy—tapped a beautiful gold snuff-box and offered it to me. The supper quite simple but served on beautiful silver. Everything had the air of the greatest refinement. I thought myself back in France again. I will speak to father to-morrow and beg him to approach Monsieur Pascault—with a view of my paying my addresses to his daughter.

SEPTEMBER 27

I have written to father, who is in New Geneva, telling him that I wish, if she consents, to make Miss Pascault my wife. Frances had a letter from him to-day which is most amusing. He gives a description of the home. The architect is some local man who never built a house

* Jean Charles Marie Louis Pascault, Marquis de Poléon. His father married a Mlle Dupuy—daughter of a naval surgeon. It was considered a mésalliance, and he was given a large estate in St. Domingo. He died in 1766. His son escaped with his family during the massacre of St. Domingo. As France was in such a disturbed state he sailed to Baltimore.

before. He had no idea of Grecian architecture but a style of his own which is Hiberno-teutonic. The outside is like a French barracks with port-hole windows, the inside ornamentations like those of a Dutch tavern, so that the French marble chimney-pieces, mirrors and papers which he sent out are rather out of place. The workmen are still there and live and board in what Lucien calls "The Château." The approach to the house is hidden by a log-cabin which is occupied by Monsieur, Madame, Mlle and the petits Bouffé family. Albert has taken possession of the only parlour in the old brick house. This young gentleman has four guns, a pointer, three boats, two riding horses, and a pet colt smaller than a jackass. His wardrobe is distributed about the parlour. A billiard-table with Albert's old stockings for pockets. "So, my dear daughter," he adds, "we will pass the winter in Baltimore." This is a respite for us. I am delighted, for this will give me an opportunity for pressing my suit with Miss Pascault. I am anxiously awaiting father's answer to my letter. I know it would be wise.

SEPTEMBER 29

I have again called at Mr. Pascault's, and was received most kindly. I had some conversation with Mlle Josephine; she is so absolutely gentle and sweet, I am certain I am not good enough for her. We dine at the Pattersons' again to-morrow. Madame Bonaparte has written to her father to be most civil to us. Madame Reubel and Mlle Pascault are to be of the guests.

OCTOBER 25

Father has returned, and called yesterday on Monsieur Pascault. He gave his consent to my paying addresses to his daughter. Father was so kind, he said her want of fortune should not stand in the way. Alluding to his first marriage he added, "She had nothing, but we loved each other." Mamma has been left a nice little fortune,

so we are now well off. Mr. Pascault has another daughter
married to a Mr. O'Donnell, the son of a rich Indian nabob.
She was married when she was fifteen, and had a child
before she was sixteen. She is very beautiful like a full-
blown rose, but seems to have but little brain or education.

NOVEMBER 2

My suit is progressing. Josephine likes to hear about
France. She plays delightfully both the harp and the
spinet. I talk all sorts of nonsense which all lovers do.
It has cheered her up as her youth has not been very
cheerful.

DECEMBER 6

All is settled. Mlle Pascault has consented to be my wife
and we are to be married early in the New Year. Mamma
and Frances are delighted with her. She is so gentle and
innocent. Mamma says she is like a beautiful lily.
She is beautiful, there is no doubt about that. Madame
Reubel rather astonished me by appearing the other day
in a bright red wig. It seems she has wigs of every
colour to go with her frocks. A Bonaparte fashion and
not certainly adopted by the ladies of the Restoration,
as I never saw such a thing in Paris. General Reubel
is horrible, has not a penny in the world, stops in bed
nearly all day, and lives on Monsieur Pascault's bounty.
Does not attempt to do any work. His daughter will be
very handsome. A brother of Monsieur Pascault's lives
in a lodge at the gate but nobody ever speaks to him—
the reason I do not know.

DECEMBER 24: CHRISTMAS EVE

Madame Pascault insisted on our coming to them.
They all dine with us to-morrow. We have a very
good house in Charles Street for the winter. Father
will be much in Washington.

Joséphine Marie Henriette Gallatin
née Pascault

DECEMBER 31

To-night we all sup with Monsieur Pascault to see the New Year in. It is father's first visit to the house. I am anxious to see how he treats Reubel.

JANUARY 2, 1824

The entertainment at Monsieur Pascault's was of the greatest elegance. Father was much pleased and I noticed his astonishment at the fine plate, also the quantities of family portraits, &c. &c. I fear there is going to be delay with regard to our marriage. Josephine is a Catholic, and that is one thing father is adamant about. He will not allow (if we have any children) that they should be brought up in that religion.

JANUARY 5

Father was forced by his party, but much against his will, to accept the candidature for the Vice-Presidency. Mr. Crawford's stroke of paralysis required another candidate. All this is most annoying. Father does not wish to enter into public life again. When he left America seven years ago, I believe he vowed never to return. He has given the best part of his life and all his energies to his adopted country; no one knows better than himself that he is disliked, but that they still want to pick his brains and make use of him. He goes to Washington to-night.

FEBRUARY 18

I had hoped to be married this month, but still this question of religion. The Archbishop of Baltimore declines to marry us if there is a Protestant ceremony.

MARCH 18

At last all is settled. Monsieur Pascault is disgusted with the behaviour of the Archbishop, and has written to him to the effect that he will entirely dispense with the services of the Church of Rome, that his daughter

will be married in the Protestant Church. He added
that a wife's first duty was to obey her husband.

MAY 5

We are back from our honeymoon and leave shortly
to join poor mamma at New Geneva. Father still in
Washington. The Archbishop has excommunicated
Monsieur Pascault.

MAY 10

The French Minister intimated to us that he has an
important package to deliver into one of our hands, or
accredited servants. As Lucien was returning here from
Washington, father sent him for it. Imagine my surprise
when I found it was addressed to me. It was from the
Duc and Duchesse d'Angoulême—a most beautiful silver-
gilt vase with their arms on one side—a wedding present.
It was more than a surprise considering all they have
been through, on account of the King's death, to have
given me a thought. Josephine is delighted with it.
Monsieur Pascault was greatly overcome when he saw it.
I must consult father in what form to acknowledge it.
We go in a few days to try the new house at New Geneva.
It is all ready for our reception. In all events we will
pass the summer there. It is getting intolerably hot
here.

JUNE 8

We have been here for some time. The place itself is
delightful. The views superb. Air as pure as air can be,
but not a soul to speak to—not a neighbour, with the
exception of some totally uneducated farmers, their
wives and daughters. We are all here. Frances has a
pony. Josephine is not allowed to ride at present.
So I ride a huge farm-horse—who is as thin as a knife;
no roads, so we risk our lives every moment. Albert
sometimes rides in front of us, and when we are ap-

proaching a dangerous spot he blows a horn. I wish some of my Paris *intimes* could see us—how amused they would be. Mamma attends to all our personal comforts. We have many too many servants. Frances has named it "Castle Solitude." Our greatest friends are the mosquitoes, who certainly keep us company. Father reads all day as he is compiling some work. It is too hot for him to go to Washington at present. Mr. Crawford is no better.

SEPTEMBER 20

Josephine and myself return to Baltimore shortly. Monsieur Pascault is very ailing and they seem worried about him. Our home is empty, so I think Josephine will not suffer too much from the heat. There is a rumour about a mission to France. I dare not think of it. When we leave, Frances says she will take to her bed. It is awful for her. I am certain mamma will not stand the winter here. Father will have to be in Washington on account of the elections.

OCTOBER 15

Greatly to the relief of us all, greatly to the relief of father himself, he has been able to withdraw from the candidature of Vice-President. It really was nothing more than a hope of his party that should Mr. Crawford have been elected President his health would have obliged him to withdraw, and father would have been head of the State. Of course his birth disqualified him for standing for the Presidency, and this was the only means of putting him in that position. Now they are worrying him again with offers of the Treasury, but I am certain he will not accept any post of any kind or description. I had always heard Carrol-town, the seat of the Carrolls, spoken of with almost awe as to its magnificence. Josephine told me it was nonsense. So to see it we went. I really could not help laughing.

Merely a square wooden house with a piazza all around it. The interior most ordinary. It seems the original Carroll, who called himself Carroll of Carrol-town, was the natural child of somebody. This I fear is very much the habit of the Americans of the Southern States— vain boasting. They of course have large plantations and slaves; but miserable houses, and live in the most untidy manner. To my astonishment I hear there are no schools in the Southern States and that all the children of the better class have to be sent to the North to be educated. Father has decided to remain with mamma, Frances and Albert for the winter at New Geneva. Of course I am obliged to remain in Baltimore.

DECEMBER 1824

My father-in-law is very ill and we are all in close attendance. Reubel found the air did not agree with him and has betaken himself to New York, much to the relief of all. Madame Reubel is a delightful woman and has suffered much. To be here in Baltimore without money, dependent on her friends, must be most galling to her, having lived at Court all her life, and particularly at the Court of Westphalia, where she was the first lady-in-waiting on the Queen. She often describes to us the splendours of the Palace at Cassel, which was built by the Landgrave of Hesse in imitation of Versailles. His son has it now and I believe the whole of his vast fortune intact. When she was there and King Jerome reigned, she says nothing could equal the extravagance of living. She was not at all surprised at the Westphalian troops being quite useless to Napoleon, as they were never manœuvred. All was a life of pleasure there, from morning until night. We will have, I fear, a sad Christmas. I am sorry for Josephine's sake.

DECEMBER 23

Monsieur Pascault has recovered wonderfully and insists upon having a dinner of all the family on the 31st. He says it will be his last year, and he wants to have them all around him. I am sorry I will be away from my father and mother, but my duty is by my wife. We expect our child in the New Year.

FEBRUARY 7, 1825
My dear wife was safely delivered of a fine boy this morning. We are going to call him Albert.

APRIL 15
Monsieur de Lafayette has arrived and has been received with the greatest enthusiasm. His progress is a triumphal one. His cause is the emancipation of the Spanish Colonies and of Greece. Both of which are dear to the hearts of Liberals of all nations. When in Paris father received the thanks of the Greek Governor for his efforts on their behalf. Now that I am on the subject it seems so unfair that father was never allowed to accept an order of any kind or to retain any of the superb presents that were given to him—all of which are now in Washington. All that he did keep was a superb set of glass, some eight hundred pieces, that the Emperor Alexander gave him as a purely personal gift.

MAY 15
Father has just written to me that I must be present at Uniontown to help him receive Lafayette, who is going to stay a couple of nights with him at Friendship Hill. So I am off to-morrow. Josephine is quite well and so happy with her baby. I do not mind leaving her.

MAY 16
Detained until Thursday, as I have just received a list of things which will be wanted by mamma for the 25th: it is a mile long.

MAY 27
The meeting at Uniontown and the reception of Monsieur de Lafayette far surpassed anything I have

ever seen in this country. People came from miles
away and camped out, bringing their tents. Lafayette
is the nation's guest so was surrounded by a huge mounted
bodyguard. He spoke just after father had introduced him. Father spoke after him and I really think
he must have been inspired. His French accent seemed
to leave him as he became excited. The subject was
the critical position of the Greeks. He must have inspired his audience, as I have never heard such an outburst of genuine enthusiasm and cheering; it lasted
quite half an hour. Monsieur de Lafayette embraced
him publicly. We returned to Friendship Hill and
quite a thousand sat down to supper in relays. Mamma
had arranged everything wonderfully, rows and rows of
tables in the garden. Hundreds of niggers all dressed
in white to serve. Yesterday we passed in comparative
quiet, but there were callers all day for Monsieur de
Lafayette. We had a quiet dinner which Monsieur de
Lafayette said reminded him of the Rue de l'Université.
I do not think he was the only one who was reminded
of it. He left this morning as he has a prolonged tour
to make and a very short time to make it in. I go back
to-morrow to bring Josephine and my son here for the
summer.

JUNE 20: FRIENDSHIP HILL

We are all very happy here. The country is beautiful and
mamma certainly has the art of making everybody
comfortable. Josephine is delicate but loves the good
air here, particularly for our boy who is growing apace.
Father worships him at a distance. A few days since
I told father for the first time of Mr. Adams' letter to me
of February last. I had written privately to Mr. Adams
informing him of father's reasons for refusing the
Treasury under his administration. Father has always
been above suspicion and I may frankly say (although
he is my father) that he is the only one of either party

who has not fallen into some error which has cast suspicion on their motives. This Mr. Adams frankly acknowledges in his letter to me. When I read this paragraph I could see father's evident gratification at the opinion held of him by a political opponent—and that opponent the actual President of the United States. We drifted into reminiscences of Paris. Father's heart is there and in Geneva, but only stern duty keeps him here.

AUGUST

Father at last acknowledges that he made a mistake in building this house, and that we will never inhabit it after this summer. He has commissioned me to find a house in Baltimore for the winter as it is quite near enough to Washington for him in case he is obliged to go there. I was much gratified at receiving a beautiful silver bowl from some of my friends in Paris for my son. Albertine de Staël sent the most beautiful baby clothes. The first clothes my boy wore were those of Napoleon. The Queen of Westphalia gave them to Madame Reubel when her boy was born, and she gave them to Josephine. He still wears the little dressing-gown that was made by Madame Mère.

MAY 1826

I cannot realize what has happened. We are actually going to England. Mr. Rufus King's (our Minister in London) health has broken down. Most important matters have to be negotiated. The President has begged father to take his place. He has accepted but on the condition that he goes on a special mission and not as a resident Minister; that he is at liberty to return in a year; that an ample sum is to be put at his disposal, as he knows that outward show has a great effect on the English people. This has all been agreed to privately. These are the most important negotiations and can only be placed in the hands of a very strong man. The whole of the commercial questions to be finally settled. The most important are the North-Eastern and North-Western Boundary questions. Also the Commercial Convention which father negotiated in 1815 in London, and again in 1818 to last ten years.

MAY 25

I am torn both ways. I know I could be of the greatest use to father. It is impossible to take our child at his age across the ocean, as the discomforts, particularly where food is concerned, are so great. Josephine is quite willing for me to go, in fact urges me to do so. I will leave the matter entirely in father's hands.

JUNE 7

It is finally decided I am to accompany father, but only for six months should I be wanted at home. For many reasons this is thought to be for the best. As now arranged we sail on July 1. I am doing all I can to provide for more comfort for the voyage. I often wonder how father has stood so many of these disagreeable crossings of the Atlantic. The horrible cramped feeling. The misery of a gale when we can barely crawl about, and the absolute horrors of a fog. We are to take a very southerly course this time. Both father and mother are very much annoyed. At the last moment an application was made to father asking him to take a Miss Bates to England. It seems she is to marry a Monsieur Van der Weyer, a Belgian *avocat*. The latter made himself very useful to Prince Leopold, the husband of Princess Charlotte. None of us know or ever heard of the Bates family; they are very rich and extremely vulgar. Father could not refuse.

AUGUST: LONDON

We sailed on July 1, and arrived here a few days since. We have a beautiful house in Seymour Street.

I have seen to the carriages and horses, all jobbed but very fine.

AUGUST 20

The King received us last week and was most gracious. But what a change since I last saw him. He is fat, very red in the face and unwieldy.

SEPTEMBER

As nearly the entire Cabinet had left London, including Mr. Canning, father thought it a good opportunity to pay a visit to Paris. He particularly wished to consult Pozzo di Borgo on several very important matters. He finds that Bonapartism is nearly extinct. He found Monsieur de Lafayette in a far more peaceful frame of mind than when he paid his visit to America. He spoke to him in the most forcible language of his love of petty plotting. He seems now to realize that such things are futile. His one wish now is to see the Duc d'Orléans on the throne as a constitutional Monarch. I fear this is in the dim future. Lafayette is strongly in favour of the Duke's disputing the legitimacy of the Duc de Bordeaux. We had an interview with Monsieur de Vilèlle, who seems much annoyed with the President's message, particularly with regard to Hayti. I do not think father gave him much satisfaction. A funny incident I must record. When we crossed to Boulogne mamma had to dress on board for a reception at that port, which was being given to Monsieur de Lafayette. On our arrival it was low tide and as is the custom fishermen came out to the pacquet in shallow water to carry us to the shore—fisherwomen for the ladies. Mamma was mounted on the back of a fat Boulognese. Not thinking the woman was going fast enough she prodded her with her heels. The woman lost her temper and dropped mamma in about a foot of water. We could not help laughing to see her sitting up to her waist in water. She was in red velvet with a huge turban covered with white feathers. The more we laughed the more enraged she became. At last she was rescued and carried, dripping, ashore. She had to be taken at once to an inn and dried. She will never forgive us.

I find Paris delightful, but few of our friends here as all are at their châteaux or by the sea. I visited all my old haunts and have registered a vow that the moment I am in a position to do so I will return here to live and die.

OCTOBER: LONDON

We have now returned here and are seriously at work, and plenty of it.*

ALBERT GALLATIN *to* J. Q. ADAMS

LONDON, *October* 18, 1826

DEAR SIR,

I had intended next spring, before my return to America, to have an excursion to Paris once more to see some of my friends. Mr. Canning's absence and the dispersion of the other members of the Cabinet having left me literally without anything to do here, I embraced what was the most favourable opportunity of making that journey, from which I have just returned. My letter of yesterday to the Secretary of State contains the substance of the information I was able to collect there; and I will now add some particulars which, as they involve the names of individuals, I did not wish to remain on record in the Department of State.

In the course of a long conversation with Pozzo di Borgo the state of our relations with Great Britain was alluded to. I told him that the Emperor's decision in the case of slaves carried away and the convention relative thereto had not been carried into effect by Great Britain in conformity with what we considered their

* James Gallatin went to America in 1826 and returned to London in March, 1827.

real intention and meaning; that the British Government had offered to compromise the matter by payment of a sum of money which fell short of our expectations; but that we were nevertheless inclined to accept it, principally on account of the reluctance we felt to trouble the Emperor by an appeal, asking from him further explanation of his decision. Pozzo immediately expressed his wish that we might compromise or otherwise adjust the matter without making such an appeal, which, particularly at this time, would be, as he thought, extremely inconvenient to the Emperor; and speaking of the Maine Boundary question, with which and its possible consequences he appeared well acquainted, he appeared also desirous, though he did not express himself as positively as on that of slaves, that Russia should not be selected as the umpire. I only observed that if there was any inconvenience in being obliged to make decisions which might not please both parties, that inconvenience was less to Russia than to any other Power, and that a compensation for it was found in the additional degree of consideration accruing to the Monarch in whom such confidence was placed. All this, however, corroborates what I have stated in my official letter respecting an approximation between Russia and Great Britain, and the disposition of the Emperor to interfere less than his predecessor in affairs in which he has no immediate interest.   .

The most remarkable change discoverable to France is the extinction of Bonapartism, both as relates to dynasty and to the wish of a military Government. This, I am happy to say, appears to have had a favourable effect on our friend Lafayette, who was very ungovernable in all that related to petty plots during my residence at Paris as Minister, and to whom I had again spoken on the same subject in the most forcible manner whilst he was in America. His opinions and feelings are not changed; but he appears to be thoroughly satisfied of the hopelessness of any attempt to produce a change at present; and he confines his hopes to a vague expectation that, after the death of the present King and of the Dauphin, the Duc d'Orléans will dispute the legitimacy of the Duke of Bordeaux and become a constitutional King. This is such a doubtful and distant contingency as is not likely to involve Lafayette in any difficulties. Mr. de Villèle complained to me of those expressions in the President's message which declared Hayti to have placed herself in a state of vassalage to France, as calculated to increase the dissatisfaction amongst the people of the island at the late arrangement. He said that he was aware of the objections of a very different nature which we had to a recognition of the independence of Hayti, but did not see the necessity of alleging the reason alluded to. As I did not wish and did not think it at all proper to enter into any discussion of the subject, I answered, as if in jest, *"Qu'un tribut, imposé à une colonie comme le prix de son indépendance, était contraire aux grands principes."* I forgot to mention the circumstance to Mr. Brown, and do not know whether the thing had already been complained of to him. If so, its being repeated to me—and they were almost the first words Mr. de Villèle addressed to me—shows that it must have made a deep impression on the French Government. This reminds me that I received here a communication from a respectable quarter stating that, a few days before the publication of the order in council of July last, one of the King's Ministers had complained to a confidential friend of the general tone of the American (United States) diplomacy towards England, still more so as respected manner than matter, and added that it was time to show that this was felt and resented. As to manner, the reproach cannot certainly attach either to Mr. Rush's or Mr. King's correspondence; and I know, from a conversation with Mr. Addington, that in that respect Mr. Clay's has been quite acceptable. On looking

at your own communications, I am satisfied that those
to the British Ministers can have given no offence whatever, and that what they allude to and which has offended
them is your instructions to Mr. Rush, printed by order
of the Senate, and which have been transmitted both to
Mr. Canning and to Mr. Huskisson; a circumstance,
by the by, not very favourable to negotiations still pend-
ing.   That they. have no right to complain of what you
wrote to our own Minister is obvious; still, I think the
fact to be so.

I forgot to mention in my letter of yesterday to the
Secretary of State that there is some alarm amongst
the legitimates about a plan of Metternich to change
the line of succession in Austria, or a plea of the presumed incapacity of the heir presumptive; and that the
King of the Netherlands has at last, by his unabated and
exclusive attention to business and by his perfect probity
and sincerity, so far conquered the prejudices of the
Belgians as to have become highly respected and almost
popular amongst them.

I have the honour, &c.,

ALBERT GALLATIN

NOVEMBER 14

Yesterday the Convention of 1818 was renewed and
signed; a meeting again to-morrow. Mr. King left
yesterday.   Mr. Lawrence is expected to-day.

DECEMBER

Father is anxious that the Emperor of Russia should
act as arbiter on the North-Eastern Boundary question,
but Prince Lieven thinks it will not be convenient for
him to do so.

DECEMBER

Frances is enjoying herself amazingly and is I think a great
favourite.   She is at present paying some visits in the
country with mamma.   The Marchioness of Stafford has

been most gracious.   She has bidden us all to Trentham
in January.   They say it is a most magnificent palace,
and that wonderful state is kept up.   The Duke of
Devonshire, whom we knew in 1818, has been most atten-
tive.   He is not married and never will.   It seems he is
the son of the Duke ——: that at nearly the same time
the Duchess had a daughter, the Duke's mistress had a
son—as they were most anxious for an heir the babies
were changed.   For a long time the deception was kept
up, but somebody in the end confessed.   This Duke
was then in possession of the title; as he was so much
beloved it was agreed that he should retain all his honours
but that he was never to marry.

The Barings were most cordial in their greetings to
us.   We dine with them on Christmas Day.   At times I
feel very low in my mind and feel that after all I should
not have left my dear wife and child.   I was torn both
ways.   It seems to take such an unconscionable time to
receive any news from home.   The King goes openly
everywhere with Lady Conyngham.   Scandal says she is
getting all the money and property that she can for her
children, before the King dies.   She wore the other night
at Princess Lieven's all the Crown Sapphires.   They say
the King has given them to her.

DECEMBER 15

There is not much entertaining.   The King is at Brighton.
I met Mr. Greville* the other night.   He is Clerk of the
Council.   I was amused to see him making notes of the
different things I told him.   Rather a pedantic person.
Princess Lieven is the Ambassador: Prince Lieven is
absolutely a nonentity.   Lord Goderich is always the
same delightful gentleman, it is a pleasure to meet him.
Lord Grey I suppose means to be civil, but his manners
are not what they should be.   Mr. Canning is always

* Charles Greville, author of Journals of the reigns of George IV and
William IV.

most gracious to father, who likes him very much but does not think him a very strong man. Lady Wellesley (Mrs. Robert Patterson*) has been in London. We dined with her. Of course now she is a very great lady, and does not forget it. She has asked me to come to Dublin after Christmas. She says I will be much amused at Dublin society and the Viceregal Court. I will certainly go if there is not too much work here. There is that horrible Irish Channel to be considered and the very long journey. Mamma arrives to-morrow. We have to entertain some Americans, there are a great many in London at present. Father has declined to present any at Court. He is not resident Minister only a special Ambassador.

I ride every day as I fear I am getting fat; Mrs. Baring has just told mamma that she has invited every available member of the Baring family to her Christmas dinner. We are to be the only outsiders.

DECEMBER 20

Looked in at White's. All intent on gambling. While I was there a sum of £8000 changed hands. Had some supper; a thick fog, had to have a link man to show me the way home.

DECEMBER 21

Dined at a large Diplomatic dinner at Prince Jules de Polignac's at the French Embassy; all men—we sat down thirty-six. I was delighted to meet Montmorency; we had a good talk over our old days in Paris. He says things are much changed now, and that the King is much disliked. Our successors are not at all well received and do not entertain at all. After dinner, Mont-

---

* Mrs. Robert Patterson, widow of Robert Patterson, who was a brother of Madame Bonaparte Patterson, married, some years after the death of her husband, the Marquis of Wellesley, Lord Lieutenant of Ireland, elder brother of the Duke of Wellington.

morency and I went for a short time to White's and had supper late. London unutterably dull. Mamma is very happy as she has a perfect riot of churches to go to. It will be gayer after Christmas, but only among the Corps Diplomatique. We are booked for several visits. I was delighted with a long letter from my dear wife. All are well and seem very happy. Father will have to have some sort of reception for the Americans in the New Year. We really make quite a show. We are using all our old French State liveries—which are perfectly fresh.

DECEMBER 26

We had a delightful Christmas with the Barings, who are hospitality itself. There are Barings of all shapes and colours, all sizes—tall ones, short ones, lean ones, fat ones, but all are so nice and cheerful; they seem indeed a united family. We played all sorts of silly games and became children again. I could not keep my thoughts from home. Mr. Baring would drink my wife and boy's health, this nearly broke me up.

We have a big reception of Americans on January 2.

DECEMBER 29

Driving home late last night near the top of Park Lane, we heard cries for help. I jumped down and found a hackney-coach which had been stopped by footpads. Two lonely females were in it. They had stunned the jarvey. I at once escorted them to our coach and we drove them home. They lived quite close to us. A Lady Lucy and her daughter. We had just come upon them in the nick of time and had disturbed the robbers. We never go out at night without at least two footmen and generally father's *chasseur* as well. It is extraordinary how unsafe London is at night, and in the very best quarters.

DECEMBER 30

Rumours of a change in the Cabinet, but nothing definite. The King comes to Buckingham House in a few days. There is a report that Lord Liverpool is ill—not confirmed. . . .

JANUARY 3, 1827

The "rout" for all of our compatriots last night was as successful as any "rout" can be; to be several hours sitting in a coach before arriving at the door of one's destination; then to crawl up about three or four steps every half-hour; to be stifled and toes trodden upon; to make a bow to your hosts; to edge one's way through the crowd; to drink hot champagne and secure an ice down one's back. Then to start one's journey back again. If this spells pleasure, then a "rout" is pleasant. We indeed take our pleasures oddly.

"Crockford's," the magnificent new gambling-hell in St. James's Street, was opened yesterday. Pozzo di Borgo, Prince Esterhazy, the Duke of Wellington, Talleyrand, &c. &c., all belong to it. Pozzo took me under his wing. It was very fine. Supper lavish. It is to be the fashionable gambling resort of the aristocracy.

JANUARY 6

The Duke of York died yesterday quietly seated in an arm-chair. This of course puts the Court into deep mourning. They say he never recovered from the shock of the Duchess of Rutland's death—his mistress. She induced him to build that huge palace in the Mall called York House. He incurred huge debts. I only saw him once or twice in 1818. He was a great contrast to the then Prince Regent—coarse and very loud in his manners; a *viveur* in every sense of the word. He had the reputation of being a most loyal friend, and never forsook anybody who was in trouble. Peace to his ashes! I will have to go to the funeral as father's health does not permit him to attend such ceremonies.

JANUARY 20

We have had some difficulty with our coachman. He committed an assault outside the Embassy but took refuge when they were about to arrest him in the Embassy. Of course no officers of the law can enter an Embassy. Father was informed of the matter. He inquired into the facts of the case and absolutely refused to give the man up. It has caused a good deal of correspondence and the matter is not yet closed.

Our visit to Trentham was a great success. It is a palace indeed, and such magnificence I have never seen outside a royal residence, either here, in France, or in Russia. Lady Stafford received us in her usual dignified and gracious manner. She has always liked father, I believe, because Madame de Staël was so fond of him, and she had a cult for her. My room was quite beautiful, looking out on a fine sheet of water. In summer it must be perfectly beautiful. Then it stands empty as all the family come up to London. The reception rooms, state rooms, &c. &c., beggar description, full of superb works of art. We were sixty guests, a large portion of the Corps Diplomatique and Mr. Canning. Great ceremony for dinner, but the rest of the day we were allowed to do exactly as we chose. Horses to ride, coaches of all sorts at our disposal. Dancing and music in the evening. I thoroughly enjoyed it. So did Frances.

JANUARY 25

We are going on apace with the negotiations for the absolutely final settlement of the Commercial Treaty. Of course delays are inevitable in so important a matter. Lord Liverpool has seemed very odd in his manner lately as if he were half dazed. Walked in the Mall this morning with Frances, the inevitable footman following us. Lord Cassillis called to-day with his charming wife; she was a daughter of Mr. and Lady Mary Watts. Lady Mary was brought up in America as she and her sister, Lady Cathrine Duer, were the daughters of Lord Stirling. Mamma had known them well.

FEBRUARY

There is a Cabinet crisis which has kept everything at a standstill—very annoying. We dined with the Duke of Devonshire yesterday, at his house in Piccadilly. He is a most gracious host. Snappy Charles Greville, always asking questions and taking notes, was there. A book called "Vivian Grey," published by Colburn and immensely puffed, appeared last year. There were many surmises as to who the author was. Great names were mentioned and there was much speculation on the matter. It now turns out to be by a quite unknown youth called Disraeli, a Jew. Greville had the audacity to say that he knew who the author was from the first. Father thought well of the book. Lady Conyngham appears in the depth of mourning for the Duke of York. This causes much amusement. I do not think we will remain here much longer. I am most anxious to return home.

Father is really despondent, everything goes at a snail's pace. Mr. Adams after promising him an absolutely free hand is evidently irritated by Mr. Clay's continual interference and also influenced by him. Father looks upon Mr. Clay as simply an obstinate firebrand who is not capable of grasping or dealing with a subject without prejudice. The present negotiations are of a most delicate nature and have to be treated as such. Here it seems the custom for statesmen to conceal the truth. In France they do not pretend to tell the truth. The President has written a private letter to father begging him to remain in England. It is flattering to his vanity,

but he has none. He is determined after this mission
is fulfilled to give up political life altogether.

FEBRUARY 28

Lord Liverpool had a stroke on the 17th, and died yester-
day. Father does not think this will make any difference.
He hopes that Mr. Canning will not be Prime Minister.
It will be some time before anything definite is decided.

MARCH

We seem to be slowly creeping toward the end. Patience
is the only thing and we want a sack full of it. Supped
at Crockford's last night. Talleyrand was opposite to me
and looked more like an ape than ever. The absolute
silence of the gambling-rooms is extraordinary. I cannot
realize the passion for gambling. I suppose it is a disease,
like everything else. Father has little dinners of his
beloved cronies, Humboldt, Pozzo di Borgo, Baring, &c.
I really enjoy their delightful conversation—their
contempt for the world amuses me.

MARCH

The weather, which has been dreadful, is a little better.
No entertaining to speak of. Desperately dull. I am
glad I have plenty of work to do. Mr. Lawrence seems
very capable and father is much pleased with him.

APRIL 10

Mr. Canning is now Prime Minister. It seems to have
put him into a good temper and he is far more gracious,
although his temper at times is very trying. Father,
much to his disgust, has been summoned by the King
to Brighton—I go with him.

APRIL 15

We only stopped one night at Brighton. Rooms had been
prepared for us at a house close to the Pavilion, which

the King keeps for his guests. We were received by his Majesty, who was lying on a divan—he could hardly hold himself up. Lady Conyngham was present at first, but at a nod from the King, retired. She looks as if she had something of a temper. The King spoke on several political subjects, and for a wonder with great lucidity. He said suddenly, "Canning is a damned old woman." We were bid to sup with the Royal circle. I could see that father could hardly dissemble his disgust. The conversation was boisterous and indecent. Cards after supper, and on a plea of being very fatigued father begged leave to retire. He and I went for a walk by the sea. The only remark he made was, "And that is a King." We left in the morning without seeing His Majesty.

APRIL 24

Mr. Canning's temper has become most uncertain. At dinner last night father was sitting next to Baron Humboldt; after dinner, Mr. Canning came up to father and said, "The opinion universally entertained abroad and generally in England is that the Government is an aristocracy—it is not, it is a monarchy." Both father and Baron Humboldt were much surprised at this extraordinary outburst. They could not explain it. Some of the gentlemen sitting near, too, heard this remark and seemed much astonished. Later on the Duke of Wellington had a chair brought and placed between father and Humboldt. He made himself most agreeable, but seemed worried about something. He suddenly said, "Do you find anything odd in Mr. Canning's manner?"

ALBERT GALLATIN *to* HENRY CLAY

LONDON, *April* 28, 1827

. . . At the dinner of the 23rd, Mr. Canning came near Baron Humboldt and me and told us, "You see that the opinion universally entertained abroad, and very generally indeed in England, that this Government is an aristocracy, is not true.   It is," said he emphatically, "a monarchy.   The Whigs had found it out in 1784, when they tried to oppose the King's prerogative of choosing his Prime Minister.   The Tories have now repeated the same experiment, and with no greater success." He appears certainly very confident, and speaks of any intended opposition in Parliament as if he had no fear of it.   As all the leading newspapers are in his favour, I enclose the only pamphlet of note that has appeared on the other side.

An infusion of Whiggism in the Ministry, by the accession of such a man as the Marquis of Lansdowne, might perhaps, after a while, have produced some favourable change in the policy of the Administration towards the United States.   For the present, none can be expected.   I do not believe that there is a single question between us in which the Ministers will not be supported by the public opinion of the country in taking rank ground against us.   Our dependence for friendly arrangements rests solely on the superior sense of the Ministers. Unfortunately Mr. Huskisson * is less favourably disposed towards the United States, principally on the commercial subjects, than towards any other country.   And, having to meet in other respects a formidable opposition to his plans, he may be disposed to regain some popularity with the shipping interest to pursuing with the United States measures inconsistent with his avowed general principles on that subject.   If there is any reaction as relates to us, it must come from the West Indies, and perhaps, at last, from the manufacturing interests.

I have been compelled to remain perfectly quiet for the last months; but now that a temporary Administration is formed, which will last at least as long as this

* William Huskisson, Colonial Secretary 1827, responsible for the repeal of the Navigation laws.

session of Parliament, I will ascertain in the course of next week whether it is intended that our negotiations should be resumed. Mr. Canning, on the 23rd, again expressed great regret that they should have been so long interrupted, and intimated his intention of having, within a few days, a special conversation with me.

I have the honour, and &c.,
ALBERT GALLATIN

MAY

People are returning to London, and it promises to be a very gay season. Already we have several invitations, but we are here for too short a time to make really any friends. The Court returns to Buckingham House in June, but there will not be any Court entertainments, which is a relief. London is looking her best now; the Park is gay with flowers. I ride out to Kew and Richmond in the early morning—before anybody is stirring. Lady Kensington has been most kind to mamma and Frances. Miss Edwards and the latter are inseparable. I go sometimes to Holland House, which is very beautiful.

JUNE

Took Frances to Kew Gardens this afternoon. Flowers and plants beautiful. Dinner at the French Embassy. Glad to see some of my old Paris friends. Mr. Canning more and more odd in his manner. Lord Goderich had a long interview with father this morning.

JUNE 4

Took Frances to Eton for the 4th of June. A fine company, a very charming sight. The procession of boats delightful and very English. We are stopping at the White Hart Inn, directly opposite the Castle. Lady Kensington, her son and daughter, are of our party.

JUNE 10

Matters are going on very well, and father has great hopes of a speedy settlement. A splendid banquet at the Duke of Wellington's last night. A wonderful display of gold plate. A rout at Lady Lansdowne's. It took me exactly one hour to get from the top to the bottom of the stairs. I was wedged between Charles Greville and an immensely fat Dowager. We all three moved step by step together—and this is called pleasure. Dinner at Devonshire House to-night. The Court is at Buckingham House, but no entertaining.

JUNE 15

Frances has just come in from a walk in the Mall. She made us guess whom she met—fat Miss Bates whom we brought from America with us. The King was in a wheeled chair; Lady Conyngham walking along side of him. The weather intolerably hot. Good news from home. All are well. Plenty of work for me to-night.

JULY

Work, work, work, nothing but work, copying dispatches, preparing drafts of treaty, only to be torn up and new ones made. Weather intolerably hot. I will be glad when all is signed and sealed and we can have a little breathing time. Mamma and Frances in their element as they are dining out every night, and routs and balls following. Mrs. Baring is most assiduous in her attentions and insists on chaperoning Frances when mamma is tired.

AUGUST

Bad rumours of Mr. Canning's health; some say he cannot possibly live.

AUGUST 10

Mr. Canning died on the 8th. Lord Goderich, much to father's delight, is Prime Minister. All will now be plain sailing. When this treaty is signed it will be a final and we hope a lasting one. Certainly nothing has been left to chance, every detail has been discussed, assuring peace for years to come.

ALBERT GALLATIN *to* HENRY CLAY

LONDON, *August* 14, 1827

SIR,

It is now understood that the new Administration of this country is to be but a continuation of that of Mr. Canning, to act on the same principles, and no new appointments to be made but those that are strictly necessary.

Lord Goderich is First Lord of the Treasury. Lord Harrowby, President of the Council, retires from office, principally on account of a domestic affliction. Marquis Lansdowne, Lord Dudley, and the other Ministers, with the exception perhaps of Mr. Huskisson, remain in their respective offices. The Duke of Wellington may resume his place of Commander-in-Chief, but without a seat in the Cabinet, which he could not with propriety have accepted, since his fellow-seceders were excluded. Mr. Peel, and this is the greatest loss to the Administration, cannot at this time come in, having so lately committed himself by his solemn declaration that his reason for resigning was that he could not make part of an Administration at the head of which was a friend to Catholic emancipation.

The places to be filled are: (1) the President of the Council; and I have not heard who is intended, perhaps the Duke of Portland; (2) Colonial Department, vacant by Lord Goderich's promotion; (3) Chancellor of the Exchequer, an office which as a peer he cannot fill. It is probable that the option of these two places will be given to Mr. Huskisson, now on the Continent, where he was to remain three months, but whom the late event will probably bring back. The last place is that for which he is best qualified, and to which he is called by public opinion—but his precarious health will probably induce him to take the Colonial Department, as less laborious and, above all, as requiring less public speaking. In that case Mr. Herries, the principal Under-Secretary of the Treasury, and a capable man, but without political influence, will probably be the Chancellor, though Lord Palmerston is also spoken of; and Mr. Grant, now Vice-President, will naturally become President of the Board of Trade.

The great difficulty is who shall succeed Mr. Canning as leader of the House of Commons. Mr. Peel, who would have more of their confidence than any other man, is out of the question; and all that can be hoped is that, agreeing on almost every subject but that of the Catholic emancipation with the members of the Cabinet, he will not become the leader of an opposition. Without him there hardly can be one in the House of Commons; and the return of the Duke of Wellington to the command of the Army would go far to paralyse that in the House of Lords, whilst it would add to the weight of the Administration abroad. Mr. Brougham is undoubtedly the first man in the House of Commons, superior to Mr. Canning in force and logic, at least equal in sarcastic powers, far more consistent in his political opinions; but these are much too rank for the House, and, perhaps for the nation. Not even a moderate Whig would do for the present, and Mr. Brougham is, besides too harsh, better calculated to drive than to lead. Mr. Huskisson is, therefore, the only man; and he is accordingly looked on and intended as the Ministerial leader in the House.

This place, for it is one united to the superiority of his talents and energy over his colleagues, would make him in reality almost Prime Minister, if he was not rather a sensible than an eloquent speaker, and if it was not that he must govern through at least two of his associates—Lord Goderich, who besides all the patronage of his office, must be considered as the head of the moderate Tory Party, and Marquis Lansdowne, who is the head of almost the whole Whig Party; both also greatly and justly respected, and men of sound judg-

ment and solid, if not showy, talents. Power will be
more divided than under Mr. Canning. I think that the
influence of Marquis Lansdowne would be greater if
he could be transferred to the Foreign Office. As matters
now stand, the great political questions will be decided
by the Cabinet. Mr. Huskisson will have more weight
in those affecting the finances of the country; he will
direct almost exclusively (with the exception of the corn
question) the commercial regulations, whether interior
or in their connexion with foreign relations.

There will, therefore, be no change in the policy of
Great Britain towards us. The question of Colonial inter-
course was decided almost entirely by Mr. Huskisson's
influence. He adheres to that decision, and immediately
before leaving the country again committed himself in
that respect by positive assurance to merchants interested
in the subject. All the difficulties in renewing the commercial convention, and the determination not to renew
it unless it might be rescinded at will, also originated
with him. He has an undue and not very liberal jealousy
of the increasing navigation of the United States. In
other respects he cannot be said to be hostile to them;
and he would wish that causes of actual rupture might
be removed. I have reason to believe that he would be
in favour of a satisfactory arrangement on the subject
of impressment.

His views in regard of the country west of the Rocky
Mountains are, on the whole, temperate, and the difficulties on the subject of the North-East Boundary cannot
be ascribed to him. Whether his reign will last is extremely doubtful, his general health is precarious, and
he has an organic affection of the throat, so serious
that he never made a long speech during the last session
of Parliament without experiencing a relapse.

The present Administration will, at all events, last till
after the next meeting of Parliament in January, and
will probably become permanent if not disturbed by
untoward events. The critical situation of affairs in

Portugal is at this moment the principal cause of embarrassment.

I have the honour to be respectfully, sir,

Your most obedient servant,

ALBERT GALLATIN

AUGUST 16

A treaty was signed to-day which continues the Commercial Convention of 1815 indefinitely. All is now entirely satisfactorily settled and we return at once to America.

SEPTEMBER

London empty. We have to go to Brighton to take formal leave of his Majesty. We sail on October 9. All left now for us to do is to settle our domestic affairs. Mamma and Frances are paying some farewell visits in the country. Father is serenely content and believes there will be peace for many years between Great Britain and the United States.

OCTOBER 9: LIVERPOOL

We embark to-morrow morning. The weather very bad. It is a bad season of the year but we must take our chance. Mr. Lawrence and Mr. Baring have accompanied us here—most kind of the latter. I leave with some regret, but long to see my dear wife and child. Now for a new life in the New World.

The following letter from Lord Ashburton to Albert Gallatin, seven years before the latter's death, is of interest as showing at once the friendly feeling between America and England which was the fruit of his labours, and also the great esteem in which he himself was held.

LORD ASHBURTON *to* **ALBERT GALLATIN**

WASHINGTON, *April* 12, 1842

DEAR MR. GALLATIN,

My first destination was to approach America through New York, but the winds decided otherwise, and I was landed at Annapolis. In one respect only this was a disappointment, and a serious one. I should have much wished to seek you out in your retreat to renew an old and highly valued acquaintance, and I believe and hope I may add, friendship; to talk over with you the Old and New World, their follies and their wisdom, their present and bygone actors, all of which nobody understands so well as you do, and, what is more rare, nobody that has crossed my passage in life has appeared to me to judge with the same candid impartiality. This pleasure of meeting you is, I trust, only deferred. I shall, if I live to accomplish my work here, certainly not leave the country without an attempt to find you out and to draw a little wisdom from the best well, though it may be too late for my use in the work I have in hand and very much at heart.

You will probably be surprised at my undertaking this task at my period of life, and when I am left to my own thoughts I am sometimes surprised myself at my rashness. People here stare when I tell them that I listened to the debates in Congress on Mr. Jay's treaty in 1795, and seem to think that some antediluvian has come amongst them out of his grave. The truth is that I was tempted by my great anxiety in the cause, and the extreme peace between our countries. The latter circumstance induced my political friends to press this appointment upon me, and with much hesitation, founded solely upon my health and age, I yielded. In short, here I am. My reception has been everything I could expect or wish; but your experience will tell you that little can be inferred from this until real business is entered upon. I can only say that it shall not be my fault if we do not continue to live on better terms than we have lately done, and, if I do not understand the present very anomalous state of parties here, or misinterpret public opinion generally, there appears to be no class of politicians of any respectable character indisposed to peace with us on reasonable terms. I expect and desire to obtain no other, and my present character of a diplomatist is so new to me that I know no other course but candour and plain dealing. The most inexpert protocolist would beat me hollow at such work. I rely on your good wishes, my dear sir, though I have nothing else, and that you will believe me unfeignedly yours,

ASHBURTON

APPENDIX I

Correspondence between Albert Gallatin and Alexander Baring; showing the state of feeling in England towards America and the possibilities of the success of the mission.

ALBERT GALLATIN *to* MESSRS. BARING BROS. & CO.

GOTTENBURG, *June 22*, 1813

GENTLEMEN,

The President of the United States having accepted on the part of the said States the mediation offered by the Emperor of Russia, Mr. Bayard and myself have been appointed, jointly with Mr. Adams, Ministers, with full powers to treat of peace with such Ministers as may be appointed on the part of Great Britain. We left the United States in the public ship *Neptune*, Captain Lloyd Jones, on May 11, arrived here on the 20th instant, and intend to proceed this evening in the ship on our way to St. Petersburg.

We are authorized to draw on you for our salaries and for the contingent expenses of the mission, and, in order to assist us with the best mode of negotiating bills, will thank you to let us know at St. Petersburg the course of exchange between London and Amsterdam.

We will also be obliged to you to have the account and date of our arrival in Lloyd's list and some other paper, as it may give to our friends in America the earliest account of our safe arrival.

Of the fact that we are appointed to treat and on our way to St. Petersburg for that purpose, as stated in the first paragraph of this letter, I should wish your Government to be informed. And we will be thankful for any intelligence connected with our mission which you may deem important and which you may feel at liberty to communicate. We sailed with a passport from Admiral Warren; and whatever may be the result of this mission, we feel anxious to return speedily and safely to America. We will detain the *Neptune* at St. Petersburg for that purpose, and may want a passport from your Government for her return with ourselves and suite on board. It is presumable that this will be obtained without difficulty. And will thank you to make the inquiry, and to cause, if necessary, such passport to be forwarded to us at St. Petersburg.

ALBERT GALLATIN

ALEXANDER BARING *to* ALBERT GALLATIN

LONDON, *July 22*, 1813

DEAR SIR,

The letter with which you honoured my house from Gottenburg has remained for a few days unanswered, for the purpose of obtaining the information necessary to enable me to make a satisfactory reply.

For the money you may require you will please to direct drafts upon us or on Amsterdam in any manner you may think expedient. Messrs. Meyer and Bruxner, bankers at St. Petersburg, by whom this letter will be conveyed to you, have our directions to obey any orders you may give them on this subject, presuming that you will prefer not to let your own drafts go into public circulation. Our present exchange with Holland is about 79 the pound sterling, which will enable you to calculate what mode of reimbursement will best answer your purpose.

I have taken care to make in the proper quarter the communications you desire, and, as you express a wish to be informed of any occurrences here, relating to your mission, some observations may perhaps be acceptable on the dispositions of Government and of the public concerning it, upon which I have good reason to assure you that you may perfectly rely.

I anticipated the most favourable result from the names which constituted the new commission, and felt confident that we should soon see an end of this senseless war. I was quite sure you would not leave your home without the powers and the disposition to do your country this essential service, and although the place fixed upon for the negotiation, and the manner in which it was proposed to conduct it, considerably abated the confidence of the public, I never entertained those doubts of the sincerity of America with which those circumstances inspired others.

The mediation of Russia was offered, not sought—it was fairly and frankly accepted. I do not see how America could with any consistency refuse it; but to the eyes of a European politician it was clear that such an interference could produce no practical benefit. The only question now seriously at issue between us is one purely of a domestic nature in each country respectively; no foreign Government can fairly judge it. A question of the relative rights and duties of Sovereign and subject between two great countries, where, owing to their recent separation, a distinction between the great masses of their seafaring population becomes almost impossible, can only exist between Great Britain and America; no other country can judge of the various positions of great delicacy and importance to which such a state of things must give rise; and even where the best understanding prevails between European courts, there are shades of difference and sometimes feelings of various sorts which must prevent any cordial mediation on such points. On the other hand, what a handle does such a subject offer for fomenting discord on points totally foreign from it! We have lately seen a threat of dragging American politics into a German congress, among Powers neither understanding nor caring for any of its interest, but merely to enable them to wrangle the more dexterously about their own.

This is not the way for Great Britain and America really to settle their disputes; intelligent persons of the two countries might devise mutual securities and concessions which perhaps neither country would offer in the presence of a third party. It is a sort of family quarrel, where foreign interferences can only do harm and irritate at any time, but more especially in the present state of Europe, when attempts would be made to make a tool of America in a manner which I am sure neither you nor your colleagues would sanction.

These, I have good reason to know, are pretty nearly the sentiments of Government here on the question of place of negotiation and foreign mediation, and before this reaches you you will have been informed that this mediation has been refused, with expressions of our desire to treat separately and directly here, or, if more agreeable to you, at Gottenburg.

I believe you may rely upon it that from this resolution we shall not here depart, not only from the sense of the objections I have already stated to a mediating negotiation, but that your persevering in such a course will be considered here as the touchstone of your sincerity. Although I trust our Government does not participate in the prevailing opinion here that a secret political connexion exists with France, yet your persevering in bringing this insulated question before the Powers of the Continent would favour those suspicions, and induce Ministers to believe that your only object was to assist France in the sort of mystification and confusion in which it often suits her purpose to envolve her diplomatic negotiations.

I trust that these considerations, duly weighed, will satisfy you that no inference is to be drawn from our refusal of the Russian mediation unfavourable to our disposition for peace, and that if we wish to remove the seat of the negotiation it is in reality for the purpose of coming at that result with more certainty. This city has, I understand, been proposed to you, and Gottenburg offered as an alternative in case you do not choose to trust yourselves so near to us.

My hopes of a favourable result would be much increased by your coming at once in contact with our Ministers. The advantages in all cases of treating this principle are obvious, but the peculiar character of the point in dispute gives them greater weight. You would find any Minister of this country very cautious in giving instructions to any plenipotentiary to treat on a subject of so much delicacy as the rights and duties of Sovereign and subject. Those instructions must remain recorded in his office, and may be called for by Parliament. Concessions might be made, securities and substitutes devised, and difficulties overcome in a direct negotiation which I should almost despair of if it were to be carried on at a distance; and I am quite sure that the mass of intelligence which your commission affords on the relative policy of Great Britain and America is more than a match for all our island can produce on the same subject, upon which the ignorance of many of our leading characters would probably surprise you. But you would naturally wish to ask the question whether, should you consent to come here to negotiate, there is a probable chance of a favourable result. Upon this I will give you my candid opinion, and I know that I can, without deceiving you, state the sentiments of Government.

That we wish for a restoration of peace with you need not be argued. Our situation, the great contest in which we are engaged, make it impossible that we should be otherwise than heartily desirous of putting an end to a contest from which we suffer considerably (though perhaps, less than was anticipated), and from which no good can result. The extent of the injury which the two countries can do each other is now pretty well ascertained, we can tease and weaken each other without any practical result, and you cannot for a moment doubt our wish to carry the resources now employed in defending ourselves against you into the more important field of European contest.

With these feelings, why has the war continued so long? The only serious point at issue may be said to be that of the impressment of seamen—a question presenting of itself serious and not imaginary difficulties. To hope for any solution of them the disposition on both sides must be sincere, the spirit of peace must animate both parties, and I will not disguise from you that when America set this question of seamen up as cause of war after the great effort for conciliation was made in the repeal of the Orders in Council, the prevalent opinion here was that the war was a war of passion with the people of America, and that concessions would only show weakness, and never satisfy them, and that therefore no alternative was left to us but to fight it out as well as we could. Whether this opinion was well or ill founded need not now be discussed; it prevented at the time any deliberate consideration of the question of seamen, which was considered merely as a pretext, to be followed by some other if once removed. This opinion I believe to be, in as far as Government is concerned, on the change. The representation of persons desirous of seeing a return of peace on honourable terms, a growing opinion that America has a real and serious interest in this question of seamen, the repeated wish expressed by your Executive, and above all, the characters appointed for the pacific mission to St. Petersburg, have excited hopes; there is a disposition to examine the question, and I am quite certain that I can now assure you that should you come here you will be received with confidence in your intentions, with great personal respect, and with a determination to come to terms of peace with you if it be found practicable to do so consistently with the safety of our maritime power, supposed to be, and which undoubtedly is, involved in this question.

So much I can confidently say of the disposition existing here. But are the difficulties, supposing the disposition on both sides to be perfect, of themselves insurmountable, or are we doomed to the necessity of perpetual war? Upon this point I will give you with sincerity my opinion: I shall not trouble you with any extensive discussion of a subject with which you are so well acquainted. The difficulties are very considerable, but, although I can hardly say that I think they can be surmounted to the *entire* satisfaction of both parties, I do think that by sincere and friendly discussions some system may be devised of practical efficiency to answer the reasonable purposes of both countries. At all events, it is the duty of both to make some arrangement, because some arrangement or perpetual war are the only alternative. It is easy on either side to dress the question out with popular attractions, but any indifferent person understanding it and considering it calmly must be sensible that on our side we could not admit your pretensions to their full extent without endangering the discipline, and even the existence, of our navy, and, on the other hand, that on your part you cannot submit to the existing system as practised by us. There is, therefore, a necessity of some settlement. If you submitted at present, the growing power and population of America would force a settlement on the two countries at no distant period perhaps after ruinous wars. Being frequently accused here of undue partiality towards America, I trust at least that I shall have credit with you for a sincere wish to see an end put to so permanent and certain a source of strife; but I must freely confess that, highly as I value a state of peace and harmony with America, I am so sensible of the danger to our naval power from anything like an unrestricted admission of your principles, that I should almost incline to think it safer to consider an American as an inevitable concomitant of a French war, and to provide for it accordingly. It is useless to discuss the abstract question of right when it becomes one of necessity, and with us I sincerely believe it to be so.

If therefore the disposition of your Government be to adhere pertinaciously to the determination to give us no better security than the Act of Congress lately passed, I should think your coming here or negotiating anywhere useless for any good purpose. I know it must be so, because I know that any Government of this country would be restrained from such an unlimited concession by its known and certain danger, by the state of public opinion, and that the best friends to the restoration of peace would not be bold enough to recommend it. But, on the other hand, if you are desirous of endeavouring, by mutual explanation and concession, to consult the security and just apprehension of both countries, I know that I can assure you that you will find a corresponding disposition here; and although I would not speak lightly of the difficulties to be overcome, I am inclined by a long consideration of the subject to anticipate every reasonable degree of success from the joint efforts of yourselves and those persons whom our Government will be prepared to appoint to meet you.

I have thus, my dear sir, ventured to suggest to you what occurs to me on the interesting subject of your mission. I should not have risked opinions without feeling certain that I was not misleading you if you think proper to trust to them. I hope they will encourage you not to return to America without at least making an experiment in the manner most likely to lead to success.

I am assured by my Lord Castlereagh that the requisite order shall be sent for permitting your cartel-ship, the *Neptune*, to carry the gentlemen composing your mission wherever they may think proper; and I trust that I shall be ere long gratified by seeing her bring with you the hope of peace to our shores.

APPENDIX I

If I can personally be of any service, I trust you will freely command me, and that I may be permitted to present my compliments to Mr. Bayard and Mr. Adams with whom I believe I have the advantage of a very slight acquaintance, which I should have the greatest satisfaction in being afforded an opportunity of improving.

I am, with great consideration and personal regard, dear sir, your very obedient servant,

ALEXANDER BARING

ALBERT GALLATIN *to* ALEXANDER BARING

ST. PETERSBURG, *August* 27, 1813

DEAR SIR,

The letter (of July 22) with which you have favoured me was received on the 17th inst. For this I return you my sincere thanks, and duly appreciate the importance of the information you have obtained, and the motives which have actuated you. Although I cannot write as freely as a person whose communications do not commit his own Government, the hope that our correspondence may be of some public utility induces me to enter as far in the subject as is consistent with my situation.

We have not received, as you suggested, the information that the mediation of Russia had been refused by Great Britain, with expressions of a desire to treat with us separately and directly at London or at Gottenburg. It is possible that Lord Walpole, who is said here to have gone to the Emperor's headquarters, may be the bearer of that communication. We have in the meanwhile been notified that the Emperor had, on the arrival of our mission, given orders that his offer of mediation should be renewed; and we will wait here the result. But if your Government should, after due consideration, persist in its absolute refusal of that offer, a negotiation with us cannot be opened, since our powers in that respect are to treat of peace with Great Britain expressly under the mediation of Russia. We have a distinct commission to treat afterwards of commerce, if agreeable to your Government, and without reference to any mediation. This was alluded to by the President of the United States in his last message, and is now mentioned as an evidence of his sincere desire not only to make peace, but to establish the relations between the two countries on the most friendly footing.

It does not belong to me to discuss the objections which your Government may have to treat of peace under the mediation of Russia; but we were altogether unaware, when we left America, that any such could exist. Russia had an interest in the restoration of peace between the two countries, since the war interrupted her commercial relations with America, and diverted a certain portion of the British force from the important object of European warfare. In the terms on which peace should be made, in the essential point at issue—a point, which, as you suggest, could not in practice arise with respect to her—she had no immediate interest. In those respects she united therefore the essential requisites in a mediating Power, a sincere wish that peace might be made, and impartiality as to the subject of the dispute. On the other hand, with Russia we had only friendly and commercial relations, but no political connexion. You had also with her relations of the same nature with ours and on a much more extensive scale. And you had at the same time an intimate political connexion, necessarily arising from your being united in a most important conflict against a formidable common enemy. You are her ally in a war which to her is an object of so much superior importance to the interest she has in the restoration of peace between you and us—that America might have hesitated to accept her mediation had it not been for the great confidence we place in the personal character of the Emperor. This we considered a sufficient pledge of impartiality; and, certain that your Government at least in that respect entertained sentiments similar to ours, we did not presuppose that if the mediation was accepted by us there could be any hesitation on the subject on the part of Great Britain, unless she considered peace as, at all events at this moment, either impracticable or undesirable. We did also believe that our accepting as a mediator a Sovereign at war with France was such a clear evidence of our neither having nor wishing to have any political connexion with this last Power, that it must remove those suspicions on the part of your Government to which you allude, and which, although altogether erroneous and destitute of foundation, might probably continue to have an unfavourable effect on its dispositions and termination.

Such was the view of the subject under which our Government acted in the appointment of the extraordinary mission; and you must at once perceive that if a rejection of the mediation on the part of Great Britain had been anticipated, the result would have been, not a direct mission to that country for which there was no preliminary foundation, but merely a declaration that the United States accepted the mediation, and would be ready to act upon it whenever it was accepted by Great Britain.

It will be a matter of regret if this frank proceeding on the part of America, this effort to re-establish peace in an honourable manner and without suing for it, should, on the threshold, be defeated by the absolute refusal of your Government of the offered mediation. Without at all entering in a discussion of the objections they have to that measure, still, so far as those objections are exhibited in your letter they do not appear to me to go beyond a belief that a direct negotiation would afford a better prospect of success than one conducted under the mediation of any third Power. This may be true; but as it does not, however, seem necessarily to imply that the attempt to negotiate under a mediation may not under certain circumstances be made, or that a mediation, where

APPENDIX I

America is concerned, is at all events and in itself inadmissible, I still indulge the hope that your Government, finding that a rejection of the mediation is, so far as this mission is concerned, a refusal to negotiate, and placing that confidence in the sincerity of our dispositions and views to which we feel ourselves entitled, will, on a due consideration of the subject, find it practicable to reconcile an acceptance of the mediation with their views and principles.

With respect to the main question, the probability of an arrangement, you are sensible that I cannot at this time and on this occasion enter into details. That I would not have given up my political existence and separated myself from my family unless I had believed an arrangement practicable and that I might be of some utility in effecting it, you are sufficiently aware. The law to which you allude is a municipal regulation, which may, however, be considered as a primary evidence of the general disposition of the American Government to advance towards a compromise. On that subject I could not be more explicit without in fact entering into the negotiation itself. I will only state that, however desirable it might be to define with precision and in a permanent manner the respective rights of the two countries on the subject of impressment, I do not hope that this can be effected at this time, that either nation can be induced to abandon its rights or pretensions in that respect. All that, in my opinion, can be done is an arrangement, by way of experiment, which, reserving to both nations their respective abstract rights real or assumed, shall be founded on mutual engagements in such manner that the failure of either nation to fulfil her engagement shall absolve the other nation from her own and leave her in as full exercise of her rights and pretensions as if the arrangement had not been made.

I have thus freely communicated as far as our relative situation seemed to permit, being well assured that what I

have said will be used for its intended purpose of assisting
in promoting the restoration of peace. I know how dear
this object is to you, and that we both have an equal
desire that not only peace but the most friendly relations
and understanding should subsist between the two
countries. I can assure you that such also is the sincere
and earnest desire of my Government, and that nothing
which can be done in that respect will be omitted on my
part or on that of my colleagues. Whatever the result
may be, I will preserve a just sense of your friendly
conduct on this occasion, and remain with great consideration and sincere regard, dear sir, your very obedient
servant,

ALBERT GALLATIN

ALEXANDER BARING *to* ALBERT GALLATIN

LONDON, *October* 12, 1813

DEAR SIR,
The letter you favoured me with of August 27,
reached me in course of post, and if I have delayed my
reply it has not been, I can assure you, from any neglect
of the important subject of its contents. I have been
endeavouring to be useful in an object which I have very
much at heart. At this season of the year those with
whom I wished to confer are generally out of town, and
correspondence becomes necessary. In communicating to
you the result of my endeavours I am sorry to say that
they have been less successful than I could hope or than
I had at one time expected; at the same time, however,
I feel the more convinced that the existing difficulties
are more difficulties of form than of substance, and I very
much misunderstand the disposition on both sides if an
agreement were not the result of negotiation, if that
negotiation could but be once set on foot. In what I
communicate I beg leave again to assure you that you
may rely upon my not misleading you, and, without
troubling you much with the arguments that are used,

APPENDIX I

I shall confine myself principally to the results, and that the rather as little time is left me before the departure of the post, and I wish that no time may be lost. We are here resolved to abide by the principle of direct negotiation. I had hoped that an agreement might have been so far advanced and ascertained that the mediation would have been a mere matter of form, and in that case it might have been adopted for the purpose of keeping your powers alive, and although I could of course attain to nothing like certainty as to this probability of agreement, I am still inclined to infer it from the general expression of your letter and from what I have collected here. But it has been resolved here not to depart from the first resolution of entering only into a direct negotiation, and it is thought that, upon the whole, time will at last be saved by this mode, even though it should oblige you to have recourse to America for an alteration of your powers. The arguments used by you in favour of a Russian mediation are very ingenious, and no inference of insincerity is drawn from America's adopting this mode, but there are circumstances connected with the nature of the question which makes it ineligible, when in any common political dissension it might be the most rational and satisfactory course to pursue. But whatever may be the weight of argument on either side, you may be assured that the determination is here irrevocable, and before this reaches you it must have been communicated to you in some authentic shape. As at the same time a readiness for direct negotiations will be declared, this must save entirely any feelings of pride that America may entertain, as the advance for direct negotiation comes from hence in return for a step on her part of much less concession. What you will think proper to do in this case—whether to wait for new powers, to return yourselves, or to come here in the expectation of those powers being sent—will remain with you to determine; perhaps, indeed, you have determined before this reaches you, as the Baltic will probably be closed for navigation by the end of this month. The omission of Mr. Adams' name in the passport was quite accidental, and must have been my fault. I have no recollection of the circumstance, but I probably concluded at the time that as he was the resident Minister at St. Petersburg he would not return. I trust, however, that he will not have hesitated to accompany you on account of this omission, which he may be assured will be of no consequence, and that the vessel, with any person belonging to the mission, will be suffered freely to pass our fleets.

On the subject of the probability of an agreement between the two Governments I am sensible that you must necessarily write with reserve; but as I am under no such restraint, I will state to you fairly what you may expect here, and I do it because this may influence your determination on other points, and because I always think that between States, as between individuals, where the intentions are honest, plain language is always preferable to artifice. We wish for peace. The pressure of the war upon our commerce and manufactures is over; they have ample relief in other quarters; and, indeed, the dependence of the two countries on each other was, as it usually is, overrated. But the war has no object; it is expensive; and we want to carry our efforts elsewhere. Our desire of peace, therefore, cannot be doubted, and you may quite rely upon it. With respect to the only question really at issue, we are disposed to concert with you the most efficient means of confining the seamen of each country to their respective services; but we do not believe in the practicability of so doing without a reservation of a right of search for them, or rather without a continuation of the practice, for we do not want from you a recognition of right. This practice we are ready to regulate in any manner consistent with its object, and I feel an entire conviction that it may be regulated in a manner to do away

APPENDIX I

almost everything that is objectionable in it. On this point you will find us reasonable and liberal, but very firm upon the question of not giving up the practice of examination and search, and indeed with every desire not only to see peace restored, but to see satisfaction given to America on this point—which I always thought she had a right to—I cannot see how we can under our present system of manning our navy do more. All the Acts of Congress or Acts of Parliament that can be framed would be ineffectual without this, and I am sure that when you come to the details you would be of the same opinion; and it is for this reason that I infer from the cautious wording of your letter that you would not be disinclined to an arrangement upon this principle, where every precaution would be taken, and taken, I think, effectually, to remove everything that is vexatious in the present practice, and to subject it to the responsibility towards both Governments, under which alone it can be made consistent with a state of peace. I shall not trouble you with any detailed examination of this point; the general principles of our Government you would find as I have stated, and if they are not repugnant to your instructions I think you would soon complete the work of peace without the help or hindrance of any mediator.

I have not yet had a good opportunity for America to send your letters for Mrs. Gallatin; they are now here, but a cartel is expected to sail in a few days, and they shall be taken care of. We have not hitherto received any for you. I beg you will believe me at all times happy to be useful, and with great esteem and regard, dear sir, your sincerely devoted servant,

ALEXANDER BARING

APPENDIX II

9 *Février*, 1761.

Voici la plus belle occasion, mon cher ange, d'exercer votre ministère céleste. Il s'agit du meilleur office que je puisse recevoir de vos bontés.

Je vous conjure, mon cher et respectable ami, d'employer tout votre crédit auprès de Monsieur le Duc de Choiseul; auprès de ses amis, s'il le faut après, de sa maîtresse, etc. etc. Et pourquoi ose-je vous demander tant d'appui, tant de zèle, tant de vivacité, et surtout un prompt succès? Pour le bien du service, mon cher ange: pour battre le Duc de Brunswick. M. Gallatin, Officier aux gardes Suisses, qui vous présentera ma très-humble réquête, est de la plus ancienne famille de Genève. Ils se font tuer pour nous de père en fils depuis Henri Quatre.

L'Oncle de celui-ci a été tué devant Ostende; son frère a été à la malheureuse et abominable journée de Rosbach, à ce que je crois; journée où les régiments suisses firent seuls leur devoir. Si ce n'est pas à Rosbach, c'est ailleurs; le fait est qu'il a été tué; celui-ci a été blessé. Il sert depuis dix ans; il a été aide-major; il veut l'être. Il faut des aides-major qui parlent bien l'allemand, qui soient actifs, intelligents; il est tout cela. Enfin vous saurez de lui précisément ce qu'il lui faut; c'est en général la permission d'aller vite chercher la mort à votre service. Faites-lui cette grâce et qu'il ne soit point tué, car il est fort aimable et il est neveu de cette Madame Calendrin que vous avez vue étant enfant. Madame sa mère est bien aussi aimable que Madame Calendrin.

APPENDIX II

February 9, 1761.

Here, my dear angel, is the finest occasion for using your heavenly ministration. I am asking for the greatest service I could receive from your kindness.

My dear and honourable friend, I implore you to use all your credit with the Duc de Choiseul, with his friends, and if that fails, with his mistress, etc. Why do I ask for so much support, such zeal, such determination—above all for a speedy and successful issue? For the good of the service, dear angel—to fight the Duke of Brunswick. M. Gallatin, officer in the Swiss Guards, who will present my humble request to you, belongs to the oldest family in Geneva. They have shed their blood for us from father to son since the time of Henri Quatre.

The uncle of this Gallatin was killed before Ostend; his brother was, I believe, at the unhappy and accurséd day of Rosbach, the day when the Swiss regiments alone did their duty. If it was not Rosbach it was somewhere else. The fact remains that he was killed—this one was wounded. He has served for ten years, has been staff-major —which is the post he wants. We need staff-majors who speak German and who are active and intelligent; he is all of that. But you will learn from him the exact nature of his wants: generally speaking, it is leave to seek a speedy death in your service. Do him this kindness and see that he be not killed, for he is very amiable and a nephew of the Madame Calendrin whom you saw in your childhood. His mother too is as amiable as Madame Calendrin.

APPENDIX III

TRANSLATION OF DECISION OF THE 5TH AUGUST 1810

Whereas the above report made in the Council of Commerce and Manufacture, with the following results:

(1) That the Government of the United States is not bound by her act of the 1st March 1809—by the order dated 20th May following that the French Ships and Merchandise therein contained, which enter their ports should be put under sequestration, but that the confiscation of the aforesaid ships and merchandise has been ordered.

(2) That it has been established by the same Act that when the relations with France have been re-established the confiscations will continue to have their effect.

(3) That the Act of the 1st March 1809 has been put into execution on every occasion that has presented itself, not only against the Cargoes but against the French ships as well. We have ordered, and order what follows:

(1) That the funds arising from the sales of the American Cargoes which have been sold up to this date, and the total which has been placed on deposit in the Caisse of Amortisment, shall be transferred to the public treasury.

(2) That the American Cargoes that have been placed under sequestration shall be sold and the funds arising from the same shall be paid into the Public Treasury.

(3) That the American ships which up to this date, no decision has been come to, shall be sold and the funds they realize shall be paid into the Public Treasury.

(4) Taking into consideration that the Act of the 1st March 1809 made by the United States does not contain

any order as to the disposition of the Crews of our ships, and always wishing to treat the United States as fairly as possible and using only with regret our rights of reprisal against them. We agree that the Crews of American ships entering our ports shall not be considered as prisoners, but shall be sent back to their own country.

(5) The dispositions above stated shall be carried out with regard to all the American ships which have entered our ports and been sequestered since the 20th March 1808—to the 1st of May of the present year 1810—the date of the Act by which the United States has revoked the Act of the 1st March 1809.

(6) In the future and up to the 1st of November the date fixed by the letter of our Minister of Foreign Affairs to the plenipotentiary's of the United States for the revocation of our decrees of Berlin and Milan (in the case that our conditions established in the aforesaid letters are fulfilled) the American ships can enter our ports; but the unloading cannot take place without a license signed by our hand, and on a report made in the Council of Commerce stating that they have not been denationalized by their submission to the order of the Council of Great Britain and that they have not contravened decrees of Berlin and Milan.

Given at our Palace of the Trianon the 5th August 1810.

Signed NAPOLEON

INDEX

INDEX

Argental, Count d', letter from Voltaire, 295–96

Ashburton, Lord. *See* Baring, Alexander

Astor, John Jacob, and Albert Gallatin, vi *and note*, vii, 80, 174, 201, 229; manners, 167; and Mme. Bonaparte, 179

Aumont, Duc d', 241

Austria, question of succession, 261

BACHALAN's Hotel, Copenhagen, 3

Bache, Richard, letter from Benjamin Franklin to, ii

Balmat, Jacques, 215

Baltimore, 61–62, 211, 221, 237, 240, 244–46, 252, 255

Archbishop of, and M. Pascault, 249

Bank of the United States, presidency refused by Albert Gallatin, 197, 201

Baring, Alexander, letters from Albert Gallatin, vii, 3, 279–80, 287–91; negotiations with, 12, 14; friendship with the Gallatins, 72, 77, 172, 174, 203, 210, 222, 262–64, 268, 276; offer to James Gallatin, 224; letter to Albert Gallatin, 280–87, 291–94

Baring, Mrs. Alexander, 72, 203, 210, 272

Barry, Colonel, letter to the Marquis of Huntly, 52–56

Bassano, Duc de, 166, 172, 187–88

Bates, Miss, 256, 272

Bathurst, Lord, 15, 20, 30–32, 59

Bayard, Mr., vi, 1, 2, 12, 13, 15, 16, 22, 28–30, 33, 69, 75, 279, 287

Belgarde, 62

Bentham, Jeremy, 14 *and note*, 175–76

Bentinck, Mlle, 112

Berlin Decree, the, 187, 188, 298

"Berline," use of a, 87

Bernadotte, Jean, 122 *and note*, 223

Mme. *See* Sweden, Queen of

Berne, 217

Berri, Duc de, in London, 56; and Albert Gallatin, 86 *and note*, 93, 130; and the Duke of Wellington, 104–5; and the Orléans family, 106; a story of, 107–8; and James Gallatin, 135, 136, 140; the Duchesse and, 144; innovations at Court, 149; at the Elysée, 154; death of, 156–61; effect of his death on *jeunesse dorée*, 182

Duchesse de, and the Orléans family, 106, 140; hospitality of, 124, 144; death of the Duke, 156–61; accusation against Decazes, 161; at the Tuileries, 162; birth of the Duc de Bordeaux, 165–67, 177; and the bomb explosions, 180; and the Gallatins, 220–21, 236

Berthal, Mme., housekeeper, 96, 139–40, 148, 150, 151, 168, 175–76, 180

Berthe, la Reine, 50

Berthollet, 44, 45

Bertrand, Gen., in Elba, 53

Béthisy, Mme. de, 157 *and note*, 235

Bingham, Miss, of Philadelphia. *See* Baring, Mrs. Alexander.

Biron family, the, 63

Blanc, Mont, ascent, 215

Blockade in time of war, question of, 70

Boar hunts, 113–14, 151–52, 200

"Bocage," house at Pregny, 138

Boigne, Comtesse de, 58, 92 *and note*, 98, 104, 106, 139, 150, 169, 192, 208, 220, 228, 233, 239

General de, 92 *note*

Bois de Boulogne, 136; skating on the Petit Lac, 101, 119, 195, 198–99, 202, 226–27, 232

Bonaparte, Jerome, 51, 61–63, 202, 252

Joseph, ex-King of Spain, 49 *and note*, 50, 122, 190; Albert Gallatin and, 67

INDEX

INDEX

INDEX

INDEX

Gallatin, Albert—*cont.*

lations with Spain, 142; discovery of the Trianon decree, 187–90; Geneva in 1821, 191; his first marriage, 219, 247; the vice-presidency, 249, 251; conditions of English mission, 255–56; and George IV, 268–69

Letters from :

Ashburton, Lord, 276–78

Baring, Alexander, 280–87, 291–94

Bonaparte, Mme., 144–45

Humboldt, Alexander von, 44–45

Monroe, James, 84

Moreau, General, 7–10

Staël, Mme. de, 37–39

Letters to :

Adams, J. Q., 187–90, 258–61

Baring, Alexander, 3, 279–80, 287–91

Clay, Henry, 269–71, 273–76

Crawford, W. H., 15–19

his brother-in-law, 2

Jefferson, Thomas, 78–80

Lafayette, General, 19–20

Monroe, James, 81–84, 88–89

Staël, Mme. de, 40–44

Albert, his son, in Paris, 78, 94, 98, 101, 103, 125; at Fontainebleau, 113; life in America, 179, 186, 196, 207, 217, 228–29, 233, 235, 239, 247; illness of, 211; wife of, 245; the house at New Geneva, 250–52

Albert, son of James, 253

Barthélemy de, 15 *and note*

Comte de, 95, 96, 106, 118–20, 204, 223, 226

Comtesse de, 96, 106, 118–20, 204, 226; and Frances, 197; theatricals, 208–10

Count Paul Michael de, 12–13 46

Gallatin—*cont.*

Frances, 78, 82; journey to France, 85; in Paris, 87, 94, 96–98, 101, 103, 105, 115, 125, 134, 135, 144–45, 175–76, 180, 219; and Mme. Bonaparte, 91; the King's admiration for, 95; at Versailles, 103; at Fontainebleau, 113, 211; a Christmas party, 116–18; at the Opéra, 137; at the Elysée, 142; at Suresnes, 148–49; Christmas preparations, 150–51; pearls for, 152–53; début, 163, 167, 177, 184–85; and Mr. Astor, 167; *sauterie* for, 168–70; a *bal costumé*, 169–71; scarlet fever, 171–72; at the Palais Royal, 178; trick played by James on, 181–82; the Paris churches, 183; in society, 190, 192, 195, 197, 204, 206, 220, 221, 224, 225–26, 232; proposals, 193, 240; and Mamie Kitty, 205; theatricals, 208, 210; and Miss Edwards, 222, 229, 271; the Christmas play, 225–28; reception by the Duchesse d'Angoulême, 236, 238; by Louis XVIII, 240–41; present from Pozzo di Borgo, 242; return to America, 242–45; letter from her father, 246–47; and Mlle Pascault, 248; at New Geneva, 250–52; at Trentham, 266; in London, 271–72, 276

François de, 110

House, Geneva, 46

James, diary of, v; mission to Russia, 1 *et seq.*; and Alexander, 24–25; at Coppet, 58; and the Duchesse d'Angoulême, 64; portrait by David, 64–67; and Louis

INDEX

INDEX

INDEX

INDEX

INDEX

INDEX

INDEX

INDEX

INDEX

Tuileries, reception of Napoleon, 65–66; etiquette, 124; funeral of the Duc de Berri, 159; Duchesse de Berri at, 162; bomb explosion at, 177; receptions, &c., 177, 210, 220–21

Twenty years' war in Europe, 41

UNIONTOWN, reception of Lafayette, 253–54

United States, Trianon decree of August 5, 1810, 297–98

VALLIERE, Mlle de la, 126

Vaud, Canton de, address to Albert Gallatin, 50, 59

Vaux Praslin, 63

Veronese, Paolo, "Queen Esther before Ahasuerus," 67

Versailles, the Petit Trianon, 26; entertainment at, 52 *note*, 56–57, 183–84; the Lussacs at, 87; visits to, 103; the Duchesse d'Angoulême and, 211

Vestris, Mme. Le, 182

Veufflans, Château de, above Lausanne, 50

Vienna, Congress of, 37, 74, 79

Villar, Duc de, 60

Ville Juis, 55

Villèle, M. de, 227, 257, 260

Vilette, Mme. de la, 61

Vincennes, skating at, 174

Vincent, Baron, 106, 239

"Vivian Grey," 267

Vodka, popularity of, 6

Voltaire, v, 56, 59–61, 105, 184; letter to Count d'Argental, 295–96

Vosges Mountains, 60

WADDINGTON, Mme., 236 *note*

Waldorf, 80

Walewski, Count, 234

Walpole, Lord, 13, 287

Warden, Mr., 44, 45

Warren, Admiral, passport of, 2, 280

Washington, capture of, 40–41; impressions, 73; Albert Gallatin in, 83, 84, 244

President, 11, 56

Waterloo, 76; the plains of, 111

Watts, Lady Mary, 267

Mr., 267

Weald of Sussex, 132

Wellesley, Lady. *See* Patterson, Mrs. Robt.

Marquis of, 62 *note*, 222, 263 *note*

Wellington, Duke of, 28 *note*, 62 *note*, 90, 141 *and note*, 265; private notes to Albert Gallatin, 34–35; and Mme. de Staël, 39, 51; the negotiations, 59; and Albert Gallatin, 73; on the Treaty of Ghent, 74; Waterloo, 76; and James Gallatin, 93; personality, 102; attempt on his life, 104; dinner given by, 106; and the French Royal Family, 138; amours, 165; and Mrs. Robert Patterson, 194, 222, 263 *note*; purchase of the Hôtel Borghèse, 220 *note*; and Canning, 269; a banquet, 271–72; command of the Army, 273, 274

West India trade, settlement of the question, 70, 126, 133

Western Virginia, Albert Gallatin's love for, 196, 217, 219, 224; the house in, 244–45

Westmoreland, Countess of, 141 *and note*, 144, 208

Westphalia, Court of, 252, 255

Weyer, M. Van der, 256

Whigs, policy of the, 1827, 270

White Hart Inn, 271

White's Club, 132, 203; gambling at, 263, 264

Wigs, Bonaparte fashion of wearing, 248

Wisconsin, State of, 28

Würtemberg, King of, 96

YORK, Duke of, death, 265–67

York House, 265